Sir Harry Gibbs

WITHOUT FEAR OR FAVOUR

"His work as Chief Justice was of the first quality and I would rank him as one of the greatest of your Chief Justices rivalling even my good friend Sir Owen Dixon":

LORD DENNING

JOAN PRIEST

Published on the Gold Coast, Australia by

Scribblers Publishing
PO Box 501, Mudgeeraba
Queensland 4213

National Library of Australia
Cataloguing-in-Publication entry

Priest, Joan
Sir Harry Gibbs: Without Fear or Favour

Includes Index

ISBN 0 646 23693 8

1. Gibbs, Sir Harry Talbot, 1917-
2. Judges—Australia—Biography
3. Judges—Queensland—Biography

I. Title

Purchases: Copies of this biography can be
purchased for Aust $27 each from Scribblers
Publishing, PO Box 501, Mudgeeraba, Qld,
Australia 4213.

The portrait of Sir Harry Gibbs used on the front cover was painted by Sir William
Dargie and hangs in the Banco Court in the Queensland Supreme Court building.

Printed by Hyde Park Press, Adelaide, South Australia

Sponsored by the
University of Queensland
Law Graduates Association

FOREWORD

I have been fortunate in undertaking this biography of Sir Harry Gibbs to have had the cooperation of the Hon Peter Connolly CSI CBE QC, Justice of the Supreme Court of Queensland from 1976-1991. He provided analysis of the significant cases on which Sir Harry sat during his 17 years as a member of the High Court of Australia, the final six as Chief Justice. The Connolly analysis will be found in the *Appendix* under the heading: "The Years on the High Court and After". I thank him for his invaluable contribution.

My sincere thanks to all the distinguished judges and lawyers who gave me of their time and expert knowledge and made such a vital contribution to the work. To them, to Sir Harry and Lady Gibbs for their cooperation, and to the Queensland Supreme Court librarian, Aladin Rahemtula, High Court Senior Registrar, Frank Jones, and James Merralls QC for their practical assistance, I am greatly indebted. Special appreciation goes to my editor, Jim Corkery, for his dedicated and expert guidance. He was most ably assisted by Helen Fordham.

I also wish to thank my husband, Eric Priest, for his assistance throughout. Family members, Roger Priest, Helen O'Reilly, Rachel O'Reilly and Brian Halligan, and friends, Esther Roe, Elise Rathus, Gerard Carney, Christina Lau and Anthony Jefferies, also gave invaluable support.

Joan Priest
Brisbane, 20 March 1995

ACKNOWLEDGMENTS

We wish to acknowledge with thanks use of material from the *The Courier-Mail*, *Sydney Morning Herald*, *The Age*, *The Australian*, *The Financial Review*, *Bulletin*, *Queensland Times*, *Independent Weekly* (Brisbane), the former *Pix* and the Brisbane *Telegraph*.

CONTENTS

Chapter 1

THE YOUNG GIBBS

In January 1981, Sir Harry Gibbs had been a member of the High Court of Australia for 11 years. He was in Perth attending a Judges' Conference. Gibbs and his wife Muriel were at the breakfast table of the Parmelia Hotel with Queensland Judge, later Chief Justice, Sir Walter Campbell, and his wife Georgina, when Gibbs was called to the phone. The Attorney-General, Senator Durack, informed Sir Harry that he had just been appointed Chief Justice of Australia. Elated, Gibbs returned to the table. It was a moment of tremendous gratification for the Queensland quartet. They toasted the new Chief Justice with their breakfast coffee and the two men left for the Conference.

Just over 50 years before, in 1929, Brisbane was celebrating the completion of its elegant neo-classical City Hall and the sculptor, Daphne Mayo, was carving her procession of historical figures above the graceful columns of its portico. 44 kilometres away, the neighbouring city of Ipswich, which had nurtured Australia's first Chief Justice, Sir Samuel Griffith, saw its eighth Chief Justice, Harry Talbot Gibbs, about to turn twelve years of age.

He could be found, most lunch hours, at the Central State School propped against a gnarled Moreton Bay fig. Under this very tree the famous English explorer and King's Botanist, Allan Cunningham, had paused on his way to the Darling Downs to boil a billy a century before. There Gibbs discussed science fiction (especially the works of H G Wells) with his friend, future physician, Harry Wilson. The historic tree, one of several in the district credited as a Cunningham stopping place, pleased their imagination.

Young Harry Talbot Gibbs, a gangling, bespectacled, rather introverted youth, was known to family and friends as Bill. Harry Snr, his father, a popular Ipswich solicitor, had coined the nickname to distinguish the infant from himself. On returning from overseas service in World War I, and having not yet seen his firstborn, Gunner Harry Gibbs lent over the infant's cot in exuberant mood and exclaimed, "Hello Billo." Harry Jnr became Bill to his family.

Young Bill Gibbs had invented a non-hero, Hiram Fisher King Ulysses Bott, round whom he spun stories to Wilson. The enterprising boys produced a family magazine to which members of the two households contributed. Gibbs' most memorable contribution was *The Saga of Bill the Bad*, an eleven stanza, rhyming, tongue-in-cheek verse about a roguish chief who did battle with a model of chivalry known as Good Derek.

A liking for words and precocity in literary tastes was the precursor of the career ahead for the boy. Within a year or two, only 15 years old, the pair were reading the American avant-garde, "abstract" poet and writer Gertrude Stein. They had no reverence for her influential, controversial stream-of-consciousness and highly individual technique of writing. Gibbs, predating the famous *Angry Penguin*/Ern Malley Australian literary hoax, sent Stein a concoction of non-sequitur gibberish, put together from jumbled remarks made by others. He called it Ditto.

> I wonder which
> Is mad, ah.
> What
> Is it note.
> The Shakespearian prose i.....
> Precisely —quite like a
> Sheep— hark I.
> Am referring
> To you
> Not.
> Hark. Hark. Hark.
> Not....

Gibbs asked for an opinion on it, saying that it was the writing of a gifted friend. He received a serious reply from Stein's famous secretary and companion, Alice B Toklas. "Your friend has some interesting ideas," she wrote, "but he should speak more of what he sees and less of what he intends."

Bill and his young brother Wylie, who was later variously doctor, parliamentarian and pharmaceutical company director, were fourth generation Australians on both sides. Their great-grandfather, Harry Gibbs, came from Belfast in the north of Ireland. He had married there a young widow, Margaret Harlin (nee Seeds), from a centuries old legal family. They migrated to Victoria in the 1860s, taking up a Harlin[1] property, *Glenvale*.

Their son, Charles Henry Gibbs (Bill and Wylie's grandfather), moved to Queensland and bought a property at Rosewood near Ipswich. He sold this to Patrick Durack, partly in exchange for three properties in the Channel country in far south western Queensland. These were *Waveney Station*,

---

1 Family of founding Brisbane Grammar School Headmaster, Thomas Harlin.

Canterbury Plains and *The JC* (standing for John Canterbury, an English gentleman, presumably the original owner). A wattle and daub hotel was later built at *The JC,* and it became the horse changing post for Cobb & Co coaches. Charles Henry married Harriet Foote, a member of one of the two families of pioneering retail renown in Ipswich, Cribb & Foote, and took her out to *Waveney* Station. They went by steamer to Rockhampton, by Cobb & Co coach to Longreach and then by Charles Henry's own camel-drawn buggy along the Thomson and over the Cooper to the property. Out on this isolated station with its dry landscape of scattered boulders and dried up watercourses, Harriet had to cope with dirt floors and other frontier deprivations, with only inexperienced household help. She readily travelled the 1300 kms to Ipswich for the births of their children.

Bill Gibbs (third from left, second row) in Grade 3 at Boys' Central State School, Ipswich. Back row (far right) is Doug Campbell, later a Justice of the Queensland Supreme Court.

She gave birth to two small daughters. She was in Ipswich again awaiting the birth of their third child, when word reached Charles Henry (known as Harry) at *Waveney* that the birth was likely to be difficult. He set out at once, but it took some days to reach town. On arrival, he found that his 25 year old wife had died of septicaemia (blood poisoning) after giving birth to a son. Harriet had shared the fate of many women in those days of shocking obstetrical hazards. Her parents, John and Mary Ann Foote, reared the three children. Her husband, Charles Henry, eventually remarried and settled in Sydney as a "gentleman of independent means", a well-liked character given to wearing a red buttonhole and an elegant rolled-brimmed hat. His daughter by the second marriage, Sybil Gibbs, became one of Sydney's first woman barristers.

The deceased Harriet's strong and lusty infant son had been christened Harry Victor. He was later to insist in turn that his own son, though dubbed "Bill" by him, carry the family name of Harry, adding the "Talbot" from his wife's maternal family side. Harry Victor was to marry a high-spirited Sydney girl five years his senior, Flora Woods, whom he had met while she was teaching at Ipswich Girls' Grammar School. Her forebears had settled in New South Wales two generations before. Harry and Flora's son, Harry Talbot Gibbs, was born on 7 February 1917 at a hospital in Paddington, Sydney, where Flora had briefly returned to be with her family for the confinement.

Apart from delighting his returned soldier father, the baby Gibbs was doted upon by his mother. Flora, a confident, gracious personality with a lively sense of humour, observed signs of special brightness very early in her son, and later his young brother. She read them the children's comic, *Chick's Own,* and both were able to read it by age four. Both also took an early interest in the family encyclopaedia. All Flora Gibbs' geese were inclined to be swans, but, in regard to her two sons, she was right.

As soon as the toddler Bill Gibbs was old enough, he was sent off to the modern Congregational Hall kindergarten run by Miss Hancock of the Ipswich timber family. He was joined there by Dr Gilmore Wilson's son, Harry, and the little boys saw a great deal of each other, often playing together at Gibbs' home at Thorn Street. A 19th century, spacious weatherboard with wide verandahs, low-set, sloping roof, beautiful cedar doors and fittings, it had been bought by Gibbs' paternal grandparents, the Footes, in 1894. Its grounds were ideal for such games as hide and seek and cowboys and Indians. They used to leap round the diamond shaped rosebeds in the narrow front garden - the pride and joy of the gardener, a Kanaka, Tarragindi (Tarry for short) - and make for the thick bushes along the street side fence, or the big jacarandas at the back near the former carriage drive, or the grassed courtyard inside flanking another, smaller verandah. It was here that Gibbs' widowed grandmother, Flora Woods Snr, who often came from Sydney to visit, frequently sat sewing. She was a magnet for the small boy. An occasional visitor was Gibbs' cousin, Constance or Consie Holland, the daughter of Harry Snr's sister, Ida. She remarked on the bond between the boy and his grandmother. "He often turned to her," she recalled. "You would see him there, just standing beside her chair, and she would talk to him." The serene elderly woman drew him out, something which no doubt pleased his mother for she had her hands full with the new baby. The Gibbs younger son, Wylie, was born when Bill was five and was rather a delicate child. The return home each evening from his busy solicitor's practice of Harry Snr, a gentle affectionate man, was a highlight for the small family.

A tradition of the Gibbs' childhood was the yearly school holiday visit, at Easter or in September, to young Consie's country home, *Ashley*. Bill and younger brother Wylie travelled there by train, in the earlier days with their mother. They experienced plenty of rural life. It was on this dairy and grazing property that the boys learnt to ride, to milk the cows and to shell corn. Bill also picked pumpkins and the ploughed-up potato crop. Ken Holland rose early, set the fire in the big kitchen range, called Consie, her elder sister Marian, and the boys to begin the day's work. "Bill and I were up quickly," Consie recalled. "Wylie was the only one who sometimes managed to wangle out of it." Their mother outfitted the boys for the hot sun and outdoor work. They wore knee length gabardine shorts, long-sleeved shirts, long socks, boots and cloth hats.

Picnicking outside Ipswich. Bill Gibbs (far right), aged about 15 years, talks with his friend, Harry Wilson. His mother Flora Gibbs is seated far left; his young brother Wylie is centre.

At home, during the hot summers in Ipswich, they often went swimming, sometimes in the Brisbane River, sometimes in the "big swimming hole" at College's Crossing, an offshoot of the Bremer River. This was frequented as well by Harry Wilson and his brothers with whom they also learnt to play tennis. Music lessons were tried until it was clear that was not their forte, and, alternating with Christmas holidays at Southport, they accompanied their parents to Sydney to spend Christmas with their Grandmother Woods. Gibbs experienced a settled, relatively prosperous and well-rounded Australian childhood.

Summer holidays at Southport. Chariot races on the beach at Little Burleigh. Left Chariot: Bill Gibbs, two other students. Right Chariot: Brian Wilson, Harry Wilson, Roger Dark. Riders: Medical students, Eunice Dowzer (left), Esther Roe (right).

The boy went to school a year younger than most and always had to cope with being one of the youngest in his year. His scholastic achievements were good, although not startling until university. Secondary education at Ipswich Grammar School established the teenager Bill Gibbs' preference for the Arts subjects. He did only "moderately" at mathematics and science but excelled in English and history. For the latter, Wilson estimated, Gibbs averaged a spectacular 98% in examinations over four years. History master, Ben Patterson, aware of the boy's wide reading and formidable memory took "most of young Gibbs statements for gospel if he couldn't remember himself".

Ipswich is a city of seven hills and Bill, Wylie and Harry, all keen readers, said it was like Rome only steeper as they cycled over several of them to school each day. Harry Wilson called en route at the Gibbs household for the two brothers and invariably found the methodical Bill ready and waiting, but the mercurial Wylie either impatient and about to start off alone, or still asleep. Flora Gibbs was firmly behind the scholarly drive of both sons. So was Harry Snr, who was by now senior partner in the firm of solicitors, Walker & Walker, whose founders were related to his own mother Harriet. Harry Snr also encouraged sport, particularly swimming and tennis. Harry Wilson's parents had built a tennis court. Dr Gilmore Wilson, his wife Dorothy, one of Sydney University's first women Arts graduates, and their young family of future medicos, Harry, Esther, Chester and Brian, became the weekend social centre for the Gibbs and other bright young people in the town. Dr Wilson and Harry Gibbs Snr made formidable tennis partners, the former with a fierce serve, and Gibbs at net, lifting his nuggetty frame from the ground to smash overhead shots. His son, Bill, played a reasonable tennis game - much better than his efforts at rugby union against rugby renowned Nudgee College. Harry Wilson recalled that they were both in the infamous fifths, "who were beaten on one occasion by Nudgee with a cricket score of 105-nil". In the 1980s when Gibbs, as the knighted Chief Justice, returned to present prizes at the school and was reminded of the rugby fiasco by Dr Wilson, he replied: "I feel sure if the match had gone on a little longer the tide would have turned..."

Gibbs enrolled at the University of Queensland in 1934 as a law student in the Faculty of Arts. The Dean was the outstanding Professor of English Language and Literature, JJ Stable, whose advice was to prove formative. The Chair in Law was held by the authoritarian and elderly Professor Cumbrae Stewart, the founding Registrar. The University itself was still in its first home in the historic old Government House buildings opposite the Botanical Gardens in George Street. Gibbs, with his cousin Ian Walker, were in residence at the Presbyterian Emmanuel College, then sited on Gregory Terrace. He threw himself into his studies, unencumbered now by science subjects, and showed enthusiasm for university life generally. He became president of the Law Students' Society, editor of the student literary magazine *Galmahra*, vice-president of Emmanuel College, and president of the Students' Union.

In his first year he met Tom Matthews, son of Supreme Court Justice Ben Matthews, who was to prove his academic rival. Matthews' class mate from Brisbane Grammar, a part-time student and articled clerk with solicitors Fitzgerald & Walsh, the lively, outgoing Jack (later Sir John) Rowell was also to become a lifelong friend of Gibbs. Rowell found Latin an obdurate language. "In fact, I think I'd still be doing it if it weren't for Bill Gibbs," he commented recently. "We sat beside each other and he used to help me with it. They called our course, Arts with a tendency to Law." This was before the Faculty of Law was set up. Cumbrae Stewart lectured Jurisprudence and Roman Law. These were meat and drink to Gibbs. Rowell found little difficulty there, too, but he did trouble the professor who insisted that all his students wear gowns. Rowell walked in late to a lecture one day without his and attracted loud attention. "Look at you! Look at you, Rowell," the professor thundered. "You're not dressed!" Bewildered, Rowell looked down at his clothes. "I felt half naked," he recalled, and must have looked alarmed. "*Academically*! *Academically*!" shouted Cumbrae Stewart, impatiently. "Come back when you've got a gown." T-shirts and jeans were unimaginable worlds away.

Gibbs remembers two brilliant men, Professor Henry Alcock and Dr ACV Melbourne, who between them illuminated Constitutional History and Political Science for him. He is also indebted to Professor Stable who, on seeing Gibbs' first year English results, suggested that he do Honours English. Although he liked the subject, Gibbs had not considered this choice. In hindsight, that course proved to be important in his academic development. Words are a lawyer's tools and weapons and this undergraduate study of English language was to serve Gibbs well over decades of speech making and legal opinion and decision writing.

Law instructors were not numerous in Australian universities at this time. Inspirational mentors were rare indeed. "In Law," Gibbs commented, "Tom Fry was a great help. An eccentric man, probably even a figure of fun, but he did everything he possibly could for you." Dr Fry's father was a Brisbane optometrist - "Fry for the Eye" - an epigram that attached to the son. The students concocted a Commemoration song about their lecturer:

> The sillily solemnly newspaper columnly
> Frequently photographed Fry.

Fry's record was impressive. He had a BCL (Oxon), an Sc Jur D from Harvard, lectured Constitutional Law, Equity, Criminal Law, Real Property, Conveyancing and Torts, and later had a distinguished wartime career in the Middle East with the Australian Military Forces as Deputy Judge-Advocate General. His energy and talent made him a mentor for young HT Gibbs and other law students.

The country had emerged from the Great Depression by the mid-1930s. War was not yet looming, and high spirits prevailed among the young. There were around 60 students in residence at Emmanuel College. Only one of them had a car. Since its brakes did not work, the students did not vie to be passengers down precipitous Edward Street and along to the University but mostly strolled down in groups. For the return journey they reserved the matchbox trams which then regularly rattled and clinked their way up and down the hill. Student life was leisurely.

HT (Bill) Gibbs BA, in 1938, during his post-graduate student days at University of Queensland. Extract taken from Semper Floreat the University of Queenslands students' newspaper of 12 October 1938.

A longtime friend of Gibbs and president of their Students' Association, Buck (CB) Manning, headed for a journalistic career, recalled the "interminable student room discussions in which we indulged when we should have been following the counsel of the then Vice-Principal, Mos Hanger, against this sort of time wasting in lieu of study". Even then, Manning remembered, "it was clear to us lesser mortals that a bright future lay ahead for Bill". In his role as president, Manning also recalled being "a sitting duck for Bill and his colleague Ian Walker to test their knowledge of the House of Commons and legal procedure".

Flushed with his knowledge and skills in law and classics, Gibbs brought them readily into his daily speech and student activities. Orthopaedic surgeon Alexander Grant recalled:

> Bill was a contemporary and fellow student in English. In our early days at College, [he] and I put on a float in the University procession ...the theme was "The Three Muses - Mourning at the Death of Learning - Late Deceased and Beggary". The treatment was satirical and probably rude and the details are irrelevant, but the idea to my mind was pure Gibbs, for even in his moments of levity he could not escape his fondness for Elizabethan and classical allusions.

The family canvassed the possibility that Bill might attend Sydney University, with its premier reputation and long established Law Faculty. This need to travel was obviated in 1936 when the University of Queensland's Law Faculty - the T C Beirne School of Law - opened at the George St campus. A Law Students' Society formed, Bill Gibbs was elected inaugural president and "HT Gibbs" became a familiar signature on numerous letters addressed to the University newspaper *Semper Floreat*. He was a leader, too, in student humour. He discovered that the Women's Club rules stated that "all qualified students were ipso facto members of the Women's Club". He and others arranged for the Men's Club to invade the next meeting of the Women's Club and apply as "qualified students" for membership. He led the delegation to the meeting and demanded admission. The ensuing mock legal argument was conducted with elan by the women. Their chairman, Betty Stephens, later to marry Harry Wilson, flanked by Wilson's amused sister Esther (later Dr Esther Roe) and a dozen others, accepted Gibbs' point. The rule would be changed suitably at that very meeting, she assured them, so would they "be gentlemen enough to withdraw." They were.

Law student, Muriel Dunn, whom Gibbs met at the University of Queensland and later married.

Another episode created a press headline: "Students Marooned in Bay". Bill and a friend, Lex Dunn, were out sailing in Moreton Bay off Brisbane in the latter's boat with four girls from the Women's College. They included Lex's lively brown-eyed cousin, a new law student, Muriel Dunn, whom Gibbs was later to marry. Time got away. They started for home but their engine failed. Under sail they reached Bishop Island at the mouth of the river by nightfall and were given shelter in a disused shed by an old man, who appeared highly suspicious of the mixed gender group. He brought from his own hut a tarpaulin which he draped in the centre of the shed "to make a room each for the boys and girls". After he left they removed the tarpaulin and covered themselves with it for warmth. "We were cold and hungry and far from feeling romantic," the girls reported after being rescued next morning by the water police.

Students stranded in bay: Bunched in the stern of their stranded boat are four students from Emmanuel College and four from Women's College. Lex Dunn is centre back, Muriel Dunn is third from the left and Bill Gibbs is on the far right.

As editor of the literary magazine, the highly committed Gibbs regretted the traditional indifference of the student body. He commented in an editorial, with more relish than brevity:

> It is significant of our times and our University that an editor of *Galmahra* is forced to become its apologist... Unfortunately, those who contend that [its] publication achieves no useful purpose need go to but little trouble to establish, prima facie, their case...If contributions are dashed off grudgingly as an irksome duty, the writers are wasting their own time and their readers. No point can be gained by flogging a stubborn ass. A poor editor, after all his blustering, cajoling and beseeching...to win a morsel more for his hungry press, is inclined in his heart to agree with his critics. But by this time his editorial work is as good as done and he will let no philistine say his labour went for nothing.

Gibbs, in the role of apologist, clearly enjoyed his tenure as editor. The magazine was well regarded, but it did not survive the Second World War years.

In 1937, Gibbs took out a Bachelor of Arts with Firsts in English literature. Also graduating, Jack Rowell bemoaned having to stand in a state of "nervous disorder" in Professor Stable's study while the latter deliberated whether he would let Rowell through his English paper (he did). Gibbs also won the *PJ McDermott Memorial Prize for English Language and Literature.*

The pair, together with Harry Wilson and others, attended the Commemoration Practices in the University's elegant old Georgian building and the Commemoration Ball at City Hall. *Semper*, true to its era, commented on the long formal gowns of the women, among them Mary Webb, associate to her father, Chief Justice William Webb, later Sir William, (the third Queenslander on the High Court after Justice Sir Charles Powers and Sir Samuel Griffith). Una Bick, to become the State's first woman barrister, was also there. She was, at that point, a member of the Law Students' Society executive.

In his final two years, while completing his law degree, Gibbs won the presidency of the Students' Union. He conducted some involved negotiations with the University Senate seeking a place for a representative of the Union Council on that body. This was unsuccessful (it was not until 1974 that this representation was established). In 1938 he led a delegation before the Minister for Public Instruction, Harry Bruce (for whom the Bruce Highway is named) on the issue, and was a delegate interstate on the National Union of Australian University Students (NUAUS).

Gibbs liking and talent for words and the undergraduate's tendency to wordiness was apparent in his student editor days. He defended the editor of *Semper Floreat* from attack by a contributor:

> The Union and the Council has always supported the principle that utmost freedom of utterance should be allowed...and to obviate the possibility that his editorial censorship might be stilled by authority, student or otherwise, the paper has never been made the official organ of the Union. This freedom is based on a trust that every editor will remember, that it is his duty to allow his paper to express not only his own views but also the views...of all contributors, even his own detractors or opponents in belief. I would like to make it public, Sir, that in my opinion you have understood your duty and never failed in it. Articles in your paper may have at times been coloured by your opinions, when your critics would have preferred a vacuous objectivity, but this has merely been a natural and consistent

viewing of fact in the light of belief. You have never deliberately passed off
the wish for the fact or propaganda for news... In short, the Union
Executive still thinks you're O.K.

So spoke the budding barrister. In 1939 Gibbs and Tom Matthews became
the first two students to graduate from the University of Queensland Law
School with First Class Honours (Matthews beat Gibbs for the University
Medal). Because they had taken their law degrees with first class honours,
the pair were entitled, under Rule 35 of the Rules Relating to Admission of
Barristers, to a waiver of the 55 guineas fee normally exacted for admission
to the Supreme Court. Uncertainty over the meaning of Rule 35 was settled
by the Full Court on a specific application prompted by the appearance, after
years of drought, of these two potential beneficiaries.[2] (HH Henchman, later
a Supreme Court judge, had been the only first class honours graduate to have
been dealt with under Rule 35 previously.)

Gibbs had developed his talents and skills well in benign pre-War Brisbane.
The Students' Union, in an au revoir to "Bill...H.T.Gibbs" in *Semper,*
described him as "an old stager with a long career of public spirited
enterprise behind him";

> He finally brought his legal mind to bear on the problems...of the Union and
> conducted Union affairs with the same bland, unhurried precision which
> has...marked his progress through university...He is now going on to adorn
> the legal world with his gently ironic presence. Good wishes from the
> undergraduates, Talbot!

---

2 Reported at [1939] Case 32 QWN 52.

Chapter 2

SECOND WORLD WAR YEARS

In May 1939, the Gibbs family gathered at the Supreme Court in Brisbane to see their elder son admitted to the Bar by the Chief Justice of Queensland, Sir James Blair. Amongst those admitted as solicitors that day was Gerald Patterson, a member of the clan of Gibbs' former history master at Ipswich Grammar School. The two had met at family holidays at Southport and were to become close, though unlikely, friends - Gibbs quietly courteous and Patterson abrasive ("I always was a difficult bastard"). They shared the same sense of humour and interest in intellectual pursuits.

In 1939, Gibbs, aspiring to be a barrister, read in chambers with a senior barrister, ET Real, a leading member of the Queensland bar. He sat in Real's chambers, participated in interviews with solicitors and litigants, drew drafts of pleadings, even wrote a few legal opinions - generally, served an apprenticeship in the law. Gibbs still views articles with an experienced solicitor or reading in the chambers of a good barrister as the best apprenticeship for a career in law, although the large number of law students makes this method impossible today. University-based postgraduate legal training courses are now the only way to cope with the rising demand. Gibbs also valued highly his training in Latin and Roman Law, the first for its invaluable training in grammatical discipline and the latter for its insights into the origins and alternative systems of law. He favours the study of continental legal systems for the comparative perspectives they bring.

Gibbs hardly had time to start legal practice. Hitler's Nazi regime in Germany had hung threateningly over Europe for two years. On 1 September 1939, German troops invaded Poland. Britain mobilised for war. The following day Gibbs enlisted in the Australian (Citizens) Military Forces (AMF). Twenty-four hours later (3 September), Britain officially declared war on Germany. Australia followed immediately in its traditionally supportive imperial role. The six long years of World War II lay ahead.

Gibbs was appointed to HQ First Military District, Northern Command (Victoria Barracks, Brisbane). This was one of the centres where staff grappled with the huge logistical task of mobilisation, work for which young lawyers were particularly well qualified. The dramatic vicissitudes of those years and Australia's progressively more direct involvement after Japan entered the war on 6 December 1941, are well documented. Gibbs' talents were soon rewarded. He moved quite swiftly through the ranks from private to temporary captain in the Adjutant-General's Department of the First Military District. After the fall of Singapore in 1942, the South-West Pacific Area became a battle zone under US Commander-in-Chief General Douglas Macarthur, with General Sir Thomas Blamey Commander-in-Chief of Australian forces. Gibbs transferred to the AIF, was promoted to captain and appointed Deputy Assistant Adjutant-General HQ Queensland Lines of Communication Area.

The city of Brisbane, previously regarded by the southern capitals as little more than a large sprawling country town, now became the centre of intense activity - a frontier town accommodating a great influx of American troops. Macarthur established his GHQ at the AMP building in Queen Street. The elegant top of town hotel, Lennons, became his personal headquarters. There a stream of US officers in "greys" (dress uniform) were constantly coming and going, and at night a US band provided up to the minute dance music. An air of excitement, of high events, of history in the making, pervaded the city.

When on leave, Gibbs' constant companion was the slender, dark-haired, brown-eyed Maryborough girl, Muriel Dunn, he had met at University. She was now completing her law degree. Muriel's father, Hector Dunn, was a son of Andrew Dunn, who had formed a newspaper company (A Dunn & Co) which published daily newspapers in Maryborough, Rockhampton and Toowoomba and eventually merged with other companies to form Provincial Newspapers Qld.

Andrew Dunn, a Scot, had married a remarkable educationist, Kate MacIntyre. The pair had migrated from Scotland in 1879 so that Kate could accept the position of headmistress at the Girls' South State School in Toowoomba in south-east Queensland. Andrew entered the building trade there. They had five sons, three born in Toowoomba. At that point, they moved to coastal Maryborough where Kate established the Central Girls' School. Andrew then quit building to go into the newspaper business. Muriel's father, Hector, and another son were born. Kate survived only five months after the birth of the last child and after her death the five little boys were sent back to Scotland to be cared for by their grandmother (the youngest boy died a year later). Andrew Dunn built up the newspaper business which would provide a livelihood for his four sons, remarried, and returned to Scotland to bring the boys home. Hector Dunn later married Lilias Fairlie of Maryborough. Lilias, who had been a clever student, nursed an unfulfilled ambition to attend university. There was then a background of scholastic aptitude on both sides of the family. When Hector and Lilias's three daughters, Muriel, Joan and Barbara, had finished their schooling at the

Central Girls' School and Maryborough Girls' Grammar, Lilias encouraged them into tertiary education. Muriel was a bright, lively, all round student, who enjoyed tennis and fishing expeditions with her father. The daughters fulfilled their mother's career expectations, Muriel becoming a lawyer, Joan a doctor and Barbara a dentist - most unusual in that era.

Muriel always had a direct, straight-speaking manner. This was shared by other members of the family, such as her cousins, Jim Dunn (later a Supreme Court judge) and Hugh Dunn (later Australian Ambassador to China). When she came to Brisbane in 1938 to attend the University of Queensland and take up residence at the Women's College at Kangaroo Point, she quickly made friends, and soon felt at ease with Bill Gibbs' friends.

Bill and Muriel were frequent guests at the flat of Gerald Patterson and his wife Marcia, a tall attractive fair-haired musician. There, Bill's brother, Wylie (final year medicine and at that time engaged to Gerald's sister) was often to be found. Gerald, an asthmatic, was frustrated at being turned down for war service. Patriotic feelings ran high. Japanese submarines had attacked Sydney Harbour, Darwin had been bombed repeatedly and the Japanese army had taken key points in New Guinea. On Gibbs' advice, Patterson subsequently volunteered for a useful stint in the District Censor's office.

Gibbs remained based at Queensland Lines of Communication Area in Brisbane for a further year. As the war in the Pacific intensified, so did the logistical work necessary to the deployment and training of the increasing number of armed services personnel.

By November 1943, as American and Australian forces drove back the Japanese in New Guinea, and General Macarthur's island hopping strategy was being implemented, more staff officers dealing with the logistics of that vast sweep north were needed in New Guinea. Gibbs at last received a posting to the war zone, as a Staff Captain, A Personnel Services, HQ New Guinea Force, at Port Moresby. He flew north by DC3 (similar to the US C47 Dakotas), the versatile aircraft for which he came to have a great respect. They carried everything from troops to supplies and were indispensable to the pursuit of the war in the area.

Like many others in the New Guinea theatre of war, Gibbs contracted bacillary dysentery. Under wartime conditions in a comparatively primitive country, it was a widespread problem. He was one of those hospitalised. The disease, by this time, was rarely fatal, thanks to the effective drug sulphaguanidine, but it remained debilitating and hard to shake. "They were as thin as sticks those boys, but never a peep of complaint out of them," remarked a former army matron on ABC Radio decades later, speaking of the cheerfulness of the rows of victims in the hospital in which she served in New Guinea. Sickness was indeed rife and, in regard to some complaints, such as bilharzia, Gibbs blamed the deceptively translucent streams of New Guinea. "You could look at a stream up there and it'd be pure and clear but it was in fact full of microbes."

During the crowded year in Port Moresby, Gibbs became familiar with the emergency wartime administration of the then Australian Mandated Territory of New Guinea. This knowledge was soon to be drawn upon, but his next posting, for a brief period, was to HQ First Australian Army at Lae. This was across the mountainous terrain so heavily fought over during the epic Kokoda Trail campaign and the battle at Buna, where Australians fought the fanatical Japanese who had bayoneted the civilian men, women and children there and at the Gona mission.

The war in the region intensified. In January, the Australians captured Shaggy Ridge, Ramu Valley and, by April, had advanced in northern New Guinea to Madang. In May, thousands of Japanese troops were trapped between advancing Australian troops from Alexishafen and US forces at Aitape and Hollandia. MacArthur's island leapfrog strategy in his advance to the Philippines had served to isolate and cut off Japanese troops from their lines of supply and communication. It was working brilliantly. By October, the Australian 6th Division began taking over from American XI Corps at Aitape. The following month, in a large scale redeployment of Allied Forces in the Pacific, Australians were given sole responsibility for the final defeat of Japanese forces in New Guinea and began pressing towards the greatest concentration of troops remaining, at Wewak (final battle, May 1945). Australian army casualties in New Guinea from 1943-1945 were: killed or died of illness: 1231: Wounded: 2867. Together with casualties in 1942, a significant number of Australian families were affected, either directly or indirectly.

In November 1944, Gibbs was promoted to Major and transferred back to Australia to the Directorate of Research & Civil Affairs Land HQ in Melbourne. But, taking advantage of his well-earned leave, he and Muriel, who was practising as a solicitor, were married at Brisbane's historic Ann Street Presbyterian Church. They were attended by Wylie, their old friend Harry Wilson and Muriel's two sisters, Joan and Barbara Dunn. Joan recalls the "yellow bridegroom " (Gibbs was taking the anti-malarial drug Atebrin). Muriel, in the excitement of donning her bridal gown, forgot to complete changing her shoes. En route to the church, she discovered she was wearing odd ones. The frantic return to rectify this has entered family legend. After a few weeks honeymoon at Surfers Paradise, then a sleepy seaside township, it was back to duty again. Gibbs' destination was now Melbourne. Muriel, after receiving permission for civilian interstate travel (a wartime necessity), was able to join him and the two found themselves an inner city flat.

The Directorate of Research and Civil Affairs HQ was at Victoria Barracks in the heart of Melbourne. Gibbs served there on a committee appointed to draw up plans for a unified government for Papua and New Guinea when hostilities ceased. The team included Colonel Hubert Murray, who had followed his renowned uncle, Sir Hubert Murray, as Administrator of Papua (1940-1942, when civilian government was suspended), and Lieutenant Colonel John Kerr, who, after a distinguished career as soldier, lawyer and judge, became Governor-General of Australia and sacked the Whitlam Labor government in 1975.

Major HT (Bill) Gibbs marries Muriel Dunn at Ann Street Presbyterian Church, Brisbane, November 1944, following his transfer from Lae, New Guinea, to Directorate of Research & Civil Affairs Land HQ, Melbourne.

The concentrated work on governmental and constitutional matters appealed to Gibbs. While off duty, he put together a Master of Laws thesis on the subject to present to the University of Queensland on his return. Meanwhile, in July 1945, just a few months after VE (Victory in Europe) Day and two months before final victory in the Pacific, Gibbs received notification that he had been Mentioned in Despatches. The citation simply read: *Services in the South-West Pacific Area*. Gibbs was not aware of anything specific. The award is made for service which is considered sufficiently outstanding and meritorious to warrant it. This was an early recognition of Gibbs' qualities that were to make his legal career so successful.

The drawing up of the unification plan for Papua and New Guinea continued at the Melbourne Directorate until mid-December 1945. By then Gibbs had also put the finishing touches to his thesis. Entitled The Laws of the Territory of New Guinea, their Constitutional Source and Basic Content,[1] it traces the British source and background of Territory Administration, its development, flaws and possibilities for the future. The thesis was used in postwar Papua and New Guinea administration and it regains some relevance in the 1990s when the Australian constitution is a matter of public debate.

In his introduction to the thesis, Gibbs spells out the principles of the application of British law to newly acquired territories. A common law doctrine was in place as far back as 1608. The Privy Council, in an Anonymous Case in 1722, reinforced the doctrine: "as the law is the birthright of every [English] subject, so, wherever they go, they carry their laws with them."

However, the colonists carried with them only so much of the English law as was applicable to the conditions of the new colony. Which English laws are so applicable has been the subject of innumerable cases considered by English, dominion and colonial courts, and, as Gibbs wrote, "has not been susceptible of an easy answer".

His thesis examined, in ten chapters, the constitutional and common law difficulties involved in Australia's administration of the Mandated Territory from 1920-1945. The Japanese invasion of New Guinea early in 1942 ended effective civil administration and the end of World War II marked the passing of a legal and administrative era. Gibbs dealt with the history of Papua New Guinea, through its days as a German Protectorate, its British Military Administration (staffed by Australians) during World War I, and afterwards, when Australia undertook, as a "trust of civilisation" on behalf of the League of Nations, the Territory's administration and the well-being of its inhabitants, including such involved legal matters as women's land rights. This is a subject of abiding interest still.

---

1 HT Gibbs, LLM thesis (1946), Central Library, University of Queensland, St Lucia, Brisbane.

Gibbs considered the application of the ever controversial external affairs power (s 51 (xxix)), remarking: "...it is impossible to accede to the view that the external affairs power is free from the restrictions and limitations for which Sections of the Constitution expressly provide..." He holds the same opinion on its application in Australia in the 1990s. His thesis concluded that the Territory had a legal system which was "obscure and confused... [T]he complexity of the law, and the fallibility of human nature" made it necessary "to adopt the only alternative...a legal system which is ex hypothesi a complete one, whether it be that of England or Queensland being immaterial." The United Nations approved Australian trusteeship over the former Mandated Territory of New Guinea in December 1946.

Gibbs' thesis was a rare achievement, since the LLM degree was usually taken through course work. The examiners in Law at University of Queensland, Dr Fry and Professor WN Harrison, praised the piece as "an outstanding contribution to systematic legal learning" on the subject.

Bill and Muriel Gibbs were back home in Queensland for Christmas of 1945, which they spent with Muriel's family at their seaside home at Hervey Bay near Maryborough. In the New Year he transferred to the Australian Army Legal Corps reserve in Brisbane and they found a pleasant old wooden "Queenslander" in the affordable suburb of Sherwood, where they could really begin family life. Muriel was pregnant and they looked forward to their first child. Meanwhile, Gibbs began setting up his practice as a barrister.

Chapter 3
THE BARRISTER

Gibbs made a slow start as a barrister. These were the vulnerable early days of his career. Briefs did not come flooding in to him. With his round dark rimmed glasses and thin face, his appearance was deceptively immature for his 29 years. He shared rooms at the first of the three "generations" of Inns of Court, built for barristers' chambers, this one in Adelaide Street. After his prolonged absence in the services, he had to pick up the threads and contacts of civilian life again.

In his first appearance at the Magistrates Court, he was opposed by an experienced solicitor, Ron Lowe, who was well used to the rough and ready atmosphere which prevailed. Magistrates were not often legally qualified in those days. "I knew them, their methods, and their various strengths and weaknesses," Lowe recalled. "This was an assault case and they were interested only in the practical evidence. Gibbs quoted a number of learned authorities. The magistrate was just unused to that sort of intellectual approach." Lowe won the case, putting it down to a triumph of local knowledge and know-how over erudition and inexperience.

Gibbs' casual meeting in town with Gerald Patterson, by this time a junior partner in the firm O'Mara & Patterson, Solicitors, renewed their friendship. Patterson promised to send briefs to Gibbs. Soon the slender, rather shy barrister began to impress. "Bill didn't inspire much confidence just to look at in those days," Patterson recalled, "but when he opened his mouth in court, then the whole situation changed. The words poured out - and he was just so good. In the Magistrates' Court, where I'd normally send a clerk, I used to go myself just for the pleasure of listening to him." Gibbs' lists of legal authorities had obviously been trimmed.

A younger barrister, Ned Williams (later Sir Edward and a Justice of the Queensland Supreme Court) had also just returned from war service and was admitted to the Bar late in 1946. He said that Gibbs did not need the usual barrister's stewardship in the Magistrates Court. During the next few years, Williams built up a very good practice as a junior barrister and often sought Gibbs to lead him in Supreme Court cases.

Before 1946 was out, Gibbs had as much work as he could cope with at the Supreme Court, had appeared in several Full Court appeal cases, one appeal to the High Court and had written many legal opinions. A glut of landlord and tenant cases, which led him into some arcane areas of land law, buoyed up his practice. Following the acceptance of his LLM thesis, he was appointed a temporary part-time lecturer in Elements of Mercantile Law and Mercantile Law Final at the University of Queensland and became increasingly involved with the Law School. The extra income was welcome, too. Gibbs started to develop his work routines and systems. He became known for his notebooks, in which he set out his heads of argument and main points of cross-examination. He did not prepare his submissions verbatim, preferring to build his argument on his feet, as any good barrister must. Confidence grew apace and his style became fluid, more polished and clearly persuasive.

Over these years Bill and Muriel had three daughters. Barbara was born while they were at their first home at Sherwood, and Margaret and Mary a year or two later, after they had moved to another more spacious old Queenslander, closer to the city, at the leafy, riverside suburb of Chelmer. "Bill always made time for the children," Muriel observed. "And Barbara, when she was a little thing, always wanted her father." This had its problems, for she was a restless sleeper and often went to curl up beside him at night. But the bond was there and the child was never turned away.

HT Gibbs appointed QC

Gibbs' reputation as an appellate advocate grew quickly. About this time, Jack Rowell, who, following the trauma of the war years as a prisoner of war in Malaya, was now in practice with O'Sullivan & Rowell, received a call from a client in Cairns instructing him to get in touch with a man named Harry Gibbs. The client had heard Gibbs was the brightest star to begin practise at the Bar since the war. "I made inquiries," Rowell recalled, "and found that he was my old mate, Bill. I told him, 'You'd better win this one, they think you're good.'" From then on, O'Sullivan & Rowell briefed him extensively for appeal or equity work. Gibbs and Rowell both bought holiday cottages at the then relatively secluded Mermaid Beach on the south coast. Rowell's attractive dark-haired, convent-educated wife, Mary, and Muriel Gibbs became friends, as did their families. The men's legacy of shared student days was to continue.

Although Gibbs was busy, the pace of life for Brisbane lawyers in the late-1940s was not hectic. Members of the relatively small profession regularly congregated at the first of the city's coffee inns - Basil's - from which the freshly ground coffee aroma floated into Adelaide Street. Gerald Patterson, one of the instigators of the coffee habit, together with Gibbs and an array of legal talent, ranging from the future Chief Justice, Mos Hanger, to the gregarious Rex King, were often joined there by music critic, Fred Rogers, cellist, Otilie Cloake and others from the Australian Broadcasting Commission's offices nearby. The proprietor, Basil, a White Russian, sought to create an atmosphere and was delighted with his habitues. "It was the sort of place he wanted," recalled Patterson, "where intellectuals came and had discussions and talked and drank his coffee - and he was a good host." Basil's Coffee Inn claimed its place in the evolving life of the city.

Chambers had not been easy to come by for any of the post-war newcomers. Gibbs initially shared rooms on the second floor of the old Inns of Court in Adelaide Street with a gifted barrister a few years his senior, JD (Doug) McGill, also from Ipswich, and a nephew of the leader of the Bar, Alec D McGill. Gibbs took adjoining rooms when they became available and, in turn, invited Muriel's cousin, newly qualified barrister Jim Dunn (later Judge of the Supreme Court), to share his chambers. Gibbs and Doug McGill, together with the big-framed, pleasant mannered George Lucas (also later a Supreme Court Judge), whose rooms were close by, spent much time together discussing legal matters. They formed, with Dunn and others, a Tea Club which became something of an institution[1] and gradually replaced, for Gibbs, the more leisurely Basil's Coffee Inn gatherings.

---

1 Members, apart from the four named, were Viv Mylne (later District Court judge), Harry Bonham, Charles Sheahan (later Supreme Court judge), W Grant-Taylor (later Judge and Chairman of the District Court).

Gibbs and Patterson sometimes also shared a morning swim at the Spring Hill baths, and met regularly at the end of the day for a beer or two, sometimes at the centrally located Ulster Hotel, in Elizabeth Street. Gibbs enjoyed these late afternoon injections of rumbustious Patterson comment. He found it the ideal way of coping with the stress which accompanied the punishing workload he had by this time set himself. He did not go without physical penalty. Although an ulcer was now diagnosed and treated, he continued to work incessantly. His wife remarked, "The law was always the great love of his life - you couldn't stop him."

Former Chairman of the District Court, the genial but measured Judge Lindsay Byth, recalls that, from the time Gibbs set up practice as a barrister in 1946, other barristers such as Doug McGill and two future Supreme court Judges, Charles Sheehan and Harry Matthews, saw him as High Court material. He was invariably on top of his brief, showed strong powers of reasoning, was unflappable, and detached to the extent that he was often found dictating an opinion on an unrelated matter a few minutes before "putting on his hat to go round and argue a case before the Full Court". Afterwards, he would often return to chambers and start on another opinion. Judge Byth commented:

> It soon became apparent to all of us at the Queensland Bar that he really was remarkable. He prepared his cases in what seemed about half the time it took most of us and he got all the hard briefs. He did not do a great deal of criminal work. I remember a murder case he had as junior counsel, and lost - the accused, a Friendly Societies' chemist, later hanged himself in jail. Criminal cases inevitably receive a lot of publicity but they are not nearly as difficult as contract, commercial and constitutional cases. And he was a marvellous appellate advocate. While most of us would argue to the Full Court and apparently not assist the judges much, when Gibbs stood up, their Honours would get their pens out and take down his precise, logical, and orderly submissions. While the amount of opinion work he got through caused McGill, who was a great leg-puller, to tease him and say that Muriel must help him with them at night.

Former Justice Harry Matthews, another contemporary, and a respected member of the Bench, remembered many shared cases "in the ordinary hurly-burly of the civil court", where he felt Gibbs was less happy than he clearly was in the Appeal Court presenting complex argument. One case neither of them ever forgot. They were in Cairns in the early 1950s, with Gibbs' junior counsel, Len Draney, acting in a big property case. This was a dispute between members of the well-known Williams family - brothers Clive, Henry, Syd (later Sir Sydney, founder of Bush Pilots), the young barrister Ned and their sister, who were disputing claims made by their cousins. The case involved a number of counsel. The senior counsel opposing was the only Queensland QC at the time, the courtly Arnold (later Sir Arnold) Bennett. Bennett presented a vast number of interrogatories (permitted, preliminary written questions). "Well over *1500*," recalls Matthews. "After we'd dealt with them, he took so long on the answers, we then had to go through another week just saying whether *we* had to answer questions that they refused to answer." When the case was finally settled they had a party to end all parties. "We were at the home of Syd Williams at about two in the morning," he recalled, "when the editor of the *Cairns Post* rang and wanted to know what he could put in the paper about the settlement. I was in somewhat better fettle than Bill or Len so I drove the pair of them in Fred Williams' meat truck to the Post Office to draft the headlines for the *Post*. All Gibbsy would say throughout that conversation was, `Yes, in heavy black type.' So, we got the headline in the *Cairns Post*, on the front page - in heavy black type."

Concurrently with his practice, Gibbs had, from 1948, extended his part-time lecturing for the University. He offered classes in Personal Property and Commercial Law, Evidence and Legal Interpretation. There were not many students. Most of the lecturers were, like Gibbs, practising barristers and the students went to their chambers for instruction. Among those who attended at the second floor of the old Inns of Court was a young student, Gerry Brennan, afterwards to become a colleague of Gibbs on the High Court. Brennan remembers the lectures in Evidence and Personal Property clearly: "We used to sit around his desk admiring the briefs, which were always piled in the natural angle of repose of briefs, as far as they could go on the side table. And apart from the splendid lectures that he gave us, he also gave us some practical experience of how to handle demanding solicitors." The hour long lectures started at 8 am and at about 8.30 the Gibbs telephone would start ringing. The calls were frequently from solicitors, anxious to know when they would get the opinion on the set of facts they had delivered to him. Brennan, with a flair for mimicry, has down to a fine art the succinct Gibbs' reply: "Yes? Yes. Yes. I have it. Yes, I have read it. Yes, I have given it some consideration. No, I haven't. I'm not sure when. I'm afraid I can't tell you. Thank you very much." The students absorbed the lessons of a busy counsel's practice. Another student to sit around Gibbs' desk a few years later, and thus begin a long association, was the young Ian Callinan. He found his lecturer in Evidence, "Very formal. Very helpful. Very lucid." Gibbs' innate reserve did not make for a warm student/lecturer relationship, yet his desire to help was evident.

Gibbs also edited the first numbers of *The University of Queensland Law Journal* (UQLJ), dedicating them to the five students of the Law School who had lost their lives in World War II. Assistant editors were Deputy

Chancellor and leader of the Bar, Alec McGill, Garrick Professor of Law, WNL Harrison and Gibbs' former mentor Dr Fry. The Officers of the UQLJ, other than Gibbs (the Editor), included two ex-servicemen and kindred spirits, with whom Gibbs was to form lasting bonds, Walter Campbell (later Sir Walter), a first class honours graduate who had just been admitted to the Bar, and the next first class honours graduate coming up, Peter Connolly (later Supreme Court judge), a fourth year Law student who was already lecturing in constitutional law. They cast their net wide for contributions to the journal. In the first number there was a foreword by Sir John Latham, Chief Justice of the High Court, and the Hon NW Macrossan, Chief Justice of Queensland. Contributors included Sir Owen Dixon (High Court Justice from 1929, Chief Justice 1952-1964), Professor GW Paton, Dean of the Faculty of Law, University of Melbourne, and Queensland's then Senior Puisne Judge, Hon AJ Mansfield (later Sir Alan, CJ). A senior Law School academic, Ross Anderson, took over the editorial duties in 1951 and Gibbs stayed as a member of the editorial board for another eight years. Gibbs, Campbell and Connolly were keenly interested. Other legal names such as Woolcock, Blair, Webb, Macrossan and Mansfield were also active in promoting the University itself and specifically its Law School. Connolly was Commanding Officer of the University Regiment for some time, while Gibbs and Campbell not only lectured extensively but were members of the Board of the Law Faculty. "Bill and I were both appointed in 1954," Sir Walter recalled. "He was not a man to push his views but he was always dogged in committee. And everybody paid great attention to what he said."

Another rising younger barrister, Kevin Ryan (later Law Professor and then Supreme Court judge), was appointed simultaneously with Gibbs to the Law Faculty Board and noted that Gibbs never missed a meeting. Ryan had taken over the greater portion of Gibbs' part-time lecturing in 1953, for Gibbs' practice as an appellate advocate was growing. He was often in Sydney and Melbourne at the High Court. He still, however, continued lecturing in Evidence, in spite of his demanding schedule, because of his involvement with the Bar as well as the University. Their students were the up and coming barristers and solicitors and Gibbs felt it important to assist with their training.

Gibbs and Campbell met frequently over these years, Campbell's strongly outgoing personality dovetailing well with Gibbs' quieter manner. They were both committee members of the Queensland Bar Association. Apart from the usual disciplinary and general matters affecting the Bar, they dealt with two particular issues of importance. First, there was the vexed question of reciprocity between the Queensland Bar and New South Wales. Opposed to the closed Queensland Bar, the State Labor Government consulted both Arnold Bennett QC and Gibbs as two of Brisbane's leading barristers.

*Arnold (later Sir Arnold) Bennett on his
appointment as QC.*

Gibbs was at first opposed to reciprocity - ie, allowing interstate practitioners ready access to each others courts. However, after consultation with members of the Bar he saw that the majority favoured reciprocity. He and Bennett, therefore, replied on behalf of the Bar that "they were not opposed to the principle of reciprocity as such".[2] Queensland legislation in 1956 allowed reciprocity of admission between the Australian States. The result was very much one way, with the disproportionately high admission in Queensland of 16 southern barristers, some very eminent. Among them was the country's greatest advocate, Sir Garfield Barwick QC. Reciprocity was soon seen as a serious threat to the Queensland Bar. The expert southerners might take the best work from the local barristers and starve Queenslanders of top experience. Bennett, Gibbs, Campbell and their fellow committee members debated the subject vigorously until the reciprocity statute was repealed by a new Country Party Liberal Coalition government in 1960. The time was not yet ripe for an Australian Bar. The other major question which concerned them was the re-establishment of the Queensland District Courts, which finally came about in 1960.

---

2 Ross Johnston, History of the Queensland Bar 18.

Doug McGill, friend of Gibbs and nephew
of former leader of the Bar, Alec McGill QC.

Throughout the 1950s, Gibbs appeared in many cases with Doug McGill and often as senior counsel to Ned (Sir Edward) Williams. One of the latter's cases highlights the problem of reciprocity with southern QCs at that time. "Bill didn't want to be in this one," Williams recalled, "but I pushed him hard. The case was *Phillott v Ballantyne*. Phillott was trying to retrieve money from a former girlfriend, Molly Ballantyne. It was connected with the wool boom and his family." It had become a matter of principle. Phillott badly wanted to win and Williams to win for him. A southern counsel had come up for Ballantyne and Harry Matthews was junior counsel. "The judge was giving me a hard time and deferring to the Sydney fellow," said Williams. Since Ballantyne had made significant admissions to him in court as to her lifestyle, this judge's partiality was beginning to upset Williams. So he rang Gibbs, who was in Sydney appearing before the High Court, and told him, "You've really got to help me, you owe it to me Gibbsy - I'm in trouble, I'm not getting anywhere at all." Gibbs agreed. On his return the next morning, he first completed a major opinion for the manager of Fairymead Sugar Mill, and was only able to listen to Williams for "what seemed like five seconds". Then he robed and went into court. "And there he was," recalled Williams, "cross-examining this important witness and he hadn't even heard the case! And it turned. Gibbs will never put a foot wrong. Never go too far. And the judge was saying, `Oh yes, Mr Gibbs?' We never looked back. It went to the High Court."

Williams tried hard, but unsuccessfully, to get Gibbs to apply for silk during these years. Williams also praised Gibbs for his nisi prius work (trial of fact before a jury, instead of judge(s) alone):

> People are inclined to say that Gibbs was only an Appellate Court lawyer - he was, he was the best. In my opinion he was better than Barwick because he had a better manner with judges. He could get his point across without being too pushy. And he didn't waste time. But you can't wipe Gibbs off as a nisi prius. Forget all the rhetoric, but in presenting the case he was terrific. As a criminal court lawyer, on factual matters I don't think he'd ever forget, and facts are the best arguments of all. Gibbs always got his facts out. Got his facts right. Got the relevant facts right. Made the point with his facts. He was a good nisi prius - a very, very good one.

The Deputy Crown Solicitor in Brisbane at this time, Andrew Menzies, later to work with Gibbs on a review of the Criminal Code, frequently briefed him for the Commonwealth government. Menzies recalled that, in major cases in Brisbane in the 1950s, Gibbs and Arnold Bennett were invariably on opposing sides. One case concerned compensation for the resumption of land from Doomben Racecourse for Eagle Farm Airport. It involved a great deal of money. In that instance, positions were reversed. Arnold Bennett (with Harry Matthews) was for the Commonwealth and Gibbs (with Ned Williams) for the individual representing Doomben racecourse. Justice Lyle O'Hagan, previously a Northern District Supreme Court judge in Townsville, was the presiding judge. O'Hagan had endeared himself to the profession and was described warmly by Sir Edward Williams as "a lovely fellow, a gentlemen, and very conscientious". It was this last quality which caused concern. He had suffered heart trouble for some years, in spite of which he insisted on inspecting the track and climbing the steward's box at Doomben to verify a point expounded upon by Gibbs and Williams. He collapsed with another heart attack. The judge made a swift recovery, but was seconded to Townsville temporarily to deal with an overload of work there and took with him his judgment on the Doomben case. Meanwhile, the Brisbane racing world, together with counsel, waited. The Doomben Racecourse management eventually received very substantial compensation.

The thrust and parry of court work fostered the mutual respect and liking Gibbs and Peter Connolly had for each other. "I often appeared against him - rather too often," recalled Peter Connolly, who was recognised for his exacting standards, penetrating analysis and sharp wit both as an advocate and later on the Bench. "Gibbs had the best mind in the business."

Gibbs' command of language, extensive knowledge of the law, excellent memory, and quickness in marshalling facts, secured his reputation. Junior counsel noticed that, when he was addressing the court and they handed him a law report with a relevant decision he had not seen before, he was capable of reading it and working it into his argument without interrupting the flow and clarity of his address or the answers to questions asked from the Bench. His colleague, Walter Campbell, remarked, "He was the only opposing counsel I feared."

It was the custom for those about to apply for silk to advise other members of the Bar that they intended to do so. Gibbs, hearing that another colleague and contemporary (from Ipswich schooldays) Douglas Campbell, later a Justice of the Queensland Supreme Court, was about to apply, was finally spurred to do so himself. They were awarded silk together in 1957. Gibbs was just 40, a comparatively young age. Five extremely busy years as a Queen's Counsel lay ahead, with more appearances before the High Court and a growing reputation in the southern states.

Chapter 4

THE SILK

One of Gibbs' appearances before the High Court as a fledgling QC in 1957 brought a comment from his junior counsel on the occasion, Harry Matthews, who felt that Gibbs' enviable reputation in southern capitals sometimes worked to his disadvantage. Counsel were being extensively briefed by transport companies to fight the Queensland Government's licensing fees. Before the Full Court of the High Court sitting in Melbourne, Gibbs and Matthews were appearing for Brown Transport of Toowoomba, and Sir Garfield Barwick, also with Matthews, for another Toowoomba-Brisbane trucking firm, Downs Transport, a subsidiary of Cobb & Co. "Bill and I worked very hard on it; we had 15 authorities," Matthews recalled. "Barwick didn't arrive in Melbourne until Sunday afternoon and the case was being heard the next morning." Barwick simply dropped in to discuss the case with them, produced a piece of foolscap and made a few notes, knowing that he could rely implicitly on Gibbs' work, and departed. Barwick was the first to make submissions in the morning and there was the whole meat of the case, competently and persuasively arranged. "A marvellous advocate," Matthews smiled at the recollection. "Barwick really stole the march on Bill that day. He quoted only one authority, otherwise thoughout his argument he was content to rely on all the propositions of law Gibbs had put up." In the event, they lost their case, but Cobb & Co eventually forced a settlement from the government. Barwick and Gibbs were destined to become High Court colleagues.

Gibbs and his friend, Doug McGill, were often briefed together on difficult cases, in one instance by O'Mara & Patterson on behalf of Stadium Pty Ltd, building owners of the recently built Festival Hall. The main contractor had gone bankrupt leaving sub-contractors "holding the baby", as Gerald Patterson put it, and inundated by claims under the Workmen's Lien Act, the validity of which they questioned. "We won our case before Justice Philp in the Supreme Court and, when the sub-contractors contributed to a fund and went up to the High Court, we won it there too," recalled Patterson with satisfaction. He had managed to hire or retain Gibbs just minutes ahead of the solicitor on the opposing side.

In April 1958, several Queensland counsel found themselves in Sydney waiting for cases to come before the High Court. The major case, *Attorney-General of Queensland v Wilkinson*,[1] concerned trading regulations on

---

1 [1958] Qd R 415.

petrol. The Full Court of the Supreme Court of Queensland had ruled against the new regulations (which prohibited the sale of petrol and oils etc before 7 am and after 6 pm from Mondays to Fridays, before 7 am and after 2 pm on Saturdays, or at all on Sundays) on the grounds that the Industrial Court of Queensland did not have jurisdiction to make the variation. The Attorney-General applied for special leave to appeal to the High Court. Feeling was running high in Queensland and many petrol vendors were flouting the law. It was a complicated matter, since union industrial regulations were involved. Ned Williams, who was representing several of the vendors, had asked Gibbs to lead him, while the Queensland Government had enlisted their favourite team, senior counsel Arnold Bennett, with Harry Matthews as junior.

Gibbs' friends, George Lucas and Lindsay Byth, both to appear in a sugar industry case, were in Sydney too. There was some delay in getting the cases before the Court. All, except the older and more sedate Bennett, went off to dine at a well-known Rose Bay restaurant built out over the water near the Sunderland Flying Boat Base. The group had a drink or two before dinner, then ordered suitable wines to accompany their three courses. Gibbs, never able to eat oysters or shell fish, found the newly available avocado with vinaigrette a good substitute. He followed this with John Dory (a favourite dish) and sweets, and sampled the various wines. Byth recalls that, before coffee and chocolates arrived, one member of the party gestured towards the large seagulls circling the Bay and shouted, "Look at the albatrosses!" It was a memorable night. Williams observed that his senior counsel was not feeling very well the next morning when the case began before Chief Justice Dixon and Justices McTiernan, Webb, Fullagar, and Taylor. "But he was perfect!" Williams recalled.

> Arnold was droning on and on, and Gibbsy stood up with a very good short point. He argued that Special Leave to Appeal should not be granted because the applicants are not persons injured by the order and had no locus standi in the matter. It really could have ended the whole thing, but the Chief Justice, Dixon, cut him off and said, "We've got to hear Mr Bennett." After the second day of this very dry argument of Arnold's, it was Gibbs' turn - he put his points up, one, two, three, four, succinctly as he always did, and Dixon leant across to Taylor, the judge on his right, and said in an audible whisper, "We should have let this fellow go yesterday, shouldn't have stopped him."

Justice Webb commented dryly, "The application was argued as fully as if it were an appeal."[2] The Supreme Court ruling was upheld, the application dismissed with costs, and Queensland drivers ceased being inconvenienced by restricted petrol sales.

---

2 (1958) 100 CLR 422 at 427.

Life was by no means all work. Bill lunched every week or so at the United Service Club with a wartime friend, Henry Becconsall, from the Commonwealth Law Office. He could also occasionally be found at a haunt of the legal profession for many years, the Johnsonian Club, or at that elegant mecca of the establishment, the Queensland Club. The Patterson friendship continued. He and Gerald used frequently to stop en route home at a quieter hotel, the Royal Exchange, at Toowong and have a drink or two in the leafy beer garden with some academic friends, Ross Anderson, Professor Gordon Greenwood and others. Summer holidays were also shared at Hervey Bay, Point Vernon on the central Queensland coast. This had been a favourite retreat of the Pattersons for some time. It was near Muriel Gibbs family's seaside home, so she decided to buy a holiday house there. This became the centre for family Christmas gatherings, and cemented their link with the Pattersons. The two families went swimming and boating and chasing the summer whiting, as Muriel loved to do. Their catches were not overwhelming but they went straight to the frying pan. As well, at home in Brisbane, Gerald Patterson was a great social organiser and the Gibbs were often to be found at lively parties, the host in full Rabelaisian swing, the hostess intermittently at the piano, English literature academics and medicos crossing amiable swords with meteorologists and the business identities who all formed part of Patterson's wide acquaintance. An occasional epigram from Gibbs remained in the memory, such as his comment on a controversial aspect of the *Voyager* sinking disaster: "Never resign in high dudgeon." Alternatively, Patterson organised tables of duplicate bridge at which total concentration was demanded in spite of the replenishment of glasses. "Sorry," a smiling Gibbs apologised for a wrong lead on one of these occasions, "a moment of aberration." It was a relaxing change from legal conferences, lectures, committee meetings and after dinner speeches.

Gibbs had, by 1960, consolidated the impression he had made on the scholarly, formidable High Court Chief Justice, Sir Owen Dixon, described by Prime Minister Menzies as "the great conductor" and by biographer Fricke in his *Judges of the High Court* as "a Bradman of the judiciary". Melbourne QC and editor of the *Commonwealth Law Reports*, James Merralls, was in 1960-1961 associate to Dixon. He recalls that Dixon said to him: "I suggest that you go down to Court today as there's a man called Gibbs appearing - Fullagar thinks he's pretty good." This was Dixon's way of saying that he thought Gibbs was pretty good. He often attributed his own views to other people whom he respected, rather than stating them directly himself. So young Merralls went down to hear Gibbs' submissions; it was a case about the jurisdiction of the Industrial Court of Queensland. "I was greatly impressed by his presentation," he said. "In the hands of anybody else, it would have been very dreary but he was lucid and incisive. He didn't have a demonstrative style but he was a very persuasive advocate, rather like a Queensland version of Keith Aickin (then a leading Melbourne QC, later a High Court Justice)." Merralls has a penchant for citing Queensland versions: a racing man, he described Sir Harry's accent not as Australian, but "very much Queensland, like an educated Keith Noud"! (Noud was a well-known racing commentator.)

Cases in Queensland proceeded apace. Gibbs and his friend Doug McGill shared many in these years, including a memorable one in Townsville, where McGill often appeared. They had, as McGill's wife Gwen put it, enjoyed "yet another successful battle followed by a thanksgiving dinner with a satisfied client". At the airport on their return, her husband was clutching a red frangipani which he said he was going to plant as "a constant reminder of Bill's brave actions in saving his barrister friend from a watery grave". They had been walking off the after-effects of the dinner, strolling out on a pier on the Ross River, when McGill, who walked with a pronounced limp, lost his footing and was swaying perilously over the water until grabbed and pulled back to safety by Gibbs. The frangipani still thrives outside the McGill home at Ashgrove in Brisbane, arresting the passerby with its brilliant splash of colour.

High as Gibbs' reputation was in the legal profession, he remained essentially a shy man, who kept a low profile. Symptomatic of this was his failure to become elected to the University of Queensland Senate when he stood in 1960, a disappointment for one so dedicated to the University and its affairs.

The Gibbs moved house again, this time to St Lucia in Brisbane and another of their favourite weatherboards, set in spacious grounds where Muriel could really enjoy her garden. Two major events occurred soon after. One was the unexpected enlargement of their family with the birth of a son, Harry, the fourth of the line - to the delight of Harry Gibbs senior and his wife in Ipswich and the discomfiture of the infant's schoolgirl sisters. The other was Gibbs' first appearance in London before the Judicial Committee of the Privy Council, the British Commonwealth's highest appellate court, on which he was later to sit.

His initial experience before Britain's law lords was in 1960, on behalf of the Queensland Government, in proceedings brought by licensed victuallers to test the validity of the State government's licensing fees. If the fees were in fact an excise, then, since it was exclusively a Commonwealth power to levy customs and excise duties, the licensing fees would be invalid. The Privy Council heard the application for special leave to appeal. Also appearing were counsel for the New South Wales and Victorian governments and for hotel interests in those States. Opposing Gibbs, for the Queensland Licensed Victuallers, was his old adversary, Arnold Bennett. The High Court had ruled in favour of the States. The Commonwealth and States were ranged against the hotel interests. Sir Garfield Barwick, the Attorney-General and Foreign Affairs Minister in the Menzies Government, arrived to represent the Commonwealth. His line of argument was that the Privy Council did not have jurisdiction to hear the appeal because the question whether State legislation dealt with a matter (namely duties of excise), in respect of which legislative power was exclusively vested in the Commonwealth, was a question inter se of the constitutional powers of the Commonwealth of Australia and that of the Australian States within s 74 of the Constitution,[3] and thus a matter within the exclusive jurisdiction of the High Court of Australia. The Privy Council granted special leave to appeal.

Gibbs, Bennett and southern counsel returned to London the following year when the case was argued. The licensed victuallers presented a strong argument and Gibbs was impressed by Arnold Bennett's address. Presenting the constitutional argument, the intricacies of which formed the kind of intellectual challenge he most enjoyed, Gibbs also excelled. Bennett was impressed in return. "Listening to Gibbs' address that day made me proud to be a Queenslander." The Privy Council advised that it had no jurisdiction to hear the appeals. The judgment was written by Lord Radcliffe, by then in the twilight of his judicial career. Accustomed to brilliant argument from Sydney and Melbourne silks, particularly from Barwick, whose advocacy they had positively enjoyed over many years, the English law lords now saw the best of the Queensland Bar.

The flight home from London that weekend was Gibbs' last as a barrister. He was approached immediately by Attorney-General Munro on behalf of the Nicklin Government to take up an appointment on the Queensland Supreme Court bench. He was to miss the varied and interesting life of a barrister, the camaraderie of the Bar and the egalitarianism of life in chambers and as an advocate. That was behind him now and the more solitary and rarefied role of the judge was to come.

---

3 The Constitution (as altered to 30 April 1991), s 74 (in part): "No appeal shall be permitted to the Queen in Council from a decision of the High Court upon any question, howsoever arising, as to the limits inter se of the Constitutional powers of the Commonwealth and those of any State or States, or as to the limits inter se of the Constitutional powers of any two or more States, unless the High Court shall certify that the question is one which ought to be determined by Her Majesty in Council."

Chapter 5

SUPREME COURT JUDGE

Gibbs' appointment in 1961 anticipated the retirement of Justice BH Matthews. It was necessary that Gibbs join the bench immediately, partly owing to the absence of the Senior Puisne Judge, Sir Roslyn Philp, who was chairing the Commonwealth Wool Marketing Inquiry, and partly due to pressure of matrimonial work expected upon the implementation of the new Commonwealth divorce laws. Barwick, in his previous career as Liberal Attorney-General in the Menzies government, had initiated a major reform: the inclusion of "the irreparable breakdown of the relationship" as a ground of divorce. So, at 44, at his peak as an appellate advocate and without a backward thought (financial disadvantage was inevitable), Gibbs accepted the new challenge and the judicial role for which he was admirably fitted. The Ipswich family - Harry Gibbs Snr, in retirement, had been elected a Liberal Alderman in that strong Labor city - assembled to see him take the oath as a judge before the Full Court of Queensland (Mansfield CJ, Matthews, Mack and Wanstall JJ). Gibbs had changed little in appearance or demeanour over the years: the same quick smile and unassuming and gentle, even courtly, manner.

Justice HT Gibbs in bench wig, 1961, soon after his appointment to the Queensland Supreme Court.

At the well attended ceremony conducted by the Chief Justice, Sir Alan Mansfield, legendary advocate Tom Barry QC, was spokesman for the Bar. He greeted the Hon Harry Talbot Gibbs to the Bench with real enthusiasm, not only because of his legal and scholarly attributes but because of "the characteristic modesty" with which he wore them: this, he said, had endeared Gibbs to them. Gibbs replied graciously, concluding:

> There are all too few countries in the world today where it can be truly said that public order and private liberty go hand in hand, but Australia is one country of which that can be said. It is due in no small measure to the fact that the law, both common and statute, is administered by a judiciary whose independence is beyond question. It is with humility that I come to play my small part in the process of the administration of the law.

He was to do so for 26 years, only seven of them in Queensland.

There were 12 members of the Supreme Court to deal with the ever increasing litigation demanded by Queensland's population of 1.5 million. The health of several was indifferent, including that of Justice WG Mack (later, Sir William, Chief Justice) and the very able Justice KR Townley. Absences were frequent, and the dilapidated old court building in George Street was crowded and inadequate. There had been talk by parliamentarians as early as 1946 about making additions, but as Justice BH McPherson observed wryly in his fine history of the Supreme Court of Queensland, "Finding more accommodation in and around the Supreme Court was still exercising Parliamentary minds in 1958".[1] The situation was not redressed for two decades. So Gibbs found himself in judicial wig and gown picking his way up the tortuous staircase leading to the back of the Bench. In wet weather - as a brother judge, EJD Stanley later recorded - it was necessary "to draw one's robes close about and sidle past a torrent of water that fell through the leaking roof".[2] The Criminal Court's slate roof was badly in need of repair.

Judging suited Gibbs' skills and temperament. His near contemporary, Peter Connolly, then a barrister (he took silk at 43 years of age in 1963), frequently appeared before him and grew to respect Gibbs' grasp of legal principle and intellectual integrity.

> Bill was a true professional. He's a man with a good sense of humour but he always had himself very much under control. You have people wasting your time, flogging away at dead horses, putting up propositions which everybody knows to be wrong - and they are busy courts. He could get

---

1 BH McPherson, The Supreme Court of Queensland 1859-1960 (Butterworths 1989) 369.
2 McPherson, ibid at 367.

impatient. But not often, not like most of us. A highly disciplined man.
His self-control has always fascinated me. As a single judge of this court he
dutifully followed decisions of the Full Court with which - it became clear
later when he was a member of the High Court and able to influence these
matters - he did not agree. He applied the law. The interpretation of the
law is intellectual. To see how its application goes to the facts is also an
intellectual problem. It doesn't consist of saying who you believe. It's "On
these facts, which it is open to the jury to find, how should the law affect the
outcome?" As a strict interpreter of the criminal law, particularly of the
Queensland Criminal Code, he was one of the very best.

Both Gibbs and Connolly, sitting in criminal cases, were meticulous when
summing up. They did not simply rely on their notes. They consulted the
transcripts of witnesses' words, as Connolly remarked, "to give the jury, they
being in fact the tribunal, the precise language used", thus ensuring that "you don't
either unwittingly understate something or state it with the wrong emphasis".

A young barrister of the day, now Justice CW (Bill) Pincus of the Queensland
Court of Appeal (formerly Brisbane-based member of the Federal Court of
Australia), was a student in Brisbane as Gibbs made his name as an appellate
advocate. He felt that, by fostering the barrister's opinion work, Gibbs set
the tradition in Queensland for senior counsel to write detailed opinions.
Pincus found later that Gibbs was excellent to appear before. "He was quick
and to the point, able to absorb a complicated set of facts, rearrange them and
produce them in due order." On the resignation of Sir Alan Mansfield as
Chief Justice in 1966, and the appointment of Sir William Mack, he had the
impression that Gibbs and Mack did not get along very well. There seemed
to be a clash of temperament. This was to prove correct.

Another member of the Queensland Court of Appeal, leading corporate law
jurist and legal historian, Bruce McPherson, then a barrister newly arrived
from South Africa via the UK, also commented on Gibbs' quickness of mind
and ability to deal expeditiously with cases. McPherson also admired Gibbs'
breadth of legal knowledge and found him to be an extremely hard worker.
He recalled that late one Friday afternoon when a case had just finished and
counsel expected to go home, Gibbs, after giving judgment, called the next
case. "He used that fifteen minutes!" Reflecting on Gibbs' legal philosophy,
he added:

> A Catholic colleague of mine described Bill Gibbs to me as a Presbyterian
> socialist in his attitude to the law, in that he liked to see the law achieve
> social justice. And I think that is a fact. He didn't follow a rule of law
> unnecessarily and blindly to its rigid conclusion. He was never described
> as a black letter lawyer, as some others are who are also good lawyers and

well-informed. He wasn't like that at all. He liked to see the law work in a way that was satisfactory, according to what seemed fair and right.

Gibbs' industry and efficiency were noted. In his history of the Queensland Supreme Court, McPherson commented that in the 1950s litigants suffered through government neglect of the State's judiciary. Steadily diminishing remuneration for judicial office had led some judges to view this as implying the right to a more leisurely existence. Few of those who still managed to disappear to cricket or Queensland Turf Club meetings well before four o'clock on a Friday afternoon took a beneficent view of the exacting work schedule Gibbs set himself. He was not universally popular and some personal frictions did develop.

Outspoken Independent Labor MP for South Townsville, Tom Aikens, specifically exempted Gibbs from his wrath directed at time-wasting judges in the Parliamentary debate in committee, when introducing the Supreme Court Acts Amendment Bill in 1963. The bill sought to increase the salaries of the judges: Chief Justice from $12,800 (then in Australian pounds 6,400) to $14,000 and each of the puisne judges from $11,800 to $12,800. The Minister for Justice, AD Munro, argued the fairness and reasonableness of the proposal in comparison with judicial salaries in the Commonwealth and other States. The fine debater and Leader of the Opposition, Jack Duggan, weighed in with a wide ranging speech covering disproportionate public service salary increases and attacked "high inflation caused by the extravagances of the Commonwealth Government". Aikens' amusing contribution quoted the Lord High Chancellor of England, Viscount Kilmuir ("Justice is not a cloistered virtue: she must be allowed to suffer the scrutiny and respectful, even though outspoken comments of ordinary men") in asserting his (Aikens') inalienable right to criticise judges. Judges imagined themselves, Aikens proclaimed, "apart from and above the ordinary herd...celestial beings, begotten by the deities" and spent far too much time in the "palatial parlours of the Queensland Club". He could see no justice at all in the proposed salaries which would mean a puisne judge would receive $246 a week while a fitter, paid at the basic rate for skilled work, received $38 a week. Aikens then attacked political appointments to the Bench, alleging that Gibbs was one, alleging he had been "campaign director and booth worker for his brother Wylie Talbot Gibbs" when he stood for Parliament. This inaccurate statement incensed the Attorney-General who upbraided Aikens and declared, "Mr Justice Gibbs is an outstanding lawyer in Australia as well as in Queensland." "You and I agree on that," replied Aikens peaceably. Gibbs had never been active in any political party and had never assisted his brother in electioneering. He was, though, pleased when Wylie, who had earlier stood for State Parliament, succeeded in winning the

Federal seat of Bowman (eastern Brisbane) and remained MHR for that electorate for the next six years. The Supreme Court Acts Amendment Bill was passed in due course, salaries increased, a fitting superannuation scheme for judges included, but the publicity given Aikens' barbs and consistent criticism of judges, in particular their short-cutting of Friday hours in court, found its mark.

Gibbs' first two associates, with whom, as with others to follow, he kept in touch throughout his career, recall different aspects of his qualities as a judge, observing him with youthful clarity. The first, then law student, now Supreme Court Judge, Glen Williams, admired the humanitarian in Gibbs:

> No matter how small a case, in terms of money or similar matters, he always gave it the same meticulous consideration. Everything he saw as a legal problem which demanded a resolution by applying the law, statute or civil, he did so. Yet he was able to sum up to juries in a simple language which they understood, and these remain precedents for other judges. While there may have been an aura of being aloof or remote, he was still able to assess the character of witnesses with an understanding of human nature.

The second associate, another up and coming student, David Jackson, now a leading Sydney QC and a former judge of the Federal Court, had been "struck by his very great technical competence and quickness". A year or two later, Jackson was appearing before Gibbs frequently as a junior barrister. "[Gibbs] had a natural gift for both the intellectual and practical aspects of the law," he commented. "He presided over a criminal trial as competently as he dealt with an argument on a point of law in the Full Court." Gibbs was outstanding among the Supreme Court judges because of this ability. "His being there raised the standard because others tried to emulate him, or not to be outdone by him. It was obvious that he was a judge of the first rank."

The mild mannered, unpretentious man of intellect rose, quietly but steadily, to judicial prominence in Queensland. He was appointed by the State Government in 1963 as Chairman of a Committee of Inquiry into the Expansion of the Australian Sugar Industry. A complex situation prevailed. The suspension in 1961 of trade between the USA and Cuba (then the world's largest sugar exporter) threw the world's sugar markets into turmoil. The quota provisions of the 1954 International Sugar Agreement became inoperative. Australia now commenced a sugar export trade with the United States, in addition to its existing trade with Japan and Commonwealth countries. In 1962, with a decline in Cuban sugar production under Castro's regime and the simultaneous failure, due to bad weather, of the European sugar beet crop, the sugar demand increased rapidly. Gibbs was joined by two committee members, Otto Wolfensberger (Chairman of the Sugar Board) and Norman King (Director of the Bureau of Sugar Experiment Stations), together with senior advisers from the Industry's Prices Board, the Cane Growers' Council, the Producers' Association and CSR. Their task was to recommend whether Australia should expand production in the highly volatile industry.

Gibbs' committee sat in Southern, Central and North Queensland coastal centres to receive evidence and submissions from those directly concerned with the Sugar Cane Industry: growers, millers, members of the Queensland Cane Growers' Council, the various Harbour Boards concerning terminals, and the Chambers of Commerce. They also conferred with overseas organisations. The project interested Gibbs and he met with a wide range of people along the Queensland coast. Then he and his two Committee members set off for the necessary overseas discussions.

In their detailed 35 page report,[3] which included assessment of markets, mill peaks and pool quotas, new cane areas, storage and harbour facilities, the Committee recommended that production should be increased but costs kept to a minimum. Fortunately, "the lands at present assigned are capable of producing 500,000 tons of sugar more than they were...[previously] permitted, and in many areas suitable additional lands are available in close proximity to, and often within, the existing mill areas." Facilities could be expanded without new mills being required. They advised expansion after discussions in Rome with the Food and Agriculture Organisation of the United Nations and with economists in London, New York and Washington. Gibbs observed the different manner in which the British and Americans conducted the discussions. "The English people would take one to lunch," he remarked, "a long lunch, various courses and wines. The Americans, on the other hand, would take you to breakfast - a working breakfast." He thought that this might be symptomatic of each country's approach to world affairs today.

The Report created an immediate furore. Many lashed it as an unmitigated disaster, contended that it would cause an appalling expenditure, and asserted that, at the very least, it was premature. Within two years, though, it was working to the satisfaction of the Government, mill owners and most of the growers. Brisbane QC, Ian Callinan, then a young barrister, and soon to represent the Queensland Cane Growers Council, remarked; "In spite of all

3 Report of the Committee of Inquiry into the Expansion of the Australian Sugar Industry (Chairman HT Gibbs) 1963.

the dire predictions, it turned out to be absolutely brilliant. It was a great success. The Queensland Sugar Industry has always been prone to hiccups but Gibbs made a very, very important strategic decision - which he got entirely right."

The Brisbane legal fraternity will not let Gibbs forget a story - apocryphal he says but now an ineradicable piece of Bar folklore - which came out of the crowded few weeks of sittings at centres along coastal Queensland. In Bundaberg, Gibbs, finding his way down to the hotel laundry with an array of shirts and sundry other items over his arm, came upon a stalwart longtime employee of the establishment known as Rosie. He gave a polite good morning, and then said, "How would you like to earn a few shillings? " Rosie opened her eyes wide and replied, "Lord above, not at this hour of the morning!"

Gibbs was back on the Bench for only a few months when his judicial duties were again interrupted. He was called upon to conduct a Royal Commission which was to have considerable ramifications in Queensland for the next two and a half decades and was to prove one of the most frustrating and difficult periods of his life.

Chapter 6

NATIONAL HOTEL ROYAL COMMISSION

Queensland's frontier and old world public values struggled in the 1960s to accommodate its new commercial dynamism, a direct result of the discovery of mineral reserves in Central Queensland which had galvanised the economy. Energy and dynamism always bring excesses. The sex industry, an old one in any society, was no stranger to Queensland's political and legal scene.

In October 1963, Opposition MLA for South Brisbane, Shadow Attorney-General Colin Bennett (supported by Independent MLA, former Labor Minister, Ted Walsh), alleged in Parliament that Police Commissioner Frank Bischof and members of the Licensing Branch of the Queensland Police Force were drinking after hours and condoning and protecting a call girl service at Brisbane's National Hotel. Leader of the Opposition Jack Duggan handed Premier Nicklin a list of names, which included 88 members of the Consorting Squad, CIB and Licensing Branch. The government defended the police force in parliament. But, within a fortnight, Nicklin decided to hold a Royal Commission. He appointed Justice Gibbs of the Supreme Court to inquire into the allegations. Gibbs stood, in Ian Callinan's opinion, "head and shoulders above others" in the State in outright ability. His integrity was unquestioned. He was a logical choice for the government. Experienced barrister, later Judge and Chairman of the District Court, Lindsay Byth was appointed counsel instructing.

The terms of reference were narrow. One hotel only - the National - was to be investigated and over a specific period, from 1958. The Commission had few investigative resources. Several police personnel, including a then unknown Detective Sergeant (later State parliamentarian) Don Lane, were seconded to assist and serve subpoenas; it also lacked authority to offer indemnity from prosecution to persons giving evidence.

This was a sensational matter. Public interest was intense. In addition to Commissioner Bischof, and Chief Inspector Bauer, the publicly-prominent Detectives Tony Murphy and Glen Hallahan were among the 88 police listed.

The Government retained their favourite QC, leader of the Bar, Arnold Bennett, together with rising barrister (later Justice) Jim Dunn. The National Hotel interests (the Roberts family) were represented by Doug McGill QC and John Macrossan (later Chief Justice, Supreme Court). The police had an array of silks, headed by Walter Campbell QC (later Chief Justice) with Jack Aboud, for Bischof, and James Douglas QC (later Justice), together with experienced counsel such as Len Draney (later QC) and former Rhodes Scholar (later QC) Cedric Hampson.

Gibbs and the counsel were shown over the National Hotel one morning before sittings commenced. It stood at Petrie Bight at the far end of Queen Street, with a dramatic view of the twin steel peaks of Story Bridge and Kangaroo Point cliffs. The hotel had previously been one of the pleasant old-fashioned, white damask tablecloth variety favoured by country people visiting town, but had recently been modernised and was painted a garish pink. *Pix* magazine described it at the time in its full evening glory - pink bars with cigarette girls in mesh tights to match, piped music, steak house and a floor show featuring befeathered and bespangled dancers. It attracted a lively clientele. The accusation was that the police, whose duty it was to inspect the premises regularly, in fact frequented the hotel, indulged in illegal after hours drinking and condoned and encouraged a call girl service. The hearing lasted 34 sitting days, over the summer of 1963-1964. *Pix* described the courtroom scene in its 1963 Christmas edition:

> In a stuffy old-fashioned courtroom in the big Supreme Court building, sits Royal Commissioner Mr Justice Gibbs crowded amongst a pile of law books and papers...He is neither wigged nor gowned...and before him as the case opens are a score of legal men representing parties in the case...In the public gallery, reached by a tortuous climb of 59 steps, spectators unable to obtain seats sit crouched on the mat covered steps intent on peering through an iron grille.

From the beginning there were difficulties. Colin Bennett had made his allegations in Parliament. His 30 minute speech attacked the administration of the Queensland Police Force generally. He thought the Inquiry's terms of reference were too narrow and simply a "face-saving" exercise for the Government. When he was called in a preliminary hearing as a witness, he retained Gerard Brennan to appear for him. Bennett had decided he ought not to give evidence and sought the Commissioner's ruling that to compel him to do so would constitute a breach of parliamentary privilege, since he had been asked to attend to give evidence based on his comments in the House. "Sir Harry's ruling on that, upholding the view which Mr Bennett was advancing," said Brennan, "was regarded as perhaps one of the most important constitutional rulings that have been made in Queensland."

It also made getting at the truth more difficult. The Secretary to the Commission and Gibbs' associate at the time, David Jackson, remarked, "I have no doubt that it suited the Government of the day to put Colin Bennett in a position where the public felt that he should `put up or shut up'...but at the time his refusal to substantiate his allegations made it seem that there was not likely to be much in them. To my mind that was a turning point in the Inquiry."[1]

Gibbs had also decided, in abundant fairness to the police against whom inaccurate testimony was to be expected, to adhere to strict rules of evidence: "Although in my inquiry I was not bound by the rules of evidence...I did endeavour to adhere to those rules as far as possible...As a general rule, I did not allow hearsay statements.". He thus adopted, as Queensland historian Dr Ross Fitzgerald commented in 1990 in a detailed analysis of the Inquiry,[2] "a judicial ethos". Fitzgerald argues that it was inappropriate. Judged in the bright light of retrospect, Gibbs was fighting a rather substantial war with duelling weaponry only.

Commissioner Gibbs and counsel leave the National Hotel after making their inspection. Foreground (left-right): Gibbs' associate, David Jackson, Doug McGill QC, Instructing Councel Lindsay Blyth, Commissioner, Justice HT Gibbs. Background, centre: Walter Campbell QC. (Photo courtesy of The Courier-Mail)

---

1 See, generally, The Independent Weekly, series on National Hotel Enquiry, 16-29 April 1993.
2 Prasser, Wear and Nethercote (eds), Corruption and Reform, The Fitzgerald Vision (UQP).
See Ross Fitzgerald's chapter at 61-80, "Judicial Culture and the Investigation of Corruption: A Comparison of the Gibbs National Hotel Enquiry 1963-64 and the Fitzgerald Inquiry 1987-89".

Ian Callinan was senior counsel assisting the Fitzgerald Inquiry. He put a similar view in a comprehensive paper delivered to the Tasmanian Bar Association in 1988 entitled: "Commissions of Inquiry - A Necessary Evil?". But the much broader Fitzgerald Inquiry was twenty-five years on, and in a different era. A better educated public, spurred by media revelations of corruption - specifically Phil Dickie's articles, beginning in January 1987, and the ABC Chris Masters' award-winning television program, "The Moonlight State" - were demanding action. By 1974, Glen Hallahan had again been the subject of an inquiry. This followed revelations by the controversial prostitute Shirley Brifman that she had lied at the Gibbs Inquiry. Author Peter James wrote and published a critical analysis of the National Hotel Commission of Inquiry entitled "In Place of Justice". He commented:

> Whether a similar enquiry would be allowed to proceed today, with as much lack of critical journalism, is open to debate. So, too, is the question of whether the same conclusions would be drawn from the same evidence. We stand, now, on the superior knowledge of official duplicity, political secrecy, Vietnam atrocities like sacrifices to a false god, preferential shares to Cabinet Ministers, company salting of drill cores, Watergate...[3]

In the early 1960s, an easy going Queensland public, including its most literate and well-informed segment, had heard rumours that Police Commissioner Bischof was prepared to blink an eye at the activities of Queensland's Starting Price (SP) bookmakers and knew that in Brisbane, as in any city, indeed township, in the world, prostitution was practised. But there was no widespread suspicion of institutionalised police corruption. The public were wary of politicians but generally held members of the police force in high regard. Sadly, revelations and allegations, fair and unfair, were to undermine this fine reputation.

The Commission, as is the nature of commissions, was inquisitorial. Bischof, Bauer, Murphy, Hallahan and others, were required to give evidence. So, too, were Shirley Brifman, a key witness, and several other prostitutes. A feature of the Gibbs Inquiry was the adversarial quality of the proceedings. This was brought about by the large number of Queen's Counsel, "the weight of silk", as David Jackson put it, representing Cabinet, police and the National Hotel. They examined and cross examined witnesses rigorously. So did Gibbs' Counsel Instructing, Lindsay Byth, and counsel (later Justice) Brian Ambrose, representing the principal witness, former National Hotel waiter, David Young. The other dominant, and finally defeating, aspect was the solid wall of silence preserved by the police.

---

3 The Weekend Independent 5 March 1993 at 14-15.

"[Commissioner] Bischof, after giving evidence himself, sat each day at the back of the court and conferred in murmurs with others," Jackson recalled. The police had evidently closed ranks and, as Lindsay Byth remarked, "were just not talking". He expanded on this in his farewell speech as Chairman of the District Court Bench in 1987:

> I remember I called more than ninety witnesses, but whenever a line of enquiry looked promising a brick wall seemed to descend. One witness said he had stayed in the hotel during the relevant period. I asked him whether he ever saw girls there, who might be call-girls. Answer: No. Question: Did you ever see any activities between girls and possible customers? Answer: No. Question: Did you ever see any policemen with girls? Answer: No. (And so on). Eventually I asked, "Don't you want to assist His Honour?" "No."

Predictably enough, the evidence was conflicting. David Young, who had initially come forward with allegations of police corruption, proved an inconsistent witness. He contradicted himself on a number of occasions, and was further discredited by Brifman. She committed perjury, stating, falsely, that Young had performed an abortion on her. In 1971, she admitted on ABC television that she had lied to protect Detectives Murphy and Hallahan. Six months later she was found dead in suspicious circumstances. John Komlosy, an emotional Hungarian, who had briefly been employed as a night porter, supported Young in his allegations but proved an even more unreliable witness. Gibbs, in his *Report*, found that his evidence,

> contained violent inconsistencies, was a curious compound of fact, hearsay, exaggeration, theory and invention...sometimes truthful in substance, although not altogether accurate in detail...he sometimes borrowed an idea from the evidence of David Young and developed it to fit his own story.

A then little known member of the Licensing Branch, Detective Sergeant Jack Herbert (the infamous "bagman" who later featured at the Fitzgerald Inquiry as an indemnified witness), also committed perjury and testified that Komlosy, the former night porter, had told him he made the allegations to "get even" with the National Hotel for dismissing him. Komlosy announced that he had once seen the Police Commissioner at the hotel at 1 am: "Police were being served liquor and prostitutes were all over the place." Other witnesses stated that Commissioner Bischof was a personal friend of the licensee, Max Roberts, which explained his presence at the hotel on several occasions: he was not a frequent visitor. The compere of the hotel floor show, John Bernard James, kept a straight face and stated, "I wouldn't know a prostitute if I saw one. Nobody told me about prostitutes being there." Several prostitutes, including Dona Youse, testified to having used the hotel "a number of times". McGill, counsel for the hotel interests, became testy with another who could not remember ever having seen the night porter Komlosy. Others who might have given evidence had fled across the State border and so were outside the Inquiry's jurisdiction.

Gibbs, when in doubt, was cautious and legalistic. He remarked in his *Report* that he had refused the application of counsel Brian Ambrose that it be ascertained whether the National Hotel was mentioned in any of the forms required to be lodged by medical officers under the State's venereal disease regulations. Also, when a witness whose credit was attacked named another person as having been involved in illegal or improper conduct and the assertion was not corroborated, Gibbs ruled against allowing its publication on the grounds that it might do unwarranted damage to that person's reputation.

Compounding the difficulties of narrow terms of reference, lack of investigative resources, legislative constraints and an inability to offer indemnities, was a strictly formal approach. This, Callinan said, was "not likely to be effective". Ross Fitzgerald put it more bluntly: "Continuing to play the game is not the way to get corrupt players off the field." In hindsight it is clear that the Inquiry's scrupulous attention to fairness made it ineffective: its method was too legalistic and unadventurous for the task.

In February 1993, the University of Queensland newspaper ran a series of five features over several months on the National Hotel Inquiry, with headings such as "Analysis of a Failed Inquiry" and major articles by the journalist and, later, Reader in Journalism at the University, Evan Whitton. These are supplemented by substantial comments from others, such as Dr Ross Fitzgerald, writer Peter James, former parliamentarian Colin Bennett, the Secretary to the Gibbs Inquiry, David Jackson QC, and key witness David Young. Gibbs himself gave short answers to questions put to him.

This series is even-handed but offers harsh judgment. Sir Thomas Hiley, who eventually "blew the whistle" on Bischof in 1965, and former Deputy Premier Bill Gunn, who was later responsible for initiating the Fitzgerald Inquiry, alone receive any praise. Whitton makes no secret of his dislike of the Australian, English-based, judicial system, preferring the inquisitorial European method. This dislike extended to one of the more conservative exponents of it. His anti-Gibbs bias led to weak journalistic gambits. Gibbs was not simply appointed, but "gained employ on the High Court in 1970" and received the "relatively inferior" knighthood, KBE, that "went with the job". When Gibbs was appointed Chief Justice of Australia, he had been awarded a very high honour - the GCMG. Whitton referred to it as "God Calls Me God". Whitton, however, concedes that Gibbs' reason for applying judicial rules of evidence in the 1964 Inquiry was to ensure scrupulous fairness to the police.

During the 34 sitting days of the Inquiry, prime witness Young complained that he himself seemed to be on trial. His health suffered when he received threatening phone calls. The highly strung Komlosy gave evidence which was not sufficiently consistent to corroborate Young's. Gibbs permitted him to return to Europe before the end of the Inquiry. Colin Bennett and his wife were also harassed by threatening phone calls, while at the Gibbs home at St Lucia, Muriel Gibbs fielded a number of nuisance calls.

It was a bleak period. The lack of any sort of breakthrough from police witnesses began to weigh on Gibbs. At the Johnsonian Club for lunch one day, when asked how things were going, he replied dryly, "I'm beginning to wonder if there is a National Hotel." Public discussion freely included phrases such as "set up" or "whitewash". "We got nowhere," Gibbs commented later:

> The police just turned up - they were simply not talking. There was no evidence at all that there was a call girl service. There was some slight evidence that prostitutes had been seen in the hotel occasionally. But prostitutes can be seen in any hotel occasionally. We had no investigative staff, no means ourselves to go out and find evidence. Moreover, we had no power to give anyone an indemnity, which is an effective way of making people talk.

He handed his *Report* to Premier Nicklin - whom Whitton dubbed "Honest Frank Nicklin" - in April 1964. Gibbs found that the liquor laws had been breached at the National Hotel from 1958 without the detection of the police (he made recommendations for the tightening of these laws). But there was insufficient evidence of a call girl service being conducted or condoned and "no acceptable evidence that any member of the Police Force was guilty of misconduct, or neglect or violation of duty in relation to the policing of the hotel".

The denouement is a matter of history. Between 1964 and 1988, no less than seven inquiries were held on police corruption, several initiated by Police Commissioner Whitrod, and several involving either Detective Murphy or Detective Hallahan (who were both cleared). It was not until the Ahern government's appointment of Tony Fitzgerald QC in 1988 (a move initiated by Deputy-Premier Bill Gunn) to head a comprehensive inquiry, with wide powers, that the extent of police corruption became known. Indemnified witness, corrupt policeman, Jack Herbert testified that he "had actively sought to become involved in corruption after joining the licensing branch in 1959".[4] It was subsequently revealed that corruption was endemic under Commissioner Bischof's administration. Justice Harry Matthews commented in 1989, "We were all amazed at the breadth and depth of the corruption." The upheaval, trials and convictions that followed the disclosure of those 29 years of corruption are now well reported. Is it possible that the 1964 Inquiry could have succeeded if different rulings had been adopted? Could a more interventionist-style Commissioner have proved the catalyst and provoked a police witness into talking? Opinions remain divided.

Critics contend that Gibbs was miscast in the role of commissioner for that specific inquiry, but still consider that the outcome at the time was inevitable. Sir Edward Williams, who led the Queensland contingent in the Australian Royal Commission into Drugs (1977-1980) and on his return conducted an inquiry, commented: "I would defend Sir Harry to the hilt in regard to the National Hotel Inquiry. That was a case without possibility. You can only find on the evidence. In the 1980 drug inquiry, with just two Federal Police assigned to us, we didn't crack any of the witnesses either. [Former Detectives Murphy and Hallahan, by then a farmer, were among them.] We didn't have any outside evidence, and we didn't have any indemnities." The 1964 Inquiry which, by convention, lacked investigative staff and indemnities, had little chance of success. "The prospect of digging anything out was remote", said David Jackson. "The times were not right," added Sir Walter Campbell, who withdrew as counsel halfway through the Inquiry because of other commitments. Journalist and academic, Evan Whitton, disagrees and so, to some degree, do Dr Ross Fitzgerald and Ian Callinan QC.

Replying to queries in April 1993, Gibbs said he felt the terms of reference in 1964 were adequate for their purpose, but admitted that, in light of the Fitzgerald Inquiry, "there may well have been evidence which was not disclosed to my inquiry but which, had it been available, might have led to a different result. The Fitzgerald Inquiry was able to offer indemnities to witnesses which I could not." Gibbs clung to his principles doggedly. "I should add, however, that opinions differ as to whether it is desirable for any inquiry to offer such indemnities."

Whitton apportioned "blame" almost equally to Mr Justice Gibbs and Arnold Bennett QC, the latter for not insisting on a wider brief from the Government (Callinan also notes that Bennett QC, treated the Government and Police

---

4 Courier-Mail report of on-going Fitzgerald Inquiry, 1 September 1988 at 4.

Force as "monolithic") and both for accepting the "defective legislation" setting up the inquiry without question. Whitton remains convinced that Gibbs did much to bring the negative result upon himself.

Tony Fitzgerald QC, later President of the Queensland Court of Appeal, judged Gibbs more sympathetically. "It is easy to understand those findings," he commented in his own Report.[5] "Nothing in the terms of reference or structures of the Royal Commission, including the range of parties represented before it, the assistance and facilities available to it, and the evidence which it received, or the social and political environment of the time, would have alerted it to the possibility that it confronted an orchestrated cover up based on, and supported by, institutionalised police attitudes and practices."

---

5 Report of a Commission of Inquiry into Possible Illegal Activities and Associated Police Misconduct (GE Fitzgerald Chairman) (1989), known asThe Fitzgerald Report. See p 34.

Chapter 7

CHANGE OF SCENE

After those frustrating months, Gibbs was relieved to return to the Supreme Court Bench and resume his duties as a judge. He drew strength from his stable and contented family life. Emeritus Professor Reg Gynter, a neighbour at St Lucia, recalled the Guy Fawkes' celebrations and gatherings in the Gibbs garden, and how much Gibbs enjoyed them.

> Bill took charge, an occasion when he could release his many pent up frustrations and inhibitions. There were bangs, explosions, sparkling displays and joyous whoops of encouragement to his young son Harry. This was in marked contrast to the quiet and serious judge his court would receive next day.

Gibbs was able to relax in his leisure hours. He remained a voracious reader, some work of literature or history could always be found on his desk or bedside table. His tastes range widely. It would be as likely to find a modern satirical novel brushing shoulders with Hardy or Flaubert, or a book of contemporary collected poetry with John Donne, Gibbon with Manning Clark or Blainey. He also played tennis fairly regularly, and had become an energetic amateur photographer, with an uncanny talent, his friend Patterson complained, for presenting his slides - "of the Colosseum or whatever" - upside down.

That year, 1964, a new college, International House, opened at the University of Queensland. The tall, distinctive pagoda-style building creating a central focus for the growing number of Asian, American and other overseas students. Gibbs was asked to accept the ancient office of Visitor, "with power to issue admonitions, decrees and instructions", an office of last resort for internal university complaints and conflicts. He found it to be a sinecure at the college. It was smoothly run under Warden Ivor Cribb and Gibbs has never had to resolve any disputes.

A tragedy marred the year. The Gibbs were at Hervey Bay, out in their dinghy fishing, when a signal from the shore brought them swiftly in. News had been received that Gibbs' close friend, Doug McGill, had been killed in a car accident. A badly shaken Gibbs returned immediately to Brisbane to be with Doug's wife, Gwen, and their children. The families' friendship went back to the immediate post-war years, the sharing of crowded chambers and the building of their practices at the bar, and had strengthened over the years. McGill's death ended one of the happiest associations of Gibbs' barrister days.

During his seven years on the Supreme Court, Gibbs sat on a number of appeals. One criminal appeal, *R v Pollard*,[1] concerned a charge of unlawful use of a motor vehicle. The accused claimed that he held an honest belief that the owner would have consented to the use if asked: an honest claim of right. The District Court judge had ruled that "on the evidence presented there did not arise for the consideration of the jury the question whether the accused's acts were done in the exercise of an honest claim of right without intention to defraud". (Section 22 of the Criminal Code provides, inter alia, that "a person is not criminally responsible, as for an offence relating to property, for an act done or omitted to be done by him with respect to any property in the exercise of an honest claim of right and without intention to defraud"). The jury returned a verdict of guilty. The appeal was heard by the Criminal Court of Appeal (Stanley, Hanger and Gibbs JJ). The question was whether the honest claim of right should have been left to the jury. Gibbs' judgment, agreed to by his brother judges, displays a lucid style:

> At his trial in the District Court the accused gave evidence that he resided at a boarding house in which one Birt, the owner of the vehicle, also resided and that he and Birt became friends and often took their recreation together. On the night in question the accused wished to go to a speech night function at the Wynnum High School, and being unable to claim a taxi took the keys of Birt's vehicle from Birt's bedroom, and drove the vehicle, although he had no license to drive a motor vehicle and although he had not asked Birt (who had gone out for the evening) for his consent. He said that he did not think that Birt would have any objections to his taking the vehicle and that he took it because he believed that if he had asked Birt he would have consented.

Gibbs continued: "It is well settled that a claim of right sufficient to relieve a person of criminal responsibility need only be honest and need not be reasonable". He concluded that the question should have been left to the jury: "It is not to the point that the accused had no right to take the vehicle. If he had honestly believed that he was entitled to take it, or if the jury had a reasonable doubt whether he had such a belief, he should have been acquitted, however wrong his belief may have been, and however tenuous and unconvincing the grounds for it may seem to a judge." The accused was acquitted.

In August 1966, Naida Haxton, the first woman to practise at the Queensland Bar, was admitted. Others, such as Una Prentice, had been admitted much earlier, but had practised either as solicitors or in Crown employment or in

1 [1962] QWN 13; 3 QJPR 45.

another State. Some of these practised later at the Queensland Bar. Gibbs sat on the Bench the day Haxton was admitted - and subsequently observed her career with interest. She practised for some years, creating her niche in Queensland legal history, and later moved with her husband to Sydney where she became a legal editor.

Gibbs' career ambitions were soon to take him out of Queensland and into the federal sphere. There was, indeed, as Bill Pincus (now a judge of the Queensland Court of Appeal) had observed, a lack of accord, amounting to a clash of personalities, between Gibbs and the longest serving member of the Supreme Court, Justice William Mack. Pincus described Mack as a "charming, brilliant but erratic man". In 1966, with the retirement of Chief Justice, Sir Alan Mansfield, to become State Governor, matters came to a head.

Sir Walter Campbell, then President of the Australian and Queensland Bar Associations, recalled, "Many of us thought, I certainly did - there was a strong move, a strong opinion - that Gibbs, the outstanding lawyer, should be appointed [Queensland] Chief Justice. However, he was very much junior and eventually Mr Justice Mack was appointed. Bill of course was disappointed about that, and at the same time there was talk of a Federal Court being set up."

Former Queensland Supreme Court judges. (From the left) Justices Stanley, Gibbs, Townley, Walter Campbell and Stable.

Justice HT (Bill) Gibbs and his wife Muriel at a garden wedding, Hervey Bay, 1966.

Gibbs did not wish to serve under Mack for any length of time. The two brief biographies of Mack included in official histories[2] indicate that Mack's and Gibbs' attitudes to judicial duties diverged considerably, the former's somewhat flexible hours (sporting interests beckoned on Friday afternoons) being anathema to the latter. It was an uncomfortable situation. Moves were meanwhile being made in the south, with the support of the Law Council of Australia and its then president, John Kerr QC, for the establishment of a Superior or Federal Court to relieve the overworked High Court in some areas of federal law. The then Chief Justice of the High Court, Sir Garfield Barwick, and others with federal influence thought highly of Gibbs. It was intimated to him that he would be appointed to the new court, if it were

---

2 Johnston, History of the Queensland Bar (1969) 93 and McPherson, The Supreme Court of Queensland 1859-1960 (1989) 384-385.

established. Gibbs and the Queensland judiciary generally were of the opinion that the jurisdiction of the State Supreme Courts should be expanded to relieve the High Court, but it was clear that this was not the course the federal government intended to take. Therefore, if a Federal Court were soon to be set up by Act of Parliament, then it was necessary to be pragmatic. In the interim, Gibbs could be appointed to the Bankruptcy Court. He immediately resigned from the Queensland Supreme Court, displaying a decisive readiness to gamble on his ability. It also highlighted his grander ambitions which, in his low key style, were nonetheless firm. He now wanted to play out his talents on the national stage. With the move towards uniformity and national laws, he saw that the federal courts were going to be busy and influential.

His departure for Sydney in 1967 was a significant loss to the Queensland Supreme Court. For him personally it was hard. The Gibbs family were dedicated Queenslanders. They did not want to leave, and the timing could hardly have been worse. The children (aged 19, 17, 15 and 8) were at formative levels in their education.

In 1967, Gibbs took up an appointment as a Federal Judge in Bankruptcy and as a Judge of the Supreme Court of the ACT. He bought a house in Sydney's North Shore suburb of Killara. It was a leafy area, reminiscent of Queensland, but there was little room for even a makeshift cricket pitch for their son Harry, to whom his father continued to bowl an over or two each day.

Several frustrating years followed for Gibbs. His hasty departure from Brisbane began to look like folly. The new Federal Court did not eventuate as expected (it was not established until 1974), and the ACT component of the appointment involved only a 21 day period several times each year in Canberra. After the diversity of his Supreme Court years, Gibbs found interminable bankruptcy proceedings very dull. "It nearly drove him mad," said Muriel. "Fortunately, John Kerr and his first wife, Peggy, were very kind to us." They had known each other since their Melbourne days in 1946, when the men had worked together at the Directorate of Research and Civil Affairs, shaping laws for post-war New Guinea. John Kerr was then a highly regarded judge of the Commonwealth Industrial Court, and a fellow judge with Gibbs of the Supreme Court of the ACT. Kerr's friendship was most welcome in the comparatively formal atmosphere among the federal judges Gibbs met at Temple Court.

Another bright spot was the new character who became an integral part of Gibbs' life for 13 years. Soon after his appointment, Gibbs rang the Repatriation Department and asked them to find him a tipstaff, to assist in the smooth running of complicated court procedures, arrangements for travel between courts, and so on. Gibbs interviewed an ex-Navy and ex-policeman, Jack Davis. He had been injured during naval action in World War II. Physically big and an extrovert, he was a devoted family man and father of seven children. He had risen to police sergeant, but had been "booted out", as he put it, after sustaining a serious back injury in a car accident. He liked "the Judge" immediately and the feeling was mutual. When the phone call came telling him he had the position he was overjoyed. Arriving at Gibbs' Chambers at Temple Court, he felt obliged to warn Gibbs that he was indeed something of a physical wreck, with "only about six discs left in [his] spine" and persistent problems, sinus and asthma. "That's alright, Mr Davis," said the judge. "I'm employing you. Anytime you're sick, I accept it." And so began a lasting and fruitful relationship.

Gibbs made a practice of introducing Davis to whomever might come in, something the tipstaff greatly appreciated. Davis was to meet a galaxy of Australian and overseas judges and politicians. He recalled that, on his very first day, "about quarter to five, a large white-haired gentleman burst into the Judge's Chambers", and greeted him exuberantly. Davis was introduced and was asked, "Are you a Queensland rabbit?" No. "A relation?" No. "Well, you must be good then!" said John Kerr, who then went with Gibbs for a Scotch. After three weeks, Gibbs insisted that the formal "Mr Davis" and "Sir" be dropped and it became "Jack" and "Judge". This was acceptance and Davis became an asset in every way, taking pride in having all necessary reference books in court "crossed and ready right beside the Judge so that he needn't waste a minute"; seeing that Brisbane's *Courier-Mail* was procured early each day (Gibbs liked to keep in touch with doings in his home State); that the portrait the Judge valued so highly of Sir Samuel Griffith by an unknown artist (Gibbs had bought it from the estate of Sir Thomas Clyne) was hanging straight above the desk; that a salad lunch was always on hand; that flights to Canberra were booked and a car (with tipstaff aboard) was outside the judge's home at Killara on the appointed day at 6 am "on the dot". Anything he could do for the Gibbs family beyond the call of duty was also done promptly and willingly. Davis stayed with Gibbs for 13 years, smoothing his path in all practical matters, including such emergencies as the disruption to court travel arrangements caused by Australian pilots' strikes. Davis' long experience made him caustic on the role of judges' associates: the bright recent law graduates who spend a year as assistants to the judges. They needed tuition on procedure from tipstaffs in their first three months, said Davis, they tried to tell tipstaffs what to do in the next six months and, "in the their last three months, when they're going out to get a job, they don't care."

Bill and Muriel Gibbs took their annual mid-winter leave, without family, in Fiji that year. Gibbs was glad to get away from insolvencies, failed finances and unhappy debtors and creditors. Nevertheless, as the then barrister Bill

The Hon Harry Talbot Gibbs, appointed a Justice of the High Court of Australia on 24 July 1970 by the Governor-General, His Excellency the Rt Hon Sir Paul Hasluck PC, GCMG, KStJ. Gibbs was knighted several months later and dubbed Sir Harry.

Pincus noted, "He even managed to make bankruptcy judgments sound like music." There was in fact a fine scholarly tradition at the Bankruptcy Court, where the learned Victorian, Justice Sir Thomas Clyne, had reigned for 25 years. A then leading Melbourne QC, Daryl Dawson (later a colleague of Gibbs on the High Court), who occasionally appeared there, saw that there would not be a falling away in standards. "Sir Harry was very pleasant in the Bankruptcy Court," he remarked. "He had a marvellous gift for putting things clearly, was obviously as bright as a button, very much to the point, and you knew you were going to be tested to the limit by him." The mot juste, it seems, had not deserted him, but it was a difficult time, compounded by the sudden death of his father with a heart attack.

Harry Gibbs Snr died at his home in Thorn Street, Ipswich, aged 83 years, on 10 August 1969. His inherent gentleness of nature had endeared him not only to his sons, family and friends but to the wider community in Ipswich. This was apparent in the obituary in the city's newspaper, *The Queensland Times*, on which he had served as a director for 22 years, providing expert legal advice during the course of his 30 years in practice as a solicitor (Walker & Walker). The obituary lauded his war service, his contribution as honorary solicitor to the Ipswich sub-branch of the RSL and subsequent granting of life membership, his

The High Court sitting in No 1 Courtroom at Darlinghurst, Sydney (1970), after the swearing in of Sir Harry Gibbs. (Left-right): Walsh J, Windeyer J, McTiernan J, Barwick CJ, Menzies J, Owen J, Gibbs J.

term as an alderman of the Ipswich City Council, and terms as president of the city's Legacy Club and United Services Bowls Club respectively. It had been a life well-lived. Bill Gibbs felt his death keenly. They had always had an affinity - there was resemblance between them in manner, appearance and attitude. Gibbs admired his father's honesty, conscientious manner, public spiritedness, firmness of purpose (as in his successful battle to win election as an alderman), and enjoyed his companionship. He would miss him greatly.

At this time, Gibbs was being widely touted as the heir to the ailing Mack as Chief Justice of the Queensland Supreme Court. He would have taken that appointment readily, but Mack hung on despite his indifferent health. The call to the High Court intervened. In Sydney, the eminent Mr Justice Kitto, who had been a member of the High Court for 20 years, decided, at 67, to resign. Attorney-General in the Gorton Government, Tom Hughes, recommended to the Executive Council that Gibbs of the Bankruptcy Court be appointed to fill the vacancy. His appointment made him the first Queenslander to sit on the High Court since the retirement of Sir William Webb in 1958. It was, for Gibbs, the pinnacle of his career and he regretted that his father had not lived to see the fruition.

The swearing in ceremony in 1970 was before the Full High Court - Chief Justice Barwick, with Justices McTiernan, Walsh, Windeyer, Menzies and Owen - at the old courthouse at Taylor Square, Darlinghurst. Attorney-General Hughes was enthusiastic, remarking, "No appointee to the High Court has brought with him such a diversity of judicial experience." By coincidence, Peter Connolly QC, was that year President of the Law Council of Australia. Speaking on behalf of the legal profession, Connolly informed the Court that their new member represented "some of the finest flowering of the university of his home State", that he came "with renowned ability to grasp with positive enjoyment the intellectual problems of the law and to take pleasure in coming to grips with them". Connolly listed Gibbs' courtesy and patience ("not given to all") as other attributes. If he were to find a fault, it would be that Gibbs had "a rather large dose of that conservatism with which the profession of the law stamps her favourite sons, and that", he concluded, "in present company, might not be found to strike a discordant note".

Gibbs spoke of the mixture of pride, trepidation and responsibility he felt at stepping into the distinguished shoes of Sir Frank Kitto and accepting appointment to a Court which "by its position as a supreme appellate tribunal in Australia and as the final interpreter of our Constitution must inevitably exercise great authority", a Court "whose members by their ability and strength of judgment" had enhanced its reputation both inside and outside Australia. It was a strong High Court that welcomed Gibbs. Both Sir

Garfield Barwick and the genial Melburnian, Sir Douglas Menzies, were highly regarded in London. The intellectual qualities of Sir Cyril Walsh were generally recognised, as was the capability of Sir William Owen, the scholarship of the distinguished Sir Victor Windeyer and the experience of Sir Edward McTiernan, then 78 years, who had served on the Court for an extraordinary period of 40 years.

It was a memorable day for the Gibbs family. Gibbs and his brother Wylie, who was no longer in politics but executive director of Australian Pharmaceutical Manufacturers, arranged for their mother, Flora, to leave Ipswich and live close

The High Court in the chambers of Chief Justice Barwick in 1970. Back row, (left-right): Walsh J, Windeyer J, Owen J, Gibbs J.Front row, (left-right): McTiernan J, Barwick CJ, Menzies J.

by her two sons' families. As is customary for High Court appointees, Bill Gibbs was knighted a few months later and dubbed "Sir Harry'" in Canberra by the Governor-General, Sir Paul Hasluck. His nickname of Bill persisted among family, friends and close colleagues, but it was as Sir Harry that he now became generally known and took his place on the High Court bench at the beginning of what was to be a turbulent decade for Australia.

Chapter 8

JUSTICE OF THE HIGH COURT

Gibbs found Australia's senior bench to be lively and its camaraderie was immediately apparent. Victor Windeyer and Douglas Menzies joked about such things as seniority and the turning to left or right of the Chief Justice as they filed into the courtroom at Darlinghurst. As in most courtrooms, the judges came on to the bench from behind a screen by two entrances, seniority determining which entrance each would use. The next in seniority to the Chief Justice sits on his right, the next most senior on his left, and so on, alternating until the seventh is reached. "To the left, to the left!" Windeyer would call. Gibbs felt quickly at home.

Sir Anthony Mason, Chief Justice of Australia in the 1990s, was at the time a member of the NSW Court of Appeal. He remarked that in spite of the galaxy of experienced judges with whom Gibbs sat, he was never afraid to dissent. "In a very short space of time after he was appointed to the High Court, Sir Harry dissented in a number of cases and [this] to my mind indicated the very great independence of mind and objectivity that he brought to the Court." While he did not dissent in *Knight v Knight*,[1] he followed the previous authority of *Kotsis v Kotsis*[2] only "with regret". "There were a series of cases in his first few years on the High Court", he added, "in which he delivered notable dissenting judgments." Attorney-General Tom Hughes QC remembered a major Gibbs' dissent in the Concrete Pipes case, which concerned the reach of the Commonwealth corporations power.

Gibbs was no centralist. He was committed to the interpretation of the Australian Constitution as "a predominantly federal Constitution, formed to set up a Commonwealth of States, dividing power amongst them, and not letting one dominate over the other". However, when an important constitutional case came before the High Court early in 1971 regarding the Commonwealth's right to impose payroll tax upon the governments of the States, *Victoria v The Commonwealth*,[3] his judgment formed part of the unanimous decision of all seven Justices that the Act did apply to the States. In this instance, his view supported the Commonwealth. James Merralls, who was junior counsel for Victoria in the case, was disappointed in Gibbs'

---

1 (1971) 122 CLR 114.
2 (1970) 122 CLR 69. See also Connolly analysis, *Appendix*.
3 (1971) 122 CLR 353.

judgment, considering that he had misunderstood Sir Owen Dixon's judgment in the Melbourne Corporation case which was central to the State's argument. Merralls, who had been an associate to Sir Owen Dixon, felt that Dixon would have held the Act invalid in its application to salaries paid by a State.

Meanwhile, on the domestic front, the Gibbs' lively trio of daughters and young son had settled into their various spheres of the Arts, university and school. Harry and Muriel Gibbs had made new friends, among them Sydney QC, Maurice (later Sir Maurice) Byers and his wife Patricia, and colleague Sir Cyril Walsh, whose scholarly attributes and judicial manner Gibbs admired, and his wife Molly. The latter liked Sir Harry very much but found it difficult to strike up a conversation with him. Gibbs remained essentially shy and uneasy with small talk. Sir Ninian Stephen, soon to become a colleague, remarked, "He's a modest fellow...A stranger first meeting him might easily think that he's a man without broad interests - a narrow lawyer. In fact, he has extraordinarily broad interests and an extraordinarily wide ranging knowledge of every subject under the sun."

Gibbs relished the new challenge and the exercise of his intellectual powers that the High Court demanded. His days were tightly packed, like those of all his colleagues. He arrived at chambers at 8.30 am. After the ritual good morning handshake with his young Queensland associate - who was Alan Stewart in 1971 - and tipstaff Jack Davis, he tackled paperwork on upcoming cases and interviews with lawyers. Following the day in Court - the luncheon break included a strenuously paced walk through the gardens or city - it was his habit to work on his judgments until 6 pm, though frequently urging his staff away earlier. When he finally climbed into his chauffeured car to drive home through the traffic to Killara, his briefcase invariably held further casework - to be perused an hour or two later. He found it a fulfilling regimen.

Labor's political slogan of 1972 was "It's time!" Gough Whitlam's triumph at the polls, with the quite remarkable upsurge of spirit across the country which accompanied it, saw the retirement from the High Court of Sir William Owen. He had struggled against ill-health for some time. The ebullient Sir Victor Windeyer also went. At 72, he felt that some leisure was overdue. The two new appointees were the incisive, silver-tongued Sir Anthony Mason, who before his years with the NSW Court of Appeal had been Commonwealth Solicitor-General, and the genial pipe-smoking Melburnian, Sir Ninian Stephen, from the Victorian Supreme Court. Gibbs found real accord with both men as colleagues and friends in the decade that followed.

That same year, Sir Harry's mother, Flora, died. Her long illness had deprived her of many of her pleasures in life, including the tending of her brilliantly colourful garden. Harry had been, temperamentally, very much akin to his father, but his bond with his mother was strong. She had been a forceful influence in the lives of both boys, spurring them on to further scholarship. Her Ipswich friends remembered her hospitality and her lively leadership in voluntary work during World War II. A mark of her strength and kindness was the continuing affection held for her by Audrey Gibbs, Wylie's first wife and mother of their family of five, who flew from Brisbane for the service.

During these years, Brisbane barristers Peter Connolly and Bruce McPherson appeared frequently before Gibbs and, as the latter remarked, saw that he was "never afraid to give the law a nudge in the right direction when he thought it necessary but had a good sense of when the law should be left as it was". Connolly points to Gibbs' ruling in a 1973 Queensland criminal law case, *Kaporonowski v The Queen*[4] (concerning a deliberate act resulting in grievous bodily harm). Gibbs established a Queensland Criminal Code precedent: that where an accused has done an act of his own volition, the intention to cause a particular result is immaterial unless intention is expressly declared to be an element of the offence. Bill Pincus, who admired Gibbs' manner of presiding, the occasional leavening of wit, and the clarity of his judgments, felt that his method of construing constitutional cases did tend to favour the States (citing the Family Law Act case, Gazzo, 1981, as an example). Gibbs' previous associate David Jackson, who had long anticipated Gibbs' appointment to the High Court, now appeared before him regularly in commercial law cases as his own career progressed.

Gibbs kept in touch with his Queensland friends. Most summer holidays still saw the Gibbs and Pattersons together at Hervey Bay. When commitments allowed, he spoke at graduation nights and Law School dinners at his alma mater, the University of Queensland. An indefatigable traveller, who must have swung some hundreds of suitcases from airport roundabouts over the years (when travelling with the Court he often beat his tipstaff to that part of the job), he enjoyed the stimulus of travel, new scenes and talented people.

The High Court's yearly sittings in the State capitals, although strenuous, brought contact with Australia's many Supreme Court judges and a great variety of counsel, among whom he found "many very good" - others quite a long way from that category. Three times a year, for three week periods, members of the High Court were to be found in Little Bourke Street, Melbourne; there were three weeks in Brisbane, and two weeks each in Hobart, Adelaide and Perth. An old saying had it that the High Court followed the sun around: after the initial sittings of the year in Sydney, it was Hobart before the cold set in, then Melbourne in its fair month of March, a

---

4 [1973] Qd R 465; (on appeal to the High Court) 133 CLR 209.

Gibbs displays his catch after a fishing expedition with the Pattersons at Hervey Bay. Daughter Barbara is on his left and son Harry on the right.

The Sydney scene. Muriel Gibbs at Rose Bay, a favourite spot for entertaining Queensland friends.

return to clear autumn days in Sydney, with Brisbane in welcome winter sun and Adelaide and Perth before their heat became too searing. The fortitude of the early justices who undertook these distances by train and ship, was matched by their climatic appreciation.

Inevitably, it was not all smooth sailing. In the so called outer capitals there was not always a warm welcome by the justices of the Supreme Courts, where the arrival of the High Court meant the sharing of their chambers. Those who had to do the sharing often resented the crowding it brought. Gibbs, who remembered his barrister days and the importance to the litigants and the Queensland Bar of the visits of the High Court to Brisbane (many local people could not otherwise have afforded to bring their cases), was mortified to find that Queensland hospitality was probably the worst. Not only were there too few reference books made available for the preparation of cases but sometimes barely enough seating in the chambers: when one judge occupied a chair, another had to stand. Sir Anthony Mason once referred to the situation with the laden remark, "This minute area of this large State which I am now occupying." Sir Ninian Stephen once provided some action by lighting up his pipe in chambers so that the smoke set off the touchy fire alarm bells in the old courthouse and brought a fire engine clanging up Adelaide Street.

Space at the Supreme Court in Adelaide was also at a premium, necessitating two or three of the justices working in one judge's chambers. The situation was tighter still in Hobart, with insufficient space for the assembling of the judges to file into Court, to say nothing of the cramped area for associates and tipstaffs in two small adjacent tearooms. In Perth, Lady Gibbs recalled, the Western Australian Chief Justice, Sir Lawrence Jackson, pragmatically sent several of his judges on circuit when the High Court was in town. Tipstaffs at one point had found problems getting photostats of reference books from the Western Australian Supreme Court Library, then some distance from the Court. This had been rectified, but there was always the time difference and the fact that the judges travelled on Sundays in order to meet their schedules. There remain to this day sharp differences of opinion over this system. Sir Garfield Barwick thoroughly disapproves of judges "going round the country like travelling salesmen". Sir Anthony Mason feels that the benefits of State contacts are outweighed by the disruption to the Court's work. Gibbs and Sir Daryl Dawson agree that occupying other people's chambers is awkward, but are firmly convinced of the system's efficacy.

Throughout Australia, the High Court saw and heard the country's finest advocates. Gibbs himself was regarded as a top advocate - reasonable, measured, well prepared, and possessed of a fine memory and a high sense of relevance. He was, above all, persuasive. Gibbs labelled Sir Garfield Barwick "one of the greatest appellate advocates of his age",[5] adding that Barwick himself attributed his skill above all to his powers of recall, so that he was able to parry and thrust in legal argument with appeal judges to win his point. Gibbs thinks that a "sense of relevance" is even more important.

> [G]iven the necessary equipment which any counsel who appears in an appellate court ought to have - a requisite knowledge of the law, an ability to marshal facts and a clarity of expression - in my opinion, the two qualities most necessary for success in appellate advocacy are a sense of relevance and tact.[6]

Citing a Quintilian[7] Latin maxim - the judge hurries to get to the strongest point - Gibbs wrote, "Fundamental to success in appellate advocacy is the ability to perceive the point or points on which the resolution of the appeal will depend and to cut a path directly to those points, without meandering to explore side issues..."[8] He also lauds "brevity and compression". Plenty of those who appeared before the High Court did not reach these standards and skills. Summarising his experience of poor barristers, Gibbs comments, "to advance a bad argument when a good one is available is the essence of bad advocacy." Again, it is the sense of relevance that comes foremost in his list of attributes.

In 1972, Gibbs was sworn in as a member of the Privy Council at Buckingham Palace. In the same ceremony, the newly appointed British Prime Minister, Harold Wilson, was sworn in as First Lord of the Treasury, the method of the swearing in of a Prime Minister in the United Kingdom. As Chief Justice, Barwick had persuaded the Privy Council to change a 600 year old practice that the Council issue only one set of reasons and allow him the right to dissent. He also had the Council reinstitute the former practice of members of the Australian High Court sitting on the Privy Council in London. Sir Samuel Griffith, whom Gibbs regarded as a role model, had done so, and others later. Sir Owen Dixon, during his 35 years as a member of the High Court, 12 of them as Chief Justice, had declined invitations to sit. He had disliked not only the inability to dissent (he found himself in disagreement with a number of the Privy Council's opinions) but also the disadvantage of being a temporary member of a tribunal without regular contact with the other members. Gibbs, on the contrary, shared

---

5 Gibbs, "Appellate Advocacy" (1986) ALJ 496 at 497.
6 Ibid at 497.
7 Quintilian wrote on the art (and sad state) of oratory in the 1st century AD.
8 Gibbs, "Appellate Advocacy" (1986) ALJ 496 at 497-498.

Barwick's views. "[In] matters of general law the Privy Council provided the most valuable service." During Harold Holt's brief prime ministership (1966-1967), Holt had suggested to Barwick that appeals from the High Court to the Privy Council on federal matters should cease. This was not set in train, however, until 1971 under the McMahon Government's Attorney-General, Nigel Bowen. Appeals on State matters remained. Gibbs was delighted to be seconded to the Privy Council for three months in 1974. Not only did it give him the opportunity of intensive work with Britain's Law Lords but of dealing with the widely divergent cases from different parts of the Commonwealth.

So the Gibbs, with their young son Harry, found themselves in a London flat just off Park Lane and at their disposal a large black Daimler together with a very large and obliging chauffeur who, inevitably, rejoiced in the name of "Tiny". Sir Harry took with him his associate, James Douglas (the son of Brisbane's Justice Jim Douglas). Douglas, now a Queen's Counsel, remembered his delight in his second year as associate, when he learned that he was to accompany Gibbs. He had intended pursuing further studies in England in any case. Now he had an airfare paid one way, several months accommodation and a chance to save towards his postgraduate university fees at Cambridge. Douglas enjoyed the understated dignity and intellectual power of the Privy Council. While counsel wore robes and wigs, the judges, sitting in committee as it were, wore ordinary suits. He noted that, in the six cases he witnessed as an associate, the Law Lords "tended to arrive at one order - one judgment of the court - and used to allocate it around for one judge to do the first draft." Australian commentators and practitioners have often wished for such unanimity from the High Court. At the time, Privy Councillor Gibbs sat with a most distinguished bench: Lord Wilberforce, regarded widely as one of the top two or three English judges of the century, Lord Hailsham of St Marylebone (former Lord Chancellor), Lord Cross of Chelsea and Lord Salmon. Douglas felt that Lord Wilberforce was the possessor of "one of the best, fairest minds you could come across as a lawyer", while Lord Hailsham was more attuned to his role as politician. Douglas also remembered an appeal from the Federal Court of Malaysia - *Lam Kee Ying v Lam Shes Tong*,[9] which gave him an opportunity to hear Lord Wilberforce once more, and with him three other Law Lords: Viscount Dilhorne, Lord Simon of Glaisdale, and Lord Kilbrandon - along with Sir Harry Gibbs. Gibbs, like Barwick, was certainly not out of his league on the Judicial Committee. A later New Zealand Privy Councillor, Sir Robin Cooke (President of the Court of Appeal of New Zealand), observed:

---

9 [1975] App Cas 247.

[Gibbs] is internationally regarded as a sound conservative Judge and his approach would be congenial to many of the English and Scottish members of the Judicial Committee. Whether he wrote any dissenting judgments I am not sure...I would be surprised if he were ever a *sole* dissentient.

He was not. Barwick, it is recalled by lawyers, did dissent on one occasion in a New Zealand case, and he himself recalls dissenting once, in company with an English Lord. Sir Owen Dixon believed that hidden dissent was not uncommon under the single reasons regime.

Lord Wilberforce has given his assessment of the differing qualities of Barwick and Gibbs.

He [Gibbs] was an excellent counterfoil to the other Chief Justice whom I remember with much affection - Sir Garfield Barwick. Sir Garfield was par excellence a proactive Judge delighting in exchanges with Counsel and fertile in interesting arguments. Sir Harry was essentially the professional Judge, patient, receptive, drawing on his considerable experience, always willing to enlighten us, the Law Lords, on features of Australian law and practice which might throw light on the case.

As so often with Australians in London, Gibbs and young James Douglas were suddenly confronted with a familiar slice of home. Among the counsel and instructing solicitors coming and going at No 9 Downing Street (the occupant of No 10 was then Harold Wilson, whom they saw occasionally), Douglas met one day his contemporary John Rowell, eldest son of Gibbs' old Brisbane friend. Rowell was working for a British firm of solicitors and about to marry an English girl in the small town of Rye, one of the Cinque Ports in Sussex. Rowell promptly asked Douglas to the wedding and extended the invitation to the Gibbs. They agreed to stand in for John Rowell's parents, who apparently were unable to come to England for the ceremony. On the day, the Gibbs' enormous, sweating, but expert, driver experienced great difficulty approaching the picturesque little church at Rye at the appointed time. In attempting to turn the Daimler in the narrow cobble-stone lanes, he finally jammed the car against the church fence. Sir Harry, in dark suit, leapt out and was standing surveying the scene when there appeared Jack Rowell himself in top hat and morning suit. He had succumbed to his wife's last minute persuasion to come. They left the valiant chauffeur juggling with the Daimler to the strains of Lohengrin. It had been a circuitous route for the two from English studies at the University of Queensland in 1933, through war experiences and post war legal briefs, and countless legal functions to this unlikely encounter in an English village.

When the Gibbs returned to Australia, events were moving towards the constitutional crisis of 1975 and in the High Court a further change was about to take place. Sir Cyril Walsh had retired and the Whitlam Government had appointed KS Jacobs (formerly President of the NSW Court of Appeal). The government was also hoping that octogenarian Sir Edward McTiernan (appointed by the Scullin Government as far back as 1930) would create another vacancy by retiring, but he showed no signs of doing so. In spirited defiance, the old man invested in new robes.

Then the unexpected occurred. In November 1974, at just 67, the universally popular High Court Justice Sir Douglas Menzies collapsed and died of a heart attack at a Bar dinner in Sydney. It was a blow to the whole Court, not least his longtime friends, the Chief Justice, Sir Garfield Barwick, who was in London at the time, and fellow Victorian, Sir Ninian Stephen. Stephen used to stay with Menzies at the Union Club when the Court was sitting in Sydney. Gibbs had appreciated Menzies' good humour, joie de vivre and his open-mindedness. Sir Maurice Byers gave a generous description of Menzies' style and qualities:

> A great man. An absolutely delightful man. It was as though he were from another age, and on the occasions when the High Court dressed in its formal 18th century garb (ie shoes with buckles, knee breeches, robes and full-bottomed wigs) he would stride in, and he had the face of a Regency rake. He was in a sense quite un-Australian - a man of the most irresistible charm.

A certain colour and flavour, not to be recaptured, went with him. Also, as Sir Anthony Mason observed, Menzies' personality ensured that a good spirit animated the Court. Menzies had provided a bridge between Garfield Barwick and the younger members of the Court and that personality link was now gone. His contribution to the mood of the Court was to be missed.

In February 1975, Whitlam, taking up a suggestion of the Minister for Social Security, Bill Hayden, appointed his boldly reformist Attorney-General, Senator Lionel Murphy, whose political stance and attitudes alone were enough to ensure an uncomfortable relationship with the Chief Justice. "Neither the Senate nor the High Court will ever be the same again," Senator James McLelland prophesied.[10] Murphy was accustomed to initiating swift change. In just three years as Attorney-General he had, apart from lifting the Senate's role and expanding the use of Senate Committees, achieved a wide range of liberal reforms. These included legal aid (which created enormous financial problems but was inevitable, since State schemes were already in force), the widely praised freedom of information legislation, and the major Family Law Act. The latter was certainly controversial. The more

---

10 See, generally, Scutt (ed), *Lionel Murphy, A Radical Judge*.

conservatively-minded considered that Garfield Barwick's earlier reform, when he was Attorney-General (the inclusion of the clause "irreparable breakdown of the relationship", Matrimonial Causes Act 1963) was completely adequate. Murphy's further relaxation would open the floodgates to easy divorce, they argued, and therefore speed up destabilisation of marriage and the family. A stormy petrel for the High Court.

Tom Hughes QC, who was president of the Australian Bar Association in 1975, described Murphy as both "a social engineer and a man of personal charisma". Gibbs, like all the puisne judges of the court, found Lionel Murphy friendly. "He tried to be cooperative. He had been very successful in changing the law and had brought about an enormous amount of change. Some of it was good change. Opinions differ about others." Predictably, Justice Murphy proved impatient of legal precedent and, as even his greatest admirers agreed, when faced with the choice tended to make decisions according to his own views and policies rather than follow established legal principles. This was diametrically opposed to Gibbs' attitude and his belief that the High Court was not intended to be a vehicle for change. "It would be hard to find two people of more different personality and views," Sir Ninian Stephen observed. "Lionel saw the Court as a major instrument for law reform, while Sir Harry took the view that the Court was there to interpret and give effect to the law as it stood. Notwithstanding that, there was never any personal animosity between them. The splendid thing was that we all were on friendly speaking terms." Murphy assumed his accustomed role as reformer, which meant dissenter on a body such as the then constituted High Court.

Journalists were by now using the phrases "States' righter" and "centralist" when referring to the various justices and their views on the reach of Commonwealth powers. The judges themselves disliked such simplistic labels, which disregarded the subtlety of their thinking on complex constitutional issues. "The expressions are silly," Barwick remarked. "Our Commonwealth gives powers to the Commonwealth under specific heads. The Constitution passes to the States what the Commonwealth doesn't get. All the High Court ever does is decide whether a Commonwealth Act is good - whether it is within power." Generally, Murphy thought there was a good deal more "within power" of the Commonwealth than did Barwick or Gibbs.

There were a number of constitutional cases before the Court in 1975. Gibbs thought the Australian Assistance Plan case, concerning grants to Regional Councils for Social Development was of particular significance. He thought that the constitutional limits on the capacity of the Commonwealth to expend Consolidated Revenue should be strictly applied. Peter Connolly in his analysis on the subject concludes, "If this view had prevailed it may well be that the Commonwealth would not have such a massive deficit on current account today."[11] State versus federal rights was a constant theme. One matter concerned representation of the federal Territories in the Senate. There were also several cases in which Victoria challenged the Commonwealth, relating to deadlock provisions between the House of Representatives and the Senate. Also in the *Territorial Seas* case the States challenged Commonwealth sovereignty over the Continental Shelf, the territorial seas and sea bed. In these vital matters, Sir Harry Gibbs made some of the most important judgments of his career.

Gibbs' judgments proved to be a bulwark for States' rights. Sir Anthony Mason commented, "In cases which involved questions as to the extent of Commonwealth/State power, broadly speaking, Sir Harry and I were on opposite sides of the judicial fence. That is, in a very general way, Sir Harry, more often than myself, would be found deciding these cases in favour of the States." This was so in the *Territorial Seas* case, for instance, in which the whole Court (Barwick CJ, McTiernan, Gibbs, Mason, Stephen, Jacobs, Murphy JJ) upheld Commonwealth exclusive rights over the Continental Shelf, and a majority, with Gibbs and Stephen JJ dissenting, sustained Commonwealth sovereignty over the territorial sea.

Solicitor-General, Sir Maurice Byers, who put the case for the Commonwealth, says Gibbs' judgment shows his propensity to approach constitutional matters from the States' viewpoint at a time when the more general interpretation of the Constitution was towards an expansion of Commonwealth power especially through the external affairs power (s 51(xxix)). Gibbs outlined what he considered the proper, and limited, federal stance. The substance of the *Territorial Seas* case, dealing as it does with the practical administration of all the States' off-shore waters (including wharves, fishing, jetties, recreation and aspects of shipping and navigation) intimately touched state concerns, and Gibbs took a stand. Connolly quotes the Gibbs' judgment in his analysis and, contradicting Byers' opinion, concludes, "Gibbs, in one of the most powerful judgments he has written, analysed the legislation rigorously and exposed the domestic power-grab lying beneath what was piously claimed as a mere acceptance of international obligation."[12]

In July 1975, Australia abolished appeals from the High Court to the Privy Council in federal matters. The fact that it had been possible for Australia's highest court to decide one way on a case and the Privy Council, on appeal,

---

11 See Connolly analysis, *Appendix*.
12 See Connolly analysis, *Appendix*.

the other way, had created a possible conflict of binding authorities and a potential problem for the lower courts. Barwick was sorry to see another link go. But his attitude had been that Australia should be free to make its own mistakes. "And we do," he acknowledged. Gibbs thought, by contrast, that the very fact that there could be an appeal from the High Court kept Australian judges in line. Sir Ninian Stephen remarked, "There is a feeling of freedom involved in the knowledge that there'll be no appeal from your judgments other than dissents from other members of the Bench." He added that the constant criticisms from legal academics and journals fulfilled a similar role. Mason commented that appeals to the Privy Council "usually meant that Australian law would follow the path of English law as charted by English judicial decisions." He added that the possibility of conflicting lines of authority - the High Court and Privy Council not necessarily agreeing - was more a problem for the State Supreme Courts. In fact, direct appeals from the latter to the Privy Council remained for another decade, as did the practice of High Court justices being seconded to the Privy Council for brief periods.

In October 1975, Gibbs attended, with Sir Ninian Stephen, the opening of the splendid Townsville Law Courts Buildings (the Russell Skerman Complex) by Queensland Premier Joh Bjelke-Petersen. The North Queensland Bar Association dated from the 19th century and the modern Law Courts building had been badly needed. It had replaced the old Supreme Court building which had been re-erected and converted from a School of Arts in 1889. Gibbs enjoyed reacquainting himself with old friends, in particular, the former northern Queensland Judge, Russell Skerman.

In the south, dramatic events were unfolding. The man who had proffered his friendship and smoothed the Gibbs' transition from Brisbane to Sydney some years before, Sir John Kerr, had been appointed Governor-General of Australia in 1974. Now, in Canberra, he became the focus of one of the most controversial and divisive political upheavals of the century: his dismissal of the Whitlam Government in November 1975. In mid-October, the devastating, hopelessly mismanaged Khemlani-petro dollars loans debacle erupted. In what became known as "The Loans Affair", Ministers had moved to bypass the Loans Council in negotiating overseas loans; Kirath Khemlani was the intermediary.[13] Whitlam dismissed his Minister for Minerals and Energy, Rex Connor, for the mishandling. At the same time, the Court handed down its judgment on the *Territories Senators'* case, allowing for the selection of four new federal senators. This was to form part of unfolding

---

13 Bryce Fraser (ed), *Macquarie Book of Events* 357.

drama. If a half-Senate election were now held, the Senate's political composition could be changed.

Opposition Leader Malcolm Fraser attacked the Government's financial mismanagement. The Opposition-dominated Senate refused to pass the budget bills, deferring supply and demanding that Whitlam advise the Governor-General to call a general election. The Prime Minister refused to do so and indicated his intention of seeking emergency financial arrangements from the private banks. Sir Garfield Barwick, as Chief Justice, became directly involved. Despite Labor Prime Minister Whitlam's objection (Barwick was a former Liberal Government minister), Governor-General Kerr consulted Barwick for legal advice as to whether Kerr should intervene. There was a precedent for this in State politics. Sir Dallas Brooks, Governor of Victoria, had sought advice from the Chief Justice of Australia, Sir Owen Dixon, in the 1950s in a not dissimilar situation. Barwick, aware of that precedent, was convinced that an Australian government, constitutionally, must have the support of both Houses of Parliament to govern. He was also alarmed at Whitlam's private banks proposal, which he saw as heralding further disaster. He advised intervention by the Governor-General. Gibbs thought that Sir John Kerr was perfectly justified in consulting the Chief Justice:

> There was ample precedent for a Governor-General or Governor to consult a Chief Justice on questions of constitutional law or constitutional convention. The Governor-General has no official legal adviser and in the circumstances in which Sir John Kerr found himself it would have been inappropriate for him to seek advice from the Solicitor General whose duty was to advise the Government.

The High Court was hearing the *McKinlay* case, in which the Attorney-General was seeking an injunction to restrain House of Representatives elections until a fair distribution of seats could be carried out (the Court found no grounds for this in the Constitution). Whitlam announced the possibility of a half-Senate election on 11 November. Kerr and Barwick consulted at Admiralty House on the 10 November. The latter, in his capacity as Chief Justice, that evening wrote an official letter to Kerr confirming his advice that the Governor-General had the "constitutional authority and duty" to dismiss "a Prime Minister who cannot ensure supply to the Crown" and would not "either advise a general election or resign". At the same time, Gibbs and his colleagues received a memorandum from Chief Justice Barwick, who had not consulted them on the matter, advising them of his advice to Kerr and his reasons for it.[14]

---

14 See Marr, *Barwick* at ch 19, esp 263-277.

Sir John Kerr's subsequent "Statement" (based on Barwick's letter), the shock dismissal of the Whitlam Government on that fateful afternoon of 11 November 1975 and the appointment of the astute and ambitious Fraser to form the caretaker Government - the rights and wrongs of which are likely to be debated indefinitely - are now matters of history. The conflict, and Barwick's role in it, did not ease his relationship with some members of the High Court, where the atmosphere became a little strained. Gibbs, and some of his colleagues, however, were now more concerned about the projected centralisation of the Court. Both the Whitlam and Fraser Governments had approved Barwick's plans to locate the much needed new High Court building in Canberra.

Chapter 9

TAYLOR SQUARE 1976 - HIGH COURT, CANBERRA, 1980

The High Court judges assembled one cold rain-drenched day in late September, 1975 by Lake Burley Griffin for the laying of the foundation stone of the majestic building planned by Sir Garfield Barwick. He had already appointed architects - Edwards Madigan Torzillo & Bribbs - and was deeply involved in plans. As Prime Minister Whitlam, flanked by the Chief Justice, wielded the ceremonial spade in the driving rain, the six puisne justices stood huddled under a giant tarpaulin. Some were filled with misgiving. On principle, the majority, Gibbs included, were opposed to the prospect of centralisation in Canberra. They worried that the move would isolate the Court, making it remote from the general populace and less accessible to litigants. Furthermore, all had their homes and families away from Canberra in the various State capitals. At one stage in the proceedings a section of one of the earth banks of the giant excavations for the Court collapsed into the water below. A fleeting hope ran through a number of the assembled justices that perhaps the whole project might be abandoned. But Garfield Barwick had not become known as the greatest Australian advocate of the century for nothing. He had brought his remarkable persuasive powers to bear to proceed thus far and was not to be deterred by a minor mishap. "Gar was enormously involved in the creation of the building," Sir Ninian Stephen recollected. "He went up almost every week to supervise it and was said to be the best building foreman that had ever existed. The National Gallery was going up next door and they were really very bitter because they didn't have anyone of the personality of Barwick pushing on the construction."

Gibbs by this time had a reputation for the analysis of established doctrine and prior authority. Sir Robin Cooke in New Zealand, frequently referred to judgments of Gibbs. He recalled a case in 1976[1] in which he cited Gibbs' discussion of the theory underlying options in a case heard by the High Court two years previously. While he had some "respectful reservation" about some suggestions in the judgment, he noted that Gibbs' views carried "great weight".

---

1 *Murray v Scott* [1976] 1 NZLR 643 at 655-656 citing Gibbs J from *Laybutt v Amoco Australia Pty Ltd* (1974) 48 ALJR 492 at 497-499.

Sir Harry and Lady Gibbs in his Melbourne Chambers after the swearing in of Justice Aickin in September 1976

High Court of Australia sitting in Melbourne, 1976. (Left to right), Murphy J, Mason J, Gibbs J, Barwick CJ, Stephen J, Jacobs J, Aickin J.

In 1977 the High Court was grappling with conflict caused by custody cases and the relative powers of the Supreme Courts and the Family Court on child welfare. Gibbs, like the Chief Justice and several others, was not particularly happy about the Family Court. He felt that its specialised nature and the sameness of cases would limit the quality of judges appointed. But it was a fait accompli, and the Commonwealth government's legislation affecting the Family Court's jurisdiction was being challenged, in particular its constitutional right to legislate on the referral of power from the Supreme Courts to the Family Court to deal with illegitimate children. The Commonwealth Solicitor-General, Sir Maurice Byers, argued that the power of the Parliament to make laws in relation to custody sprang from the notion of marriage as involving the upbringing and nurture of children. This also involved the settlement of property upon people and the dealing with children who were brought into a family, not because they were biological children of both parents of a married couple, but because they were either the biological child of one (who had previously been married), or an illegitimate child of one, or because they were adopted. "Once you had this notion of nurture," he said, "the fate of that child was a legitimate matter of legislative power. But Sir Harry wouldn't have a word of it."

Byers managed to have the Act amended, but not quite to his own satisfaction. He had wanted the phrase, in loco parentis, incorporated, but the draftsman disliked the idea of the Latin phrase. The term "a member of the household" was used instead. Counsel opposing him on the first occasion this term was litigated immediately described it as "invalid". Sir Maurice replied, "Oh no, `a member of the household' is the equivalent of in loco parentis." Gibbs, from the Bench, remarked, "Why that could include the butler!" sending Byers into a fit of laughter. Byers battled on in these cases involving ex nuptial or adopted children. "You can't confine the powers of a specialised court to biological children - it's ridiculous!" he said. "They were arguing that the child must be conceived by the wife from impregnation by the husband. They were antediluvian. Bill was antediluvian about that!"

Gibbs' expertise in criminal law was impressive. His impact was especially evident in his days on the Queensland Supreme Court. Criminal law authority, Professor Eric Colvin, thinks that "Sir Harry Gibbs has been the most authoritative interpreter of the Queensland Criminal Code in the century since its enactment." Gibbs gave several important criminal law rulings in 1977, carrying a majority of the High Court. In one case the accused's solicitor had been excluded from an interview with investigating police at which, allegedly, the accused made a verbal confession. The question was, did this not only undermine the credit of the police witness but also was it relevant to whether the confession was in fact made? Gibbs concluded that it was relevant. Some six months later, the Court dealt with the important question of self-defence in *Viro v The Queen*, a complex issue, both in itself and in regard to the Gibbs judgment. The Privy Council had previously held that a person who is attacked may defend him/herself doing what is reasonably necessary for that purpose but no more. In 1958 the High Court in *Howe* qualified this doctrine: if the defence failed only because the force used was excessive, the accused was guilty of manslaughter only. In 1971 in *Palmer* the Privy Council rejected this qualification. In 1978 High Court decisions were no longer subject to appeal to the Privy Council and in *Viro* the majority of the High Court preferred the *Howe* doctrine. Gibbs preferred the *Palmer* ruling, believing the *Howe* qualification unsound legally and likely to lead to jury confusion and error. However, as Connolly states in his analysis, "[Gibbs] agreed with the majority contrary to his personal opinion in order to achieve a measure of certainty." His judgment was to prove correct: in 1987 the Court recognised that *Howe* and *Viro* had placed "an onerous burden on judges and juries".

Meanwhile, Gibbs had been seconded again to the Privy Council in London for a three month period. Lady Gibbs accompanied him, but not his associate, Peter Rowell, who was busy in Sydney. The South African-born, Cambridge educated Bruce McPherson, was then a practising QC and in London appearing before the Privy Council on behalf of the Queensland Government. McPherson observed Gibbs in action and noted, with pleasure, that Gibbs was quite "a long way ahead" of the elderly judges "in that particular Privy Council". He remarked, too, that Gibbs' Australian accent stood out amongst their Lordships' "frightfully" British ones. Lord Wilberforce, who was not sitting at this time but met Gibbs again at various functions, spoke warmly of him. "I know that we all more than welcomed his presence here and could have done with more. I am personally the better - and the happier - for having known him."

Off duty, the Daimler, with its large chauffeur, took the Gibbs with their longtime friends, the Pattersons, who were visiting England, for a trip to the historic city of Bath. Gerald, never dull, was then in the throes of writing a monumental, fourteen volume, anti-establishment world history. (He never did approach a publisher with it). The four friends enjoyed each others company as they glided through the tranquil English countryside, and stayed at night at one or other of the atmospheric inns. The private Gibbs could be outgoing and engaging company.

Back at Taylor Square Sir Harry's calm temperament was useful. He was often Acting Chief Justice during Barwick's absences overseas. Barwick frequently sat on the Privy Council and once on the International Court of Justice (deliberating on the French Atom Bomb Pacific Tests). Among Gibbs'

High Court colleagues now was the doyen of the Melbourne Bar, the gifted commercial lawyer Sir Keith Aickin. But the atmosphere at the Court generally was not comfortable. The Chief Justice was absorbed with the new High Court now rising on the shores of Lake Burley Griffin, with its lofty nave of glass and concrete, spacious courtrooms and judges' chambers. It was to be his monument and he was determined to see it built to match his vision.

His overseeing of the building was indeed remarkable. He had observed in the early stages that one of the large concrete pillars that support the upper stories and rise in the main hall, was out of plumb, and insisted that the workmen take a theodolite to it. He was proved correct. The pillar was demolished and rebuilt. On the debit side, however, was his grab for administrative control. His colleagues felt that things had got out of hand when he announced that not only would the new High Court be administered as a separate corporate body but under the Chief Justice's sole jurisdiction. They objected. The High Court Act subsequently decreed that the Court would administer its own affairs but the powers would be exercised by the Justices in committee advising the Chief Justice, who would determine the terms and conditions of employment of its staff.

Barwick was only temporarily diverted. A few months later he announced his intention of instigating permanent residency of High Court Judges in Canberra. "It was initially envisaged that we live in some sort of enclave together near the Commonwealth Club and we had visions of our wives going out in the morning to pick up the milk bottles," Sir Ninian Stephen recalled. "Fortunately, nothing came of that, but the Government then arranged for three or four black cars to drive us all round Canberra to look at possible home sites in the outer suburbs." It was not a happy prospect. But a real crisis was reached when the Chief Justice foreshadowed his intention of closing the Court's State registries and floated the possibility of setting up a specialist High Court Bar and a separate federal court structure.

There was now open rebellion. Against all tradition, the puisne justices met, with Gibbs, as senior puisne judge, chairing the meeting. The upshot was that the Court's registries in all capitals other than Sydney and Melbourne remained (costs to litigants would therefore not increase), and, when the new High Court opened, the High Court Justices would remain in their professional home bases and commute to Canberra for sittings. The other proposals were not heard of again. The majority of the judges strongly supported the Court's appearances in other States and the opportunity for contact with Supreme Courts those hearings provided. Full support came from Sir Ronald Wilson, Western Australia's former Solicitor-General, who was appointed to the High Court in 1979. His equable temperament was welcome on the Court. He held very similar views on the preservation of the Commonwealth's original federal structure in regard to the States' status to Gibbs, whom he knew well from the Court's sittings in Perth.

Gibbs could be sure of quiet nights at home in Killara now, for their household had shrunk. Their two younger daughters were married, Margaret, a gifted mathematician, to Rod Cameron the political pollster, and Mary to Robert Hodge. Mary had graduated in science, then become a teacher/librarian. She was the only one of Gibbs' children to have considered, then eschewed, law as a career. Over the next year or two she presented the Gibbs with their first grandchildren, Suzanne and Deborah. Their eldest daughter Barbara, a lively personality with a penchant for pink hair, had toured with Circus Oz before going into film production. Their son, Harry, after experimenting with a rock band, had settled into a medical course at Sydney University. The girls maintained close contact, teasing their conservative father occasionally (an outsize, garish tie, which he loyally wore for a day or two, appeared one birthday); the father and son still saw a good deal of each other; and Muriel Gibbs had undertaken a course in Indonesian. They were a vital, varied family unit, independent but close.

Before 1979 was out, Sir Harry was seconded again to the Privy Council for several months. Meanwhile, in Sydney, Barwick's health had begun to deteriorate. Indomitable as ever, he still managed, after the Court's sittings and doctor's appointments, to fly up to Canberra every few days to superintend the final stages of the striking eight storey building. His fortitude amazed the High Court Registrar, Frank Jones. Not only was Barwick receiving laser treatment for his eyes but also medical attention for a painful ear cyst. The building was finally completed and staffed, the library equipped, and the move made early in 1980.

Gibbs, back from London, felt from the beginning that he would probably look about for a suitable cottage in Canberra, and thereby reduce the frequent commuting to and from Sydney. He needed to restore the quiet hours he habitually spent keeping abreast with the ever increasing casework. The advantages of the new large library, courtrooms and spacious Chambers were immediately apparent. In Gibbs' own Chambers the portrait of Sir Samuel Griffith looked across at a colourful oil by Queensland painter Margaret Olley, whose work he admired. Gibbs now became a familiar figure taking his brisk daily walk, during the luncheon break, along the often breezy shores of Lake Burley Griffin, clutching a hat, and sometimes preferring a paperbag of sandwiches from the Court's cafeteria to lunch with a gathering of justices in the elegant dining-room. Two or three times a week there was enough. The magnificent new building was costly. The first month's electricity bill arrived and consumption was more than double that for Taylor Square. Barwick, unwilling to substantiate the jibe "Gar's Mahal", at once issued an edict: lights must be turned off immediately upon vacating Chambers, the courtrooms or any other rooms in the building. The Court proved a practical and pleasant place in which to work. Unlike many grand buildings, it was even more effective and impressive internally than externally. This is a tribute to Barwick's intense work on the project. As a future user of the building, he probably designed from the inside looking out, rather than from the outside looking in. Some argue that the High Court would have been better placed in Sydney, Australia's greatest centre of population. But for visitors to the national capital it certainly provides an impressive symbol of the law, towering high above the lake, connected by walk bridge to the National Art Gallery and within walking distance of Parliament House.

The official opening by Queen Elizabeth II in May 1980, timed to coincide with a conference of Commonwealth Chief Justices, was a glittering international occasion. Jurists and dignitaries from various parts of the world assembled for the ceremony in the soaring entrance hall, all in full rig and wig. It was a triumph which no one, least of all Sir Harry Gibbs who for over forty years had appreciated the drive and brilliance of Garfield Barwick, begrudged the 76 year old Chief Justice. Barwick energetically escorted the Queen from top to bottom of the vast building and she admitted later to some fatigue. She paused before the Tom Roberts' painting of the Proclamation of the Commonwealth at the Melbourne Exhibition Building: the enormous painting, 20ft by 11ft, represented her grandfather, the Duke of York (later King George V), and now hangs in the new Parliament House. Sir Anthony Mason sat near her at the luncheon which followed. "The one thing that remains lodged in my mind," he said, "is that the Queen did not use the butter knife."

Before the year was out, Harry Gibbs received a personal tribute he greatly valued. The University of Queensland, honouring both his service to it and his ten years as a High Court Judge, conferred on him an Honorary Doctorate of Laws. He accepted the honour from the Chancellor, his old friend Sir Walter Campbell. The anecdotes in Mayne Hall that night went as far back as Gibbs' graduation day in 1939 when the then Chancellor, Sir James Blair, was unable to finish his speech "owing to disruption from boisterous students."

Back in Canberra, the High Court heard *O'Connor v The Queen* in 1980.[2] The Court decided, four to three, that self-induced intoxication is relevant on a charge of a criminal offence which does not involve specific intent. Gibbs

2 (1980) 54 ALJR 349; 29 ALR 449.

dissented, agreeing with a judgment by Lord Salmon in the House of Lords[3] that "if there is no penal sanction for any injury unlawfully inflicted under the complete mastery of drink or drugs voluntarily taken, the social consequences could be appalling." This was consistent with the codification of the Queensland Criminal Law by Sir Samuel Griffith. Gibbs' view was adopted in the Queensland Court of Criminal Appeal.

Later in 1980, Sir Garfield, whose eyesight was failing, retired, completing 16 years of service as Chief Justice. Prime Minister Malcolm Fraser and his Cabinet wrestled with the task of his replacement. There were only two real candidates. One was a former Solicitor-General and Attorney-General, Bob Ellicott (a cousin of Barwick), to whom the Prime Minister no doubt felt he owed a debt for his role in the 1975 political fracas. He had the ability for the job. But his involvement in the events of 1975 ruled him out, certainly as far as the federal Labor Opposition and Labor Premiers Wran (NSW) and Lowe (Tasmania), were concerned. Even the Liberal Premiers feared he would be at once too centrist and too activist. They sought a steadier, more conservative candidate and did not look far. As one newspaper put it, they found "a conservative jurist, predictable, quiet, a strict legalist, and 'nice bloke'." The senior puisne judge, Sir Harry Gibbs, with his wide experience over ten years as a member of the High Court, was an alternative with ideal credentials. "Sir Harry was the best man for the job," Sir Anthony Mason commented. "He had a proven record as an outstanding lawyer. He had the confidence of his fellow judges and he had the confidence of the Australian legal community." At 64 years when he would assume the office, Gibbs was a decade older than Ellicott, and this, too, counted in his favour (he would have to retire at 70). Ellicott declined the offer of an ordinary or puisne judge seat on the High Court. The vacancy then went to 52 year old Federal Court Justice Francis Gerard Brennan, making it a double for Queensland.[4]

The Federal Government had consulted widely. The Liberals' record in appointing people on merit to high judicial office is sound, although the appointment of ex-politicians like Barwick is bound to be controversial, no matter what their merits. Fraser's Ministers tested opinions, consulted State Attorneys-General (who, under the High Court of Australia Act 1979, must be canvassed), asked leading QCs around the country, and talked with leaders of the profession. Opinion very strongly favoured Gibbs. It was felt, not

---

3 In *DPP v Majewski* [1976] 2 All ER 142; [1977] AC 443.
4 Brennan was in turn to be appointed Chief Justice of the High Court in March 1995, making him, after Griffith and Gibbs, the third judge appointed from Queensland to that office. Brennan was born in Rockhampton (in 1928), Griffith in South Wales (in 1845) and Gibbs in Sydney (in 1917).

only by the legal profession, but Australians generally, that it was time to divorce the office from politics, a sound precedent that has persisted with the appointment, after Gibbs, of Sir Anthony Mason.

On 29 January 1981, among his peers at a Judges' Conference in Perth, Gibbs received the news of his appointment. It was the culminating moment of his career. He and his wife, together with Queenslanders also in the western capital, Sir Walter Campbell and his wife, were elated. They duly celebrated.

Chapter 10

The *Sydney Morning Herald's* headline - "Sir Harry the Healer" - set the main editorial theme throughout the country. Commentators commended the Government for choosing a lawyer of distinction who was untainted by politics, "utterly uncontroversial", and who would end the divisiveness which had reigned in the High Court since 1975. The newspaper concluded, "The *Herald* believes [the Cabinet] was right, for the sake of the unity of the country and the credit of the High Court." The *Canberra Times* pointed out: "Sir Harry has the confidence and esteem of his brother judges and a proven capacity to chair his court with confidence, authority and courtesy...and should provide real leadership."

Brisbane's *Courier-Mail* trumpeted the honour to Queensland. Sir Harry Gibbs was the second Queenslander to hold the office since 1903, the other being the first Australian Chief Justice, former Queensland Premier and

The High Court of Australia, Canberra, 1981. Sir Harry Gibbs with the first Gibbs' court after the swearing in as Chief Justice on 12 February 1981. (Left to right) Wilson J, Murphy J, Stephen J, Gibbs CJ, Mason J, Aickin J and Brennan J.

former Queensland Chief Justice Sir Samuel Griffith, "probably the greatest Queenslander ever", enthused the *Courier's* editorial. It also asserted that the appointment was the first to be made with the consultation and approval of the States. This was both "gratifying and a wise step by the Government", an opinion echoed by the legal profession. The Opposition Shadow Attorney-General, Senator Gareth Evans, was only luke warm. Gibbs would make a "safe, stop-gap...competent but thoroughly...unimaginative Chief Justice." Much more enthusiastic was Professor Tony Blackshield of La Trobe University. He not only expected that Gibbs would be "outstanding" but remarked on the potential for harmony within a High Court comprising Gibbs as Chief Justice, together with Sir Anthony Mason and Sir Ninian Stephen. The simultaneous appointment of another Queenslander, Federal Court Justice Gerard Brennan, made it, as the *Courier-Mail* reported, "a champagne day for Queensland". This made it five High Court justices from Queensland, two of whom were Chief Justices. (In 1995, Gerard Brennan was appointed Chief Justice in turn, making it three from that State.) At the time of writing, neither South Australia nor Tasmania has produced a single High Court appointee.

At the ceremony on 12 February 1981, the first swearing in of a Chief Justice in the splendid new building, the full High Court was joined on the Bench by the outgoing Chief Justice Sir Garfield Barwick, retired High Court Justices, Sir Frank Kitto and Sir Victor Windeyer, Chief Justice of the Federal Court Sir Nigel Bowen and the Chief Justices of all State Supreme Courts. At the Bar table was Sir Billy Snedden. In reply to official congratulatory speeches, Gibbs foreshadowed taking a lower profile than his predecessor - "the Chief Justice is only the first among equals". He left no doubt, said the Melbourne *Age*, "that he regarded the role of the High Court as an interpreter of the law rather than a vehicle for social change". He stated that it would eventually destroy the authority of the courts if they were to elevate social and political theories of their own over legal principle. He expressed unease at the increased costs and inconvenience to litigants from the centralising of the $50 million court building in Canberra, his hope that it would not separate the Court and the community, and also that the Court would hand down "decisions that are humane, practical and just". He called on State and Federal governments to work together to integrate federal and state courts, remarking that "no legal proceedings are more futile and unproductive than disputes as to jurisdiction". Such attitudes, *The Age* felt, indicated that Gibbs might be a more reformist Chief Justice than Barwick.

In 1977, the Constitution had been amended to reduce the tenure of future High Court justices to 70 years. This applied to Gibbs in accepting appointment as Chief Justice, so he had just six years to make his mark. As foreseen, there was greater harmony and a much less combative atmosphere in the Court itself, the domineering Barwick having gone. Gibbs' style was more consultative.

The portrait of Gibbs' inspirational predecessor, Sir Samuel Griffith, was duly transferred to his new Chambers. The Gibbs bought a small house in a leafy street in suburban Ainslie, staying there from Monday to Friday and returning to their Sydney home at weekends. There were several celebratory dinners in Queensland, one to mark the combined Gibbs and Brennan appointments, given by the Chief Justice Sir Charles Wanstall. Another was given by the Queensland Law Society, for which Gerald Patterson had penned some pithy verse:

> Of lawyers, then, who are the cream?
> Behold Creation's feat supreme,
> A dollop of primordial sludge
> Transmuted into High Court Judge!
> Who sits there high among his peers,
> Who first in verbal thrust and parry?
> None but our noble chief, Sir Harry.

Gibbs was elevated in knighthood from KBE to the Knight Grand Cross of the Order of St Michael and St George (GCMG). Governor-General Sir Zelman Cowen, whom he had known well over many years, gave a small family luncheon party for the Gibbs at Yarralumla, inviting their son, daughters and their husbands. Gibbs' first two appointed associates, Glen Williams (later Judge, Queensland Supreme Court) and David Jackson, put several months research into gathering data and memorabilia on Gibbs' career, had the resulting papers bound and issued invitations to all his associates over the years to attend a dinner at Rags Restaurant in Brisbane to present the volume to him. They came from around the nation and it was a warm tribute to a man who had always genuinely cared about his associates' careers and made efforts to keep in touch.

A copy of that volume is now with the Queensland Supreme Court Librarian, Aladin Rahemtula. He was formerly with the New South Wales' Supreme Court Library, where he came into contact with Gibbs. "Sir Harry used to shelve his own books, he had no arrogance about him. He made no demands and when he became Chief Justice, he never pulled his rank." Rahemtula also appreciated Gibbs' loyalty to Queensland and the fact that he invariably chose his associates from Brisbane, to give them experience at the High Court. Only one out of his fifteen associates was not from his home state.

The High Court heard several major cases in Gibbs' first year as Chief Justice, one in criminal law in which he successfully brought to bear strict application of the principles of the law of evidence,[1] and another a civil case on the statutory power of the Crown. An Aboriginal land claim had been made in the Northern Territory (1981, *Reg v Toohey, ex p Northern Land Council*). At issue was the legitimacy of certain land having recently been declared a town (and therefore no longer classified as unalienated Crown land). The Administrator of the Northern Territory was suspected of having made the declaration to defeat the Aboriginal claim. This complex issue of statutory authority involved a number of legal principles and may be summed up in several statements from Gibbs' judgment in which the Chief Justice asserted the supremacy of the law itself:

> If a statutory power is given to the Crown for one purpose, it is clear that it is not lawfully exercised if it is used for another. The courts have the power and duty to ensure that statutory powers are exercised only in accordance with law.[2]

The High Court held that the Crown, like any other authority, is bound in exercising a statutory power by the rules of natural justice. 1982 brought a constitutional case of vital importance.

Koowarta v Bjelke-Petersen[3] concerned the interpretation of the external affairs power (s 51(xxix) of the Commonwealth Constitution). In dispute was the ability of the Commonwealth to give effect to any international treaty to which Australia is a party, whatever its subject matter, whether it affected Australia's external relations with other nations or related to an entirely internal domestic matter. For instance, cases involving the regulation of international air traffic (1929, 1936, 1965), and those regarding the limits of Australian territorial seas and submerged lands (1976), had validated Commonwealth legislation in those spheres. In *Koowarta*, however, the treaty called for the elimination of all forms of racial discrimination within Australia - a matter of internal domestic concern. Gibbs' strongly held view was that an expansive interpretation of the external affairs power would inevitably lead to an expansion of Commonwealth power to the detriment of the balanced federal-states system of government. A slender majority of the Court - Mason, Stephen, Murphy and Brennan JJ - upheld the legitimacy of the Commonwealth's use of the external affairs power to enact the Racial Discrimination Act. Stephen J did so on a different basis to that of the other three in the majority. He said the subject of the treaty was "a matter of

---

1 *Alexander v The Queen* (1981) 145 CLR 395. See also Connolly analysis, *Appendix*.
2 (1982) 151 CLR 342.
3 (1982) 153 CLR 168; 39 ALR 417.

international concern". The other three said it did not matter what the subject matter. Gibbs CJ, Aicken and Wilson JJ dissented. Gibbs CJ required it to be a matter indisputably international in character. The danger, as the Chief Justice saw it, was the erosion of state powers and the arrogation of power to the Federal Parliament by a side door.

> If the Parliament is empowered to make laws to carry into effect within Australia any treaty which the Governor-General may make, the Executive could, by making an agreement, formal or informal, with another country, arrogate to the Parliament power to make laws on any subject whatsoever.

These concerns were to rise again in the *Tasmanian Dam* case the following year.

Longserving Court Registrar, Frank Jones, a lively well-liked personality whose duties include the timing and assembling of sittings, remembers the mannerisms of the justices as they filed in and out of the court. Sir Harry Gibbs was "distinctive, always walked with his shoulders back", Sir Anthony Mason "with his head forward", Sir Ninian Stephen "looked about with a smile", while Lionel Murphy could be seen "hitching his gown" which invariably seemed to have "gone askew". As a preliminary to filing in, Murphy was usually the one to provide a light-hearted moment or two and had long since, in keeping with his Irish nature, accepted, indeed revelled in his role as dissenter. Murphy, a gregarious man, got along well with all his colleagues. The Justices' wives necessarily attended many functions. Muriel Gibbs' friendship over the years with Patricia Mason and Valery Stephen had made this legal round companionable. They found Ingrid Murphy good company - "younger than us, and so pretty and stylish," said Muriel Gibbs. They all bore the extra strain of juggling family responsibilities with the constant commuting the centralisation of the Court in Canberra entailed.

Later in 1982, the most recently appointed justice (he sat for less than six years), Sir Keith Aickin, died in Melbourne after a car accident. Aickin was regarded as a strict constructionist among lawyers, a possible Chief Justice and a powerful commercial law influence on the Court. He had refused several invitations to the High Court and at 60 had been an elderly appointee. His death was a sad blow, particularly for his fellow Victorian and longtime friend, Sir Ninian Stephen. Gibbs regarded the patient and meticulous Aickin as one of the finest judges with whom he had served, a man of "great strength and serenity of character".

The same year, following Sir Zelman Cowen's decision to take up a post as Provost of Oriel College, Oxford, Sir Ninian Stephen was appointed Governor-General. Gibbs missed Stephen's friendship and influence in the day to day workings of the High Court. The two remained in touch. Stephen's daughter, Elizabeth, was to be Gibbs' final associate - breaking his so-called Queenslander rule.[4]

The new appointees to the High Court were William Deane, a Sydney-based member of the Federal Court, and Daryl Dawson, Victorian Solicitor-General. Dawson had taken a Master of Laws degree from Yale University; Deane, postgraduate studies at Trinity College, Dublin.

The draft judgments issued by the Chief Justice to his fellow justices were frequently adopted with few amendments. It was found in 1985 that the number of joint judgments had increased. However, some lawyers were disappointed that Gibbs did not manage to do more to streamline and expedite the hearing of cases. "In important cases you sometimes have seven opinions," said Ian Callinan in a recent interview. "[A]nd even though you have a majority one way, [the judges] had reached that conclusion by different means - which were very similar in law. You would have thought Sir Harry would have been against that."[5] Such criticism of multiple judgments is widely supported in the professional, academic and, no doubt, the commercial community which has to understand and observe the law.

The role of Chief Justice apparently suited Gibbs. He thrived on the responsibility. "He rarely turned down a request to speak," Frank Jones, the Registrar observed. "He gave a lot of papers, got out and mixed with people, and showed that the Court wasn't just going to be stuck in Canberra. A great convention goer."

He enjoyed writing papers for their legal subject matter and intellectual stimulus. He had spoken in 1980 at the University of Queensland Law School on "Developments in the Jurisdiction of Federal Courts" and at the 3rd Australasian Pacific Forensic Sciences Conference on criminal responsibility. He undertook many speaking engagements and relished the opportunity his position gave him to speak with vigor and influence.

One such paper, for the 11th Wilfred Fullagar Memorial Lecture in July 1982, concerned "The Constitutional Protection of Human Rights," which he believes is all embracing and precludes any need for considering the introduction of a separate Bill of Rights in Australia. In another, at the 7th

---

4 Sir Harry Gibbs' associates at the High Court from 1970-1987 were: Alan Stewart, Bill Heatley, John Morgan, James Douglas, Richard Vann, David Haigh, Peter Rowell, Donald Fraser, Nicholas Cowen, Khory McCormick, Marion Gibney, Douglas Campbell, Tim North, James McLachlan, Elizabeth Stephen.
5 Verge Blunden, *Sydney Morning Herald* of 21 December 1995.

A group of judges and their wives are entertained by the Governor General, Sir Ninian Stephen, and his wife, Lady Stephen, at Government House. Sir Harry Gibbs is centre front; Lady Gibbs is in the front row, fourth from the left.

Commonwealth Legal Conference at Hong Kong in September 1983, he addressed the question, "Is Civil Justice Readily Available?":

> Even when I went to the Bar before World War II, the jibe that the courts, like the Ritz hotel, were open to all who could afford them, was an old one. But lawyers...[then] were inclined to make the comfortable assumption that most people who really needed to engage in litigation were able to do so...Attitudes have changed and during the past decade there has been much discussion as to whether the individual member of society can obtain effective access to justice. The welfare state and the massive legislation which it has spawned have created many new rights for ordinary people and have given rise to greater expectations of social justice.

Gibbs was no showman, but there were glimpses of humour in his presentations. His development of theme and flow of words, enriched by classical allusion and historical illustration where appropriate, held attention. He spoke out forcefully at the Biennial Law Conventions on the "State of the Judicature", attacking the suggestion that the High Court be given power to give advisory opinions on the validity of proposed legislation.

> Persons who may be seriously affected by the proposed legislation may not be aware of that fact at the time when the application for an advisory opinion comes before the Court, so that judgment will be given by the Court which has heard argument from one interested party - the Government - but

not from those persons who in the event will prove to have a vital interest to challenge the validity of the legislation.

He also advocated a means of appeal from the Family Court, questioning the wisdom of a court of limited jurisdiction having its appeal structure within it.

Law students and teachers often sought out the Gibbs judgments, such was the lucidity of his writing. Editing the *Commonwealth Law Reports*, James Merralls also made a practice of reading Gibbs' judgments first. "I did this even before he became Chief Justice, simply to find what the case was about - the arguments were always very clearly presented: he went straight to the facts and issues."

Sir Gerard Brennan counted himself "privileged to be a member of the Court under Sir Harry's Chief Justiceship...In the judgments which [he] wrote, he identified the problems with pellucid clarity," he commented. "And if there were divergences from his opinions, his judgments assisted to sharpen the points of departure and to identify much more clearly the issues which had to be decided."

Brennan from the Bench and Merralls from the Bar, speak of Gibbs as a "superb legal technician". Merralls draws the analogy of the surgeon who might not be able to do every kind of difficult operation, but whose technique is so good he rarely makes a mistake and is thus admired by other surgeons. "Sir Harry Gibbs was like that as a judge," he concluded. "His judicial technique was probably the best on the Court - certainly since Dixon. Dixon was more subtle and had greater knowledge, but possibly the best since then."

Leading QCs, Tom Hughes, David Jackson, Ian Callinan, as well as Merralls, observed that, as presiding judge of the Court, Gibbs was invariably helpful, never unpleasant, never seeking to score points, always pushing the case along, but firm in bringing counsel back to the main track if they were meandering from it. His successor as Chief Justice, Sir Anthony Mason, was in these years senior puisne judge. "The more I saw of [Gibbs]", he said, "the more I was impressed with him as a person and as a lawyer. He is, I think, in many respects, the most naturally courteous and considerate person I know." Such personal qualities in its leader saw the Court, in the first half of the 1980s, settle to a period of relative calm and consistency.

As Editor of the High Court's official record, the *Commonwealth Law Reports*, Merralls QC, lamented that previously the editorial staff, waiting for proofs, had been at the mercy of the slowest associate of the slowest judge.

In agreement with Gibbs, to overcome their case reporting backlog, they imposed a new regime, ie, a three months limit from the end of judgment in the case beyond which the publishers would go ahead and publish. Gibbs proved to be incisive, too, when dealing with paper-happy Australian legal publishers. The publishers sought to introduce a new, second series of law reports, as has been done in Canada and the United States. The main reason for the proposal seemed to be to get new subscriptions without selling what would be the first series of the reports, which cost a prohibitive $12,000. "I felt very unhappy about it," Merralls recalled, "For one thing it would quarantine the past." Gibbs sized up the problem - "I see, spurious, is it?" He and the other justices expressed dissatisfaction with the proposal and it was not pursued.

Tax matters and the distribution of revenue are at the core of tensions between state and federal governments. The Gibbs' High Court turned to an excise duty matter in *Hematite Petroleum Pty Ltd* v *Victoria* (1983).[6] The companies extracting Bass Strait oil and using pipelines to carry the crude oil to plants for processing, were challenging the Victorian Government's right to impose a tax for the use of the pipelines. The question was whether the tax or fee could be classified as a duty of excise. Under s 90 only the Commonwealth can levy excise duties. So, if this was a true excise duty, then the Victorian Government could not levy it. The majority - Mason, Murphy, Brennan, Deane JJ - disallowed the Victorian Government's right to levy the tax. Chief Justice Gibbs and Justice Wilson dissented. The Chief Justice found that the pipeline operation fee was not a tax upon or directly affecting goods; it was simply a fee for a licence to use the pipeline and was thus not a duty of excise. He noted that the wide extension given by the High Court to the definition of excise is "one of the greatest impediments preventing the achievement of a rational and lasting division of financial powers in the Australian Federal system."

This trend towards the strengthening of Commonwealth and central power was furthered in the *Tasmanian Dam* case (1983)[7] with its expansive interpretation of the Commonwealth Government's external affairs power (s 51(xxix) of the Constitution), using its signing of an international treaty to support its own legislation and override State legislation on an internal matter. During Gibbs' term as Chief Justice, environmental issues moved from the wings to centre stage. A plan to flood a river valley in Tasmania to generate hydro-electric power brought "green" issues before Gibbs and his colleagues. The High Court upheld by 4:3 majority (Justices Mason,

6 See Connolly analysis, *Appendix*.
7 See Connolly analysis, *Appendix*.

Murphy, Brennan, Deane; with Chief Justice Gibbs, Justices Wilson and Dawson dissenting) the validity of Commonwealth legislation to prevent the Tasmanian Government building a dam on the Gordon River. The Commonwealth Government, influenced by demands from the increasingly vocal environmentalists, had invoked the international Convention for the Protection of the World Cultural and Natural Heritage, to which it was a party, and declared a 800,000 hectares area of the south western Tasmanian wilderness, which included the dam site, to be on the World Heritage List. This use of the External Affairs Power on an internal matter expanded Commonwealth power to the detriment of the States' legislative powers and responsibilities. It was a case of much significance.

The reach of the Commonwealth's Corporations Power (s 51(xx)) was also being tested. James Merralls presented that part of the case on behalf of the Tasmanian Hydro-Electric Commission. The Commission, a statutory authority established to produce and distribute electric power, also included trading amongst its activities. The point being argued was whether it should be categorised as a public authority (as held by both Wilson and Dawson) or as a trading corporation and therefore within the reach of the Commonwealth's corporations power (a view held by the majority). Merralls was receiving what he described as "a very torrid time" on the point from Sir Anthony Mason, when Gibbs stopped him and asked a question. He had the impression that the Chief Justice was in his favour and thought, "Ah relief! At last I'll get a friendly hand from the Bench." The question however was "absolutely devastating" - and against him. He thought subsequently, "Well, you should never forget he's a true judge. He's going to test your case to its foundations."

The *Tasmanian Dam* case heightened concerns about whether the High Court was being influenced by the judges' own views or perception of community values. Gibbs robustly expressed the contrary view in an address, "Law and Government," he gave some time later:[8]

> This may be discussed by reference to three of the most important cases decided in Australia during the last half-century. In 1948 the High Court decided that legislation whose purpose was to nationalise the banks was invalid. Was that decision influenced by a belief on the part of the judges that private enterprise was better for the community than a government monopoly of banking or by a belief that the community was opposed to nationalisation or by the fact (if it was a fact) that the political philosophy of the judges was conservative? In 1951 the High Court decided that

---

8 *Quadrant*, University of NSW publication, October 1990.

legislation designed to ban the Communist Party was invalid. It can hardly be suggested that the judges of that Court held values sympathetic to those of the Communist Party, but were they influenced by a feeling that the public generally thought that a ban would be unnecessarily restrictive of freedom? In 1983 the High Court held that legislation whose purpose was to prevent the building of a dam on the Gordon River in Tasmania was valid. Was this decision influenced by a belief that the detrimental effect on the environment of the building of the dam outweighed its economic benefits, or by a belief that the community strongly opposed the building of the dam?

Anyone who attempts the rather formidable task of reading the judgments in those cases will not find a word that suggests that the High Court in deciding them had been influenced by anything other than legal principles developed by legal reasoning...and not by its opinion of the wisdom or unwisdom of the legislation in question. Indeed, in the *Dams* case, the Court went out of its way to say that it had not been concerned with whether it was desirable or undesirable that the construction of the dam should proceed. The Court said that the assessment of the possible advantages and disadvantages of constructing the dam, and the balancing of the one against the other, were not matters for the Court, and that the Court's judgment did not reflect any view of the merits of the dispute.

...There is no reason to believe that, of the Justices who decided the *Dams* case the four who formed the majority thought that the building of the dam would be more harmful than beneficial and that the three in the minority held the converse view or that the four were, and the three were not, sensitive to contemporary political opinion. The difference of opinion manifested in the various judgments in that case were differences regarding legal principle, not political policy.

Sir Anthony Mason holds a similar opinion. Sir Daryl Dawson also agreed. It was felt that the environmental issue was not central to the case. When counsel for the Tasmanian Wilderness Society, Michael Black QC, in the course of proceedings, held up photographs to show how beautiful the Gordon River was, Gibbs told him that he would only "inflame the mind of the Court" with irrelevancies: the beauty of the area could be assumed. Legal principle was being argued, not the environmental issue.

The interpretation of s 51(xxix) - the Commonwealth's external affairs power - was at the heart of the case: the legality of the Commonwealth's use of international treaties signed to override a State on an intrinsically domestic matter. The minority clearly saw a danger to the principle of federation to be at issue and, if carried to extremes, the eventual prospect of a Commonwealth government with absolute legislative power - something which was never intended. Gibbs delivered an address to the Queensland Faculty of Law ten years after the Tasmanian Dam case, and one year after the Mabo decision, warning that an amendment of the Constitution might be needed to curb Commonwealth power. Sir Gerard Brennan saw the matter somewhat differently.

> It is, I think, starting to become recognised that the exercise of judicial power is an important setting of the framework of political debate in any country...what Sir Harry emphasized there [to the University of NSW law students], and I think...correctly, is that the technique of judicial decision making is not governed by contemporary...political opinions. Not about the temporary scene. It is based on far more permanent on-going values which lie deep in the social fabric of the society and has to do with the views which judges entertain about the basic nature of society.

Brennan thought that Gibbs' view of the external affairs power was more restricted than that held by the majority of the Court, which, however, "had nothing to do with contemporary politics".

The whole issue raises the question of underlying philosophical values. Gibbs thought that these exist but should remain "in the unconscious or subconscious" of the judge when dealing with intricate legal matters. Experienced QC, Tom Hughes, acknowledges that "perceptions of high political principle must play a part in the Justices' decision making process. One of the great virtues of the High Court is strict legalism, but high principle must have a subliminal effect in Constitutional questions." Sir Anthony Mason, who agreed with Gibbs' summary of the actual procedure by which the judges arrived at their decisions in the *Tasmanian Dam* case, saw more than a subliminal effect: "It is very difficult to divorce legal principle from convictions about underlying philosophy." And Sir Ninian Stephen, who was Governor-General at the time, remarked, "I think the [Gibbs'] view is too idealistic. Underlying philosophies play a big part and, even if only partly consciously, views on what is best for society".

In the *Tasmanian Dam* case Justice Lionel Murphy, as pointed out in a survey of his judgments, "closely linked his broad view of the Commonwealth external affairs power (i.e. that it extended to the implementation of any international treaty whatsoever) with his nationalist and centralist views."[9] He also, they suggested, "avoided in his customary way the fine points of precedent".
Some perspective on the *Tasmanian Dam* case is offered by Sir David Derham, the foundation Dean of Monash Law Faculty and subsequently

---

9 Jean and Richard Ely (eds), *The Rule of Law* 259-260.

Vice-Chancellor of the University of Melbourne.[10] He admired the judgments of the minority, recalling Gibbs' clarity in setting out the issues and the relevant law and facts, and the incisive analysis of authority by Justice Dawson. But Derham thought that the case might be seen to be less important with the passage of time than it appeared to be when it was decided, and that Australians will one day see this contentious case "merely as one step, however wildly aberrant in its logic, on the long path from the day when we were six quasi-independent competing self-governing colonies, to the day when we become one great nation in an international world".

Since Federation our system of government has served Australia well. Any extension of Commonwealth power that threatens the vigour of the nation's constituent parts, should surely be resisted. Diversity has meant strength. For very nearly a century, premiers, chief ministers and governments of this large country's states and territories have energetically and effectively managed the practical administration of their huge areas, incurring little real rancour or discord with Canberra. The federal system, so strongly espoused by Gibbs, has maintained our sense of national identity while at the same time providing a highly satisfactory sense of regional identification, balance and belonging: Australians first, but also, and importantly, New South Welshmen, Victorians, Queenslanders, Western Australians, South Australians, Tasmanians and Territorians.

---

10 See "Mere Surface Reflections", July 1984 *Victorian Law Institute Journal*.

Chapter 11

By the end of 1983, the Gibbs were glad of the Christmas break and set off with various members of the family for their Hervey Bay retreat and New Year celebrations with their Queensland friends. The Patterson, Connolly and Matthews families had gathered at the peaceful holiday spot, and swimming and boating were leavened with Guggenheim, a challenging word game involving homonyms. Mary Matthews on one occasion, and to much hilarity, beat all the legal brains present to the combination of tort, taut and taught.

The High Court year had been a demanding one, compounded by more mundane law and order problems. The Chief Justice's high profile and their frequent absences in Canberra had made their Killara home a target of burglaries. Locked doors and barred windows had little effect. On one occasion, the Gibbs had returned to find nearly all their furniture other than the kitchen suite removed. "At least, I could get dinner", Muriel Gibbs remarked.

The Gibbs relax at Hervey Bay. A game of cards with Gerald Patterson at his holiday home.

Justice Peter Connolly, Queensland Supreme Court, who joined the group at Hervey Bay that year, is pictured here just before his retirement from the Bench in 1991.

Sir Harry was barely back in Canberra and in harness when, in February 1984, a controversy brought the High Court into the centre of public debate again and was to test Gibbs in an unprecedented manner. This was the emergence of *The Age* tapes, NSW police phone tap material published by *The Age*, Melbourne. The tapes seemed to implicate High Court judge Lionel Murphy in misconduct affecting the 1981-1982 trial of his friend, Sydney solicitor Morgan Ryan, in the *Korean Immigrants'* case. In August 1981 Ryan had been charged with falsification of documents, and in November 1981 of conspiracy, in regard to applications from Korean national applicants for permanent resident status. In January 1982 Kevin Jones SM committed Ryan for trial on both charges. Later, the forgery charge was dropped, but in July 1983 a District Court jury convicted Ryan on the conspiracy charge: that conviction was quashed 12 months later by the NSW Court of Appeal and a new trial ordered. The publication of *The Age* tapes resulted in allegations that Justice Murphy had, during Ryan's committal hearing between December 1981 and January 1982, attempted to pervert the course of justice. For anyone, let alone a judge of the High Court, it was a very serious accusation and there were some who thought that an immediate resignation by Murphy would best serve the Court's interests. That particular course was far from Murphy's mind: rightly so, felt many of his friends, including NSW Premier Neville Wran and Acting Commonwealth Attorney-General Gareth Evans. But two disruptive years of inquiries, trials and retrials lay ahead. The Hawke Government initially considered a full Commission of Inquiry (a course opposed by Attorney-General Evans). Then, it appointed a Select Senate Committee to inquire into the question of whether the tapes were authentic and if so whether Murphy's conduct involved "misbehaviour", one of the grounds for his removal from office under s 72 of the Constitution. Ian Callinan QC was appointed counsel assisting the inquiry, assisted by a senior barrister Nicholas Cowdery and others. Tom Hughes QC was one of the number of Queen's Counsel - also Ian Barker, Sir Maurice Byers, Marcus Einfeld, Roger Gyles, Alec Shand - who represented Murphy at this and one or other of the series of hearings and trials which were to follow.

Gibbs was anxious above all about damage to the reputation of the High Court. As the drama unfolded, the press, in particular the *National Times*, seized on every detail, fuelling widespread public controversy. It was a nightmare scenario for a Chief Justice to have a colleague of the High Court under investigation. Gibbs' calm demeanour belied what was for him a bad dream.

The Select Senate Committee heard damaging evidence from Chief Stipendiary Magistrate Clarrie Briese regarding alleged approaches to him by Justice Murphy in 1981-1982 seeking favourable treatment for Ryan during Ryan's committal for trial. The phrase from the tapes - "And what about my little mate?" - was headlined around the country and has passed into Australian folklore. The police gave evidence and Murphy supplied a written statement but refused to give evidence himself. The Committee was unable to make a unanimous finding. Murphy maintained that for a High Court judge to submit to questioning by a Senate Committee would infringe the constitutional separation of powers and violate the independence of the judiciary. Nevertheless, a second Senate Committee, assisted by two former judges, was appointed. Murphy declined to appear before it. When the Committee, having heard allegations from Judge Flannery who had presided at Ryan's trial in 1983, concluded that on the balance of probabilites Murphy had attempted to influence the course of justice and that there "could" be a case of "misbehaviour", he stood down from the bench. The High Court faced a protracted and controversial period, functioning now with six instead of seven judges.

The Director of Public Prosecutions, Ian Temby QC, "taking into account public disquiet", announced that Justice Murphy would be prosecuted on two charges of attempting to pervert the course of justice. The Hawke Government a few months later (March 1985) appointed Justice Donald Stewart, head of the National Crimes Authority, to make a full inquiry into *The Age* tapes.

The affair had started with a great burst of publicity, now it assumed the proportions of an incipient Greek tragedy. Muriel Gibbs felt keenly for Ingrid Murphy, while all members of the High Court, particularly those such as Sir Daryl Dawson, who had found Lionel Murphy very companionable and generous in his recognition of the ability of others, were deeply concerned. Gibbs, personally sympathetic, had to defend the integrity of the nation's top court. At the Australian Legal Convention that year, he spoke of the "public disquiet".

> It is a matter of sadness to those concerned with the state of the courts that three judicial officers, one a member of the High Court, have been charged with offences concerning the administration of justice. Two have been convicted, but have appeals pending, and one is awaiting trial. But I am sure that no one who knows anything about the working of the law in Australia has any doubt about the complete integrity of the judicial system as a whole.

Sir Harry Gibbs (centre). Clockwise from top left, Sir Ninian Stephen, Sir Anthony Mason, Sir Daryl Dawson, Sir Gerard Brennan, (captured by Sid Scales, NZ).

Meanwhile, during 1984, Gibbs instituted a major procedural change to ease the Court's excessive caseload. The Commonwealth Government, at the Court's request, amended the Judiciary Act (s 35A), abolishing the automatic right of appeal to the High Court and substituting special leave to appeal in both civil and criminal cases. Gibbs was keen that the Court itself determine which appeals should be heard. General guidelines for granting Special Leave were indicated: that the case be a matter of public importance; or that it concern differences of opinion in other Australian courts as to the state of the law; or that it concern the interests of the administration of justice. Some senior members of the Bar, such as Ian Callinan, were unhappy with the abolition of the automatic right of appeal, particularly because it was known that the cessation of appeals to the Privy Council from State courts in non-federal matters was being mooted. It was also felt that the inauguration of Special Leave to Appeal could rebound unfairly on many litigants. In civil cases, if a litigant's case could mean the advancement or reduction in money or property by a considerable sum, it would be heard.[1] The Law Council of Australia opposed the change. Its introduction, however, was now a fait accompli and counsel were required to supply written submissions and materials.

In carrying out this new policy, Gibbs stuck to his strong sense of justice for all and equality before the law, even at the expense of procedural and administrative pain. The Chief Justice, together with Brennan and Deane, were of the opinion that in criminal cases, special leave to appeal should be granted where the High Court hearing the application formed the view that a substantial miscarriage of justice may have occurred. Mason, Wilson and Dawson were of the opinion that if the court from which it was sought to appeal itself had not made a finding of miscarriage of justice, then the High Court should refuse special leave, unless it could be shown that the case was one with a point of general importance in questions of law. Sir Daryl Dawson commented recently:

> That's where I differ from Sir Harry. He had the view that if he saw a miscarrriage of justice he had to correct it which is an entirely admirable thing but it is becoming increasingly unrealistic...[he cited the United States where there are five or six thousand applications per year]...the Court can only write so many judgments, 100 or 110 cases - obviously you can't select on the basis of righting wrongs. The High Court is not a Court of Criminal Appeal. Its duty is to develop the law and maintain procedural regularity below and that being so you must inevitably reject some cases in which you could right wrong. You can't do them.

---

1 Callinan, "The Working of the Appellate Courts", paper delivered to the Second Biennial Conference of the Australian Bar Association, July 1986.

Many Australians would identify with Gibbs and his colleagues of similar view, and might ask, if the final court of appeal in this land has not the time or it is not administratively possible to deal with perceived miscarriages of injustice in criminal cases, then should priorities be re-examined?

The administration of the Court devoured much of Gibbs' time. Legal expert, David Solomon, then legal reporter for *The Australian* and subsequently the *Financial Review* was impressed by his political nous:

> At a time when he was in the minority on what he, as well as everyone else, regarded as the most important issues before the Court - namely on the Federal-State relations question - it must have been very frustrating for him, but that never showed. He was a very good Chief Justice politically - in the sense of dealing with the politicians. He used his speeches and conferences on the law and so on, with very great political effect - to protect the Court and judges generally, but particularly to protect the Court in its relation with the Federal Government and to make sure that the Government never really contemplated cutting back on the Court's budget. He was a very good political operator. The Court worked extremely well under him. The end of the Murphy affair aside...I thought as Chief Justice he was very impressive.

It was just midway through the Murphy legal saga. In July 1985, following his first trial, at which he gave sworn evidence, he was found guilty on one count and acquitted on another. Sentence was reserved, and in the interval before Justice Cantor (Supreme Court of NSW) delivered his judgment, Murphy challenged in the High Court the validity of s 43 of the Commonwealth Crimes Act, under which the case had been brought against him. Ian Callinan, who represented the Crown, recalled the tension in the splendid, oak-pannelled courtroom with its sombre array of white-wigged, black-gowned justices, circled by portraits of their predecessors. "I'll never forget that day...There we were, we had no personal arguments - everyone was just so strained. It was an impossible situation."

Try as the Chief Justice and his colleagues might to minimise the damage to the Court, it could not escape controversy, with headlines such as "Murphy's plan rejected by brother judges", and a few weeks later, "Murphy: 18 months but will not resign" and "Words that made ALP hearts sink".[2] Justice Cantor sentenced Murphy to 18 months imprisonment, but released him on bail pending appeals. In November, the NSW Court of Criminal Appeal, with a bench of five, found that there was evidence available for a jury to convict. However, they quashed the conviction, partly on the basis that Cantor had misdirected the jury by saying that the overwhelming evidence of Murphy's

---

2 See *Sydney Morning Herald* of 15 August and 4 September 1985.

good character could not be used in considering his credibility. A new trial was ordered. Premier Wran lashed out again at Director of Public Prosecutions Temby. The press coverage generally was so omnivorous that there was some talk of law reform to curb it.

Gibbs felt the strain. Muriel Gibbs tried to lighten the load. "I became notorious on the airlines for my meat basket," she recalled. She had standing arrangements with Killara and Canberra butchers, who were happy to supply her at all hours to help smooth "the Judge's path". The Killara Post Office also cooperated, efficiently re-addressing their mail to Canberra. Lady Gibbs was on excellent terms with all these people and made her appreciation felt each Christmas, and whenever she returned with pineapples from Hervey Bay. At Ainslie, their garden featured two magnificent nectarine trees, the fruits of which the various justices and their spouses often received. "Muriel would produce these bags of fruit and we'd be delighted," recalled Sir Daryl Dawson, regretful only that he and his wife could not accept them when flying back to Victoria. The companionship of Muriel Gibbs' circle of "legal" friends made life enjoyable, but the commuting and the unremitting schedule of conferences and dinners left her exhausted. It did not occur to her that there might be an underlying medical reason for this.

Gibbs was guest speaker at the University of Queensland's 75th Anniversary and the 50th Anniversary of its Faculty of Law celebrations. His subject was "The Law Fifty Years Later". He also spoke at a dinner to mark the 25th Anniversary of the Restoration of the District Courts in Queensland where his old friend, the then Chairman of the District Court, Judge Lindsay Byth, "presided". At the first International Criminal Law Congress in Adelaide his subject was "The Role of the High Court". To the Commonwealth Magistrates' Association, at Nicosia, Cyprus, he delivered a paper on "The Appellate Structure with Particular Reference to Appeals Against Sentence"; and to a Conference of Asian Pacific Chief Justices at Penang, Malaysia, he trod on tricky ground in that country at that time to speak on "The Independence of the Judiciary". Gibbs created considerable impact on behalf of Australia on that occasion. Each of the Chief Justices present spoke on some aspect of the independence of the judiciary, although several of them were from quasi-military dictatorships. Judicial independence was little more than an ideal for them. High Court Registrar Jones, who attended the Conference, commented, "Sir Harry was the one who took over and took control and got them to [formulate a statement on judicial independence]. He really showed leadership - international standard."

Frank Jones also admired Gibbs' exercise routine each day in place of his Canberra lakeside walk. In Penang, Gibbs swam numerous laps of the pool each morning. "Up and down, up and down - he wore me down," Jones said. Although never a vigorous athlete, Gibbs had, with his friend Patterson, long recognised the need for balance between intellectual and physical exertion.

In 1985, New Zealand judge Robin Cooke, dealing with a case concerning constructive trusts as between partners in a de facto union,[3] found, as Sir Maurice Byers had some years before in child custody cases, that Gibbs, whom he holds "in high respect", took very different views from those he held himself:

> I derived a good deal of amusement from [the] judgment of Gibbs CJ...in which he expressed something like incredulity that any lawyer could hold views as heterodox as my own. But in time the High Court of Australia moved to much the same position.[4]

Another major change during Gibbs' term as Australian Chief Justice now occurred: the final severance of the Australian court system from the Privy Council. Gibbs thought that allowing litigants, on losing a case in a State court, the choice of appeal to either the Australian High Court or the London-based Privy Council was unsatisfactory. In March 1986, all the relevant parliaments -the Commonwealth parliament, the British parliament, all State parliaments - passed acts to the same effect. The Australia Act abolished appeals to the Privy Council altogether. Formal legal ties with Great Britain finally passed into history.

Gibbs has a lively sense of history. He expressed this in the foreword he wrote for Victorian County Judge, Graham Fricke's well-written and invaluable *The Judges of the High Court* (1986). The book is a set of lively biographical sketches of all the judges, no longer living, who were members of the High Court since its foundation in 1903 to the present. Gibbs wrote, "I hope his [Fricke's] prudent acceptance of the injunction *de vivis nil* will not lay him open to the reproach levelled at Lord Campbell when he wrote *The Lives of the Lord Chancellors*, that he had added a new terror to death." Gibbs had personally known 11 of the 22 judges who formed the subject of the book and had sat on the Court with four of them: Sir Douglas Menzies, Sir William Owen, Sir Cyril Walsh and Sir Keith Aickin. Their combined qualities, he commented, "could well make the ideal judge". When Fricke's book was published, its review in *The Australian* led to a feature article on 10 June 1993 by Jane Cadzow entitled "Six faceless men on the Bench", with character sketches of Gibbs and his five colleagues (Mason, Brennan, Wilson, Dawson and Deane). The article praised the Chief Justice for

---

3 *Muschinski v Dodds* (1985) 150 CLR 583 at 595.
4 In *Baumgartner v Baumgartner* (1987) 164 CLR 137, after Gibbs' time.

achieving an harmonious working relationship of "powerful intellects and strong opinions". He had displayed "firmness and...forcefulness of character", engendered universal respect, and walked a skilful line with "all the courtesy and politeness and the standards of a gentlemen, but underneath the velvet...steel". There had been several unexpected calls on the latter.

Of 80 applications heard between June 1984 and November 1985 for special leave to appeal to the High Court, some 26 (32%) had been granted. Of the applications refused, some 21 (48%) would have come to the High Court as of right under the former law.[5] Gibbs remarked, "That means the Court has been afforded moderate relief." Prominent counsel, such as Ian Callinan, were still unhappy about the new system. They were unimpressed by the various formulae for refusal used by the High Court, such as: "No matter of public importance falls to be decided in this case. The Court refuses special leave. By refusing special leave, the Court does not say that it necessarily agrees with the reasoning of the Court below."

Callinan, in a paper to the Bar Council, noted that the first two volumes of the *Commonwealth Law Reports* containing the judgments of Australia's first three High Court Justices, Samuel Griffith, Edmund Barton and Richard O'Connor, who travelled all over the country via train and ship, run to 700 pages in 1903-1904, and in 1904-1905 some 800 pages. The four volumes covering the period 1990-1991 - Volumes 170-173 - containing the work of seven Justices, who are not required to travel as much and do so by aeroplane, reach some 2400 pages of cases heard and determined during those two years. In earlier days, argument was more extensively reported and, therefore, the matter cannot, he says, be finally resolved by reference to the volume or quantity of pages of judgments written, but the exercise is an indication that under different trying conditions, fewer judges handled a very large number of appeals as of right. Why, then, he argues, limit leave to appeal? Callinan also does not believe that the criteria for special leave refusals are sufficiently objective, and concludes: "I think the abolition of rights of appeal and the substitution only of an appeal by way of special leave has been the most damaging thing in the High Court's history."

1986 was to be the most testing year of Sir Harry Gibbs' career, as he steered the Court through the turbulent constitutional crises brought about by the continuing saga of Lionel Murphy. The third ranking judge of the High Court went on trial in April at Sydney's Central Criminal Court, for the second time in a year and in a blaze of publicity. Central to the Crown's case

---

5 This and subsequent quotes from *Sydney Morning Herald* of 21 December 1985, article by Verge Blunden, "After Sir Harry, who shall be judge?"

was the longstanding friendship between Justice Murphy and solicitor Ryan and their gulf in status. Murphy, attending the court with his wife, declined to enter the witness box and give sworn evidence and so could not be cross-examined. He submitted an unsworn statement. A fortnight later he was found not guilty, a verdict welcomed by many, including Premier Wran who said he would not forgive those responsible for "the great suffering [Murphy] has been through" and announced that he no longer had confidence in NSW Chief Magistrate Briese, whose evidence in the first trial had been so damning. It seemed that Murphy would now be able to resume his seat on the High Court. Two days later, however, the Stewart Royal Commission issued its report. This authenticated *The Age* tapes and in the second volume contained further allegations. At the same time, separate allegations were made by a former federal police officer. These circumstances again put Murphy at risk of criminal charges and he cancelled his plans to return to the Bench. Gibbs wrote to him urging resignation. In Gibbs' view, Murphy ought to go so that public confidence in the High Court was not eroded further.

Rather than allowing Murphy to be charged, the Hawke Government now went about setting up a Special Parliamentary Inquiry and asked advice from the High Court on the matter. The Prime Minister also called on the Governor-General, Sir Ninian Stephen, and refrained from endorsing Murphy's return to the Bench. Legal opinion, as well as public opinion generally, was divided, often sharply. Hearn Professor of Law at the University of Melbourne, Colin Howard, was of the opinion that the "greatest service [Murphy] could render to this country would be to assist the Government to repair some of the damage done to our judicial system by retiring gracefully now. He would lose nobody's respect by so doing."[6] The High Court was in an invidious situation. Whatever the truth of all the allegations, Justice Murphy's position seemed untenable: resignation was an obvious solution. On the other hand, senior lecturer in law at the University of NSW, David Brown, argued at length that "the future of Justice Murphy should not be decided by those forces powerful enough to generate controversy from the `imputations' it is possible to draw from stale lunch conversations or the gibberish on authentic illegal tapes of doubtful reliability. He should not resile from returning to the bench."[7] Sir Maurice Byers held a similar opinion, remarking that if Justice Murphy, who had steadfastly maintained his innocence throughout, had resigned it would have implied guilt. Murphy supporters, who had set up a fund to contribute to his legal fees, felt the same, as did the thirty distinguished members of the

---

6 *Sydney Morning Herald* of 7 May 1986.
7 Ibid.

community, ranging from prominent educator and scientist Professor Harry Messel to artist Lloyd Rees, who inserted a half page advertisement in the *Sydney Morning Herald* under the title "A fair go for Justice Murphy", arguing that enough was enough and no further inquiry should be held. But the tumbleweed of public disquiet and rumour was not to be stopped.

The publicity, as Sir Anthony Mason commented, was "outrageous". Thick, black, frontpage headlines and detailed coverage of the crisis were featured in all major papers. The *Sydney Morning Herald* blazed on 7 May: "Exclusive. Gov-Gen acts on Murphy, How Sir Ninian Stephen and Sir Harry Gibbs joined in moves to resolve the constitutional crisis." Above was a Moir cartoon of the pipe-smoking Governor-General (who had interviewed Justice Murphy, but to ask his intentions not to proffer advice), a be-wigged Sir Harry Gibbs flanking a defiant Justice Murphy, and the inaccurate statement that "Sir Harry and four, possibly five other High Court judges were so determined not to sit on the Bench with him that they were ready to go on strike". Gibbs protested: "It is quite untrue to say that I said that the Court would or might go on strike, although that was widely reported, either because of misunderstanding or distortion on somebody's part." Mason, Brennan and Dawson also categorically deny that any member of the Court had even considered such a course.

An extensive 7 May *Sydney Morning Herald* article by Peter Bowers claimed that:

> It seems to have been of serious concern to Gibbs that Justice Murphy had given sworn evidence at his first trial, and had not been believed by the jury, which had proceeded to convict. In his second trial, Justice Murphy had chosen to make an unsworn statement, which had been accepted by the jury which proceeded to acquit. In the Chief Justice's view, Justice Murphy should have demonstrated a consistent willingness to submit to cross-examination at both trials.

Gibbs had contacted Attorney-General Lionel Bowen when the crisis erupted, but it was only to follow up Justice Murphy's desire to see allegations contained in the second volume of the Stewart Commission Report. Gibbs asked that copies be made available to the High Court.

The press speculated "Bowen denies that he misled public". (Opposition members had accused the Attorney-General of misleading the public into believing that the High Court judges would sit in judgment on Justice Murphy). Another paper said, "Judges' statement surprised Govt", and carried the Statement Gibbs had issued from the High Court the previous day (6 May 1986).

STATEMENT OF THE CHIEF JUSTICE

Yesterday there was a meeting of the Justices of this Court, including Mr Justice Murphy. In some way a misunderstanding of the intentions of the Justices has arisen. The Justices do not intend to conduct any inquiry or to make any finding as to the conduct of Mr Justice Murphy in order to resolve any controversy as to his Honour's judicial status, rights or duties. They did not agree to do so yesterday.

The function of the Court is to decide cases in open court and not to conduct private inquiries. The Court has no function to perform as to its own composition, though its members, of course, have an abiding concern with the preservation of public confidence in it. It was that concern which led the meeting of the Justices yesterday to consider what, if any, part it was appropriate for them as individuals to play. In the course of the discussion in that regard Mr Justice Murphy sought an opportunity to see the relevant material in the confidential volume of Mr Justice Stewart's Report and to make a public response to it. He volunteered in the meantime not to sit. The other members of the Court agreed to postpone further discussion until Mr Justice Murphy has made such response as he wishes to make.

Meanwhile, the Chief Justice's heavy schedule of duties continued unabated. He showed poise and courage in the heat of the media attention. Murphy's courage and tenacity, too, were remarkable. But by now the two men were on quite different courses. Gibbs' primary concern was the Court and its place in society: Murphy was determined to go down fighting, and was not so preoccupied with the Court's dignity and the need for his sacrifice. Murphy was feeling mortal, and for good reason. He knew the High Court would long survive him and his controversy.

The Hawke Government now went ahead and appointed three former justices - Sir George Lush, Sir Richard Blackburn and Mr Andrew Wells - to head a Parliamentary Commission to decide whether Justice Murphy should be removed from the High Court under s 72 of the Constitution. Sittings began in Sydney early in June and continued in Brisbane. Murphy challenged the validity of the Commission and sought to disqualify one of its members (Wells, whose views, it was submitted, were a pre-judgment). The Court was soon to go into its winter recess and set the hearing of this challege down for August.

Gibbs had continued with his usual round of speeches, telling an assembly of law students in Adelaide, no doubt with feeling, that from time to time the media "engages in symbolic butchery of the judiciary", and another legal gathering that though "lawyers, like the press, are often reviled" they are essential in a society tending to be controlled and regimented by bureaucracy.[8]

Matters were moving to a tragic climax. At the end of July, Lionel Murphy, who had been consulting his doctors, learnt that he was terminally ill with cancer of the colon. He resolved not to attend any further proceedings of the Parliamentary Commission of Inquiry. He then informed the High Court at its sitting on 29 July that he intended to exercise his "constitutional right" to resume sitting. Gibbs expressed his sympathy but told Murphy that he opposed this. He confirmed this two days later by letter, giving his colleague the text of a press statement he intended to release, should Murphy persist in his course.

> 31 July 1986
> *CONFIDENTIAL*
> The Honourable Mr Justice Murphy,
> High Court of Australia,
> CANBERRA   A.C.T.   2600
>
> Dear Lionel,
>
> I repeat that I am sincerely sorry to hear the news about your health.
>
> As you know, I think it undesirable that you should sit, and in the interests of the Court, as well as in your own interest, I do not propose to list you to sit. However, if you do decide to take your seat on the bench I request you to let me know (or to ask your staff to let my staff know) beforehand on what cases during this sittings you would wish to sit and I shall then make the necessary arrangements.
>
> I would propose to make a news release in the following terms:
>
> Mr Justice Murphy has informed me that he is gravely ill. He has also stated that he intends to exercise what he has described as his constitutional right to sit on the Court, notwithstanding that the Parliamentary Commission of Inquiry has not yet made its report. It is essential that the integrity and reputation of any Justice of this Court be seen to be beyond question. That being so, I regard it as most undesirable that Mr Justice Murphy should sit while matters into which the Commission is inquiring remain unresolved, and before the Commission has made its report. Nevertheless, in the circumstances to which I have referred, I do not regard it as appropriate to do more than express that view.

---

8 See *Sydney Morning Herald* 9 August 1986, article by Verge Blunden, "A mild man raising a storm."

I would not propose to say anything in court, but would make the release on the day when you first sit. I would hope that if you wish to say anything you would follow a similar procedure. In framing my draft news release in the way that I have done I have assumed that your own statement, if any, would be similarly uncontroversial and that I would not need to reply to it. I would appreciate it if you supplied me in advance with a copy of any statement you proposed to make. In your own interests, particularly to avoid any possibility of harassment by the media, I would suggest that our statements be not released until after you have gone into Court.

Murphy's persuasive response highlighted the independence of the judiciary and Murphy's right, and indeed the right of any judge, to remain active until misbehaviour was proved.

HIGH COURT OF AUSTRALIA
 Chambers of Mr Justice Murphy
1 August 1986
The Right Honourable Sir Harry Gibbs, GCMG, KBE,
Chief Justice,
High Court of Australia,
CANBERRA. A.C.T. 2600

Dear Bill,

I refer to your letter of 31 July 1986.

I find it extraordinary that you propose to make a news release, especially one in the terms set out in your letter. Although you describe it as uncontroversial, it would inevitably provoke an intense public controversy involving you, me and the Court.

If you do so, this would be the second time within weeks that such a controversy has been provoked. In May, the Government through 2 Ministers informed me that you had said that if I resumed sitting, the Court would or might go on strike. I now know that most members of the Court had not even contemplated such a course. However I have not heard any public denial by you, although the matter has been widely reported.

Your statement questions whether I have a constitutional right to sit on the Court. The plain constitutional position is that the Justices when appointed to the Court have a constitutional right to sit until death, resignation or removal under s.72 (on the grounds only of proved misbehaviour or incapacity). It is not for the Chief Justice or any Justice to decide whether it is undesirable for any other Justice to sit on the Court. It is improper for one Judge to publicly express an opinion on the desirability of another to continue as a Justice or to exercise his functions as a Justice. This is at the foundation of the independence of the judiciary.

It has been part of Australia's judicial history that a number of appointments to the High Court have been attacked, and the integrity and reputation of the appointees have been questioned in and out of Parliament, and occasionally by resolutions of Bar Councils. If your contention is correct, it would follow because the Justices' integrity and reputation had been questioned he should not continue as a Judge of the Court. Nothing could be more calculated to undermine the independence of the judiciary. It would encourage the promotion of campaigns against Judges and not only those newly-appointed.

For a Chief Justice to state that if there is a question about a Justice's reputation or integrity, or if there is an inquiry into a Judge's conduct, he should not continue as a Justice, undermines the independence of every federal judge. Significantly, you made no such suggestion when the 2 Senate inquiries were in progress, the second of which included Parliamentary Commissioners. During both of those inquiries I sat and decided cases.

You refer to the undesirability of sitting before the Commission makes its report. As I informed all members of the Court my advice is that there is no reasonable prospect of the Commission reporting by the due date of 30 September. Even if an extension were granted I am advised that the probability is that the Commission would not report before the end of this year.

I wish to avoid any public controversy with you, as this will inevitably encourage others who will be only too anxious to feed on such a controversy. But if you issue the news release I will answer along the lines of this letter, or release the letter. My present intention is that I will not make any statement from the bench or issue any statement before sitting. A copy of the statement which I intend to issue in any event is enclosed.

As you suggested, my staff have informed yours of the cases in which I propose to sit.

Yours sincerely,
Lionel

The Acting Attorney-General, Gareth Evans, expressed the government's profound distress at Justice Murphy's illness. He accepted Murphy's right to resume sitting and said that the question of the appropriate future course of the Parliamentary Commission of Inquiry would be discussed.

Justice Murphy did sit early in August and, as Gibbs and his colleagues ensured, "the sitting was dignified and went off without incident." At one point the Chief Justice leant across and offered some assistance to Justice Murphy. Tom Hughes QC, appearing in the case (*Miller v TCN Channel 9*), was appalled to see the physical change in Murphy. "It was a terrible thing to watch a man disintegrating before your eyes - dying by degrees." Hughes added: "I thought Gibbs behaved impeccably. In a very difficult situation, he went right down the middle."

The publicity continued unrestrained. Photographers and the media hounded Gibbs (one intrusive television camera captured him one morning at 6 am putting out his rubbish bin and flashed the mundane image across the country). Headlines competed for crassness: "High Court in Turmoil", "Murphy's Danse Macabre", "Bowen: I didn't call Chief Justice a liar", and, during the silence maintained by his colleagues in regard to his stance, "Gibbs becoming more isolated".

No matter what his motives, effectively Gibbs had, by his public statement, abandoned his colleague, and a popular and terminally-ill one at that. He saw that his duty to protect the Court overwhelmed personal considerations. It was a burden he largely had to bear alone. Sir Daryl Dawson remarked, "He didn't on that occasion ask for the views of the other justices. I think he felt it so strongly that those views wouldn't matter anyway. He was resolute, he never wavered." Muriel Gibbs was distressed. Her husband had wanted the support of the other justices and understood that they would give it. But publicly they were silent. Sir Ninian Stephen, looking back, commented: "I don't think the High Court handled the affair well." Legal affairs writer, David Solomon, and Gibbs' old friend, Sir Maurice Byers, felt that he had been too severe. Sir Anthony Mason, however, observed: "I have never known Sir Harry to be harsh or unfeeling in his life." In this matter, perhaps more than in any other, the steeliness underlying his mild manner became visible. He felt that a matter of high principle was involved.

The Hawke Government now struggled with the dilemma of its loyalty to Murphy and its own credibility as it drew up the Parliamentary Commission of Inquiry (Repeal) Bill. Since the Commissioners had indicated that they would need six months to complete investigations, the issue would remain on the boil. Meanwhile, Gibbs spoke to around 200 law students at the University of New South Wales on the vexed and highly relevant question of the appointment of judges. The address was featured by *The Australian* of 19 August 1986 in an article entitled, "Sir Harry wants politics off the Bench". It noted that the retirement of Sir Harry Gibbs in six months, the expected retirement of West Australian Sir Ronald Wilson, and Mr Justice Murphy's terminal illness, would recast the High Court, and quoted Gibbs' remark that: "Past political office should neither be a bar nor assist appointment to the Bench; it should be neutral." In 1987 he wrote a short piece on the issue in the *Australian Law Journal*, saying that there must be, amongst politicians of all parties, a realisation that the interests of the community require that neither political patronage, nor a desire to placate any section of society, should play any part in making judicial appointments. Merit...should be the only criterion.[9]

He defined merit as "legal excellence and experience coupled with good character and suitable temperament."

Meanwhile, the *Sydney Morning Herald* in an editorial, "Beyond Murphy a cover-up", commented:

> The Federal Government can be no more proud of its handling of the issues raised by the NSW Police tapes than the NSW Government can of its. Whatever the merits of the Parliamentary Commission of Inquiry (Repeal) Bill, its provisions making it illegal to publish allegations derived from documents gathered by the commission are indefensible...The inquiry into Justice Murphy's fitness as a judge, it can be assumed, took the commission into the jungle of allegations of corrupt power-broking in NSW...the commissioners' request for more time cannot be regarded as idle. Nor should it be seen merely in terms of Justice Murphy's personal fate.

The paper declared that history would not deal kindly with the Federal Government's act in terminating the inquiry so swiftly and "burying its remains". A political storm ensued, with adverse comment led by Opposition Leader John Howard. The Government finally accepted an amendment to allow publication of the documents in 2016AD.

This was September 1986 and Gibbs took several weeks' leave. An adventurous traveller, with a taste for out of the way places, he headed for the volcanic Galapagos Islands. He flew with Muriel to Guayaquil, Ecuador. From there, with a small group of like-minded people, they set off in a chartered boat some 1200km into the Pacific to explore the rugged islands. They were fascinated by the unique wildlife - seabirds with webbed feet (blue-footed boobies), the remarkable marine iguanas, enormous turtles and "tiptoeing" crabs - and sent off postcards to their family and friends every other day as one or other phenomenon impressed them. "He'd climb to the top of Kilimanjaro - he'd go anywhere, I don't know where he hasn't been, comfortable or uncomfortable", said his colleague Daryl Dawson.

Lionel Murphy died in late October. Prime Minister Hawke, leading the tributes said, "Lionel Murphy was a great Australian and one of our finest jurists. He made a significant and lasting contribution to the Parliament and

---

9 (1987) 61 ALJ 7 at 11.

the legal system of this country."[10] David Solomon, writing of Murphy's achievements in the *Financial Review* of 22 October 1986, noted that Murphy was "in a sense, more successful as a politician than a judge." There can be no doubt he was more suited temperamentally to political life than to the bench. He was a clever and innovative man, but was not regarded as a great jurist, although the contrary is now, in revisionist circles, becoming conventional wisdom.

Sir Harry Gibbs had now just four months to serve as Chief Justice. He found himself in the minority on several constitutional law cases, since the trend of opinion in judgments was increasingly towards extension of Commonwealth powers. But he continued to carry the Court with him on most matters of general law, which formed the vast majority of cases. One of Gibbs' last major addresses as Chief Justice was on his concern at the rising crime rate in Australia. "Not only has the crime rate risen (steeply in many instances) but offences against the person tend to be more vicious in their nature." He also launched and became patron of two new professional organisations, the Criminal Lawyers Association of Australia and the Criminal Law Section of the Law Council of Australia, at the same time accepting honorary membership, the first ever given, of the Law Council itself.

It was announced that Sir Anthony Mason would succeed him as Chief Justice. New appointees to the Court were Mary Gaudron (formerly Solicitor - General for New South Wales and John Toohey (formerly a Federal Court judge). On the day before his retirement, 5 February 1987, as he packed his books in his Chambers, Gibbs gave an interview to a journalist from the *Sydney Morning Herald*.[11] When asked about a "new Constitution", he replied: "It's fashionable to say the Constitution was drawn up in horse-and-buggy days. But it was to a large extent modelled on the US Constitution, which dates from 1776, and no one calls that a horse-and-buggy Constitution."

The High Court hosted a ceremonial farewell. Sitting with the justices, resplendent in their black silk robes, were his predecessor, Sir Garfield Barwick, several other former colleagues, the Governor-General Sir Ninian Stephen, the new appointees to the Court, all State and Federal Chief Justices and Justice Elizabeth Evatt, Chief Judge of the Family Court of Australia. Among the guests was former Prime Minister Gough Whitlam, while at and behind the bar table forty QCs were seated. After recent events, this display

---

10 *Sydney Morning Herald* of 22 October 1993.
11 *Sydney Morning Herald* of 5 February 1987 in an article by John Slee, "Don't use labels when judging the judges".

of solidarity was gratifying for Gibbs. Attorney-General Lionel Bowen, in concluding his address, said:

> During the last years of Your Honour's term as Chief Justice, the Court was placed under considerable strain as a result of accusations concerning the conduct of a judge of the Court. These accusations were such that it was inappropriate for the Court itself to deal with them, a point acknowledged by the Court...It is equally inappropriate for Parliament acting unilaterally to deal with such accusations other than in accordance with the procedures established by the Constitution.
>
> It is central to a system of justice that where accused of criminal behaviour, judges of any court, that they receive the same equal treatment as anybody else before the law. Your Honour, you have capped a great career of service in law by presiding over Australia's highest Court. In this you have manifested great professional skill and knowledge...and the willingness to state your view without fear or favour.

Roger Gyles QC, President of the Australian Bar Association, also spoke. He mentioned Gibbs' outstanding contribution to the criminal law. Ian Callinan QC, President of the Queensland Bar Association, described Gibbs' career and achievements as an inspiration to Queensland barristers. DR Williams QC, President of the Law Council of Australia, praised Gibbs' leadership, unfailing courtesy and the tremendous testimony of the law reports: "The result has been a great judge". Ian Callinan had remarked on the flexibility and effectiveness with which Gibbs had adapted to so much change in the law and in society. These were an indication of his "enormous capacities as man, lawyer and judge". Callinan ended movingly: "We thank you for your courtesy, your example and your fraternal companionship in the law."

Gibbs spoke only briefly, towards the end of his reply, of the "unprecedented difficulties" the Court had faced. He highlighted the problems of the legal profession generally and specifically of the vital role of barristers and solicitors: "The rule of law is a precious inheritance and it can be preserved only if the legal profession in Australia retains its strength and integrity." His most quoted comments concerned the volume of cases coming before the Court involving administrative law and the interpretation of statutes. "Such litigation is important," he said, "but it would be regrettable if it occupied so much time that the Court became unable to hear cases of other kinds, particularly those arising under the common law and those affecting the rights of ordinary citizens." These remarks, as *The Australian*'s John Moses commented next day, "were debated hotly...in Canberra's restaurants and hotel dining rooms by the dozens of senior lawyers and judges who came to hear the last official words of the Chief Justice." Sir Harry Gibbs, having made his challenge, affirmed his satisfaction in serving as Chief Justice, thanked all who attended his farewell, and, two days from his 70th birthday, bowed out gracefully.

Chapter 12

AN ACTIVE RETIREMENT

Retirement from such a busy and intellectual life could have been anti-climactic for Sir Harry Gibbs, but it was not. Ten days after he stepped down from the bench the Hawke Government approached him to chair a review of the Commonwealth criminal law, an area of his specific expertise and interest. The Committee included Justice Ray Watson of the Family Court at Sydney who had been working on a preliminary report on the subject for several years, and Canberra-based former deputy secretary of the Attorney-General's Department, Andrew Menzies, who had headed the Nazi War Crimes Investigation. The Commonwealth had not been given a general criminal law power at Federation. This issue needed to be resolved. The Committee, to which "Sir Harry would bring unparalleled legal skill and experience", was charged with rationalising and consolidating the complete list of Commonwealth criminal law provisions, which were presently scattered throughout various Acts of Parliament.[1] The criminal law had grown on an ad hoc basis and there were sometimes several provisions for similar offences. Bowen wanted the inquiry to amalgamate these into a concise criminal law code and examine the adequacy and consistency of penalties, onus of proof provisions, and matters such as contempt of administrative bodies.[2]

The Committee was to report by June 1988. In fact it continued over a period of three years. Andrew Menzies and his staff at the Attorney-General's Department in Canberra coordinated the project, although Gibbs himself undertook about 40% of the basic work. Andrew Menzies, a perspicacious and quietly humorous man, was a Brisbane acquaintance from Gibbs' barrister days. As Deputy Crown Solicitor, he had frequently briefed Gibbs on behalf of the Commonwealth Government.

Early that year Gibbs accepted an honorary Doctorate from Queensland's Griffith University (named after Sir Samuel Griffith). At the colourful graduation gathering of splendidly robed and tasselled academics and dignitaries, and after his presentation by the Vice-Chancellor Roy Webb, the Chancellor, the State's Chief Justice John Macrossan, awarded the Doctorate. Macrossan referred to "some controversy surrounding the High Court during

---

1 *The Courier-Mail* of 16 February 1987, "Wider look at criminal law".
2 *The Australian* of 16 February 1987, "Gibbs to head review of federal criminal law".

[Gibbs'] period as Chief Justice," and remarked: "It is a credit to him and his brother judges that despite this, the esteem and dignity of the High Court has not been diminished." Gibbs addressed the new graduates in Australian Environmental Studies on the extent to which society had changed this century:

> Sir Samuel Griffith at his graduation ceremony had to read some of the Greek and Latin verses which he had been required to compose during his course. He would have been surprised to learn that students could graduate from a University without having studied the classics, and that their studies instead included such topics as ecology, climatology and hydrology...but he had an abiding interest in the welfare of society, and, being a man of broad vision, would have commended the University for providing a course so progressive and suited to the needs of the times.

Gibbs cited High Court cases concerned with the environment which had come before the High Court in his time, and talked of the "impassioned social and political debate" behind them. He charged the graduates with a vital responsibility. Since "humankind cannot survive without putting natural resources to some use", they must ensure that "a balance is struck between conservation and use."

A month later he delivered a paper for the "Centenary of the Colonial Conference of 1887". The first Colonial Conference had been held in London and Griffith had been a delegate. Gibbs lauded Griffith's vital role in bringing about Federation and later gave to the University the portrait of Griffith which had been a companionable presence in Gibbs' High Court chambers for 17 years. This was a token of goodwill towards this relatively new University and symbolic, too, of his parting with the High Court and his absorbing career there. In a sense it was goodbye to all that.

Before the centenary speech, however, he felt the urge to get right away from legal matters, so he and Lady Gibbs set off for Borneo. There, from Sabah, they found their way to Mount Kinabalu, the highest mountain in South-East Asia. Reaching one of the more accessible levels, breathing in the fresh high altitude air and awed by the magnificence before him, he felt invigorated once again. Muriel Gibbs smiled upon the incorrigible traveller, with whom life was often too busy but never dull. On their return to Sydney the family got together to enjoy the usual post-travel jumble of talk, photographs and presents. Gibbs became a Companion of the Order of Australia (AC) in the Queen's Birthday honours of 1987, which was intensely gratifying to him.

Sir Ninian Stephen invests Sir Harry Gibbs as a Companion of the Order of Australia in the Queen's Birthday Honours, 1987, at Government House, Canberra.

He was in demand as a speaker, both at home and abroad. He interspersed the preparation and delivering of these papers with his part-time, continuing work reviewing the Criminal Code. His introductory comments to the Victorian Young Lawyers is indicative of the literary style and classical allusions he often employed:

> Your committee has asked me to speak to you on "Who Judges the Judges?" Those words echo the poet Juvenal who, writing in the 2nd Century AD, coined a phrase so pointed and penetrating that it has come down the ages in various forms, including that of the title of [this] address. When Juvenal asked, "Quis custodiet ipsos custodes?" he was not dealing with a subject as respectable as that of the judiciary but with the futility as he saw it, in the decadent times in which he wrote, of attempting to preserve the virtue of Roman matrons by setting minders to guard them. The question, "Who judges the judges?" is not a cry of similar despair, rather it seeks to resolve fundamental issues regarding the position of the judiciary in a parliamentary democracy which attempts to live under the rule of law."

Several months later, he and Lady Gibbs packed their large suitcases again (their daughters have never been able to convince them of the virtue of travelling light) and left for the United States where Sir Harry delivered the two biennial Menzies Lectures. These are given in Virginia and Australia in alternate years to honour the memory of Sir Robert Menzies and his contribution to law and to public life. Gibbs' subject was "The Appointment and Removal of Judges". In his second lecture, delivered at the William and Mary College at Williamsburg, he tackled a very different subject, "The Separation of Powers: a Comparison".

The following year, 1988, began with personal trauma. Muriel Gibbs' chronic fatigue was now being accompanied by balance problems. She became seriously ill, hydrocephalus was diagnosed, surgery undertaken and she spent some worrying weeks in hospital. Sir Harry was very anxious about Muriel's illness during this period and seemed to age visibly. His wife was his helpmate, close and totally supportive. To see her so ill was devastating. Her recovery was difficult and gradual but she insisted that he go ahead with his speaking commitments. She was able to accompany him in April to Surfers Paradise for the Second International Criminal Law Congress, where he delivered a major paper on behalf of the Criminal Law Review Committee.

Later in the year she also accompanied him to Brisbane where he became the first Anniversary Visiting Fellow for a semester at the University of Queensland. They stayed on campus at St John's College in a pleasant riverside apartment and Sir Harry lectured to the students. During that time Brisbane was en fete with World Expo '88 and the Gibbs spent some hours exploring the remarkably diverse and authentically flavoured pavilions of the 52 participating nations, enjoying such items as a copy of the Magna Carta in one pavilion and, in another, the historic collection of Vatican treasures. His view of Expo '88 as "a magnificent achievement" echoed that of the populace of Brisbane, whose city had come to life in such an extraordinary way. The Brisbane Expo generated a widespread euphoria that lasted the full six months.

On his return to Sydney, Gibbs was asked by the medical research charity Foundation 41 to conduct an in camera inquiry into allegations of scientific fraud against its founder, the internationally famous gynaecologist and obstetrician, Dr William McBride. Joining Gibbs in the inquiry were two distinguished medical scientists, Professors Robert Porter and Roger Short. Dr McBride had risen to medical fame and fortune from 1961 when his own prescribing of a new anti-morning sickness drug, thalidomide, both in private practice at Macquarie Street and as consultant at Sydney's Crown Street Women's Hospital, led to his discovery that the drug caused birth defects. Millions of women throughout the world had used thalidomide. When it was discovered that 7000 children had been born deformed because of it, the whole approach to testing and prescribing drugs under-went a major reappraisal.[3]

Dr McBride launched Foundation 41 in 1972 to conduct scientific experiments on the subject and seek publication for findings in the relevant scientific journals. By 1980 the prestige British medical journal *Lancet* had published four of his articles. In 1982, following experiments conducted on six rabbits at Foundation 41, he published an article in the *Australian Journal of Biological Science*. His own laboratory assistant (Philip Vardy) challenged this article. A public attack accusing McBride of falsifying scientific facts to suit his own theories was launched on ABC's Science Show and in the *Sydney Morning Herald* by a Sydney paediatrician-turned journalist, Dr Norman Swan. Multi-national drug companies were involved, in particular, Merrell Dow, the US Kansas City based company, which had been taken to court on 34 occasions by users of their anti-morning sickness drug, Debendox which, Dr McBride had alleged in US courts, caused birth malformations. It was a complex matter, for McBride had also put forward as evidence (in regard to the rabbit experiment) collaboration by a University of Virginia colleague who had since died: this evidence remained uncorroborated. The dispassionate analysis of this emotional case was difficult.

In November 1988, Sir Harry Gibbs found that the experiment had been conducted in accordance with proper scientific method, but that Dr McBride had "published statements which he either knew were untrue or which he did not genuinely believe to be true and, in that respect, was guilty of scientific fraud."[4] However, he also found: "There can be no doubt that Merrell Dow had a motive to discredit Dr McBride...[and] has indeed sought to have his testimony rejected in proceedings brought against them."[5] The NSW Government set up a Medical Tribunal to inquire into every aspect of McBride's career. The Tribunal sat for three and a half years, the longest period any such body had deliberated in medical history and, it would seem, an undue prolonging of McBride's personal anguish. In February 1993 the Tribunal concluded that Dr McBride had been guilty of scientific fraud. At the same time, the exhaustive investigation, which had examined records of several thousand cases in McBride's private practice, found him to be almost without blemish. However, he was now deregistered as a medical practitioner. Gibbs, who had spoken not many years before on the fatal flawing of the potentially great 19th century Queensland statesman, Thomas

---

3 See *Sydney Morning Herald* of 19 November 1988.
4 Ibid.
5 See Desmond Zwar's article, "Doctor under the knife" in *Sunday Mail* Brisbane of 23 May 1993.

McIlwraith, who in the pursuit of progress had allowed doubtful land deals and become involved in constitutional dispute, saw a similar Shakespearian dimension to the tragedy of Dr McBride.

Another case, this time involving members of the legal profession, loomed. Gibbs was back at work on the review of the Criminal Code when he received a telephone call from Tony Fitzgerald QC. Fitzgerald was now nearing the end of the massive Fitzgerald Inquiry into political and police corruption in Queensland. An impasse had been reached in the cases of Justice Angelo Vasta and Judge Eric Pratt. Both had been under investigation for their relationship with Police Commissioner Sir Terence Lewis, and Vasta for the propriety of his business dealings. Vasta had refused to continue to give evidence before the inquiry owing, he had claimed, to excessive and damaging publicity. He had requested a separate Commission of retired judges to hear his case. Following the public release by Justice Vasta of a letter to Attorney-General Paul Clauson, in which Vasta accused Clauson, together with Queensland's Chief Justice Sir Dormer Andrews and Commissioner Fitzgerald of having conspired to have him brought before the Fitzgerald Inquiry, the Ahern Government had finally agreed to a separate Commission. The upshot was that a Parliamentary Commission of Inquiry was appointed to inquire into allegations of impropriety by Justice Vasta (Supreme Court) and Judge Pratt (District Court), both of whom had stood down from office. The Commission was chaired by Gibbs, with retired justices, Sir George Lush (formerly Victorian Supreme Court and Chairman of the Commission of Inquiry into Lionel Murphy), and Michael Helsham (formerly NSW Supreme Court and its Chief Judge in Equity).

The Gibbs Commission held preliminary proceedings in November 1988. Counsel assisting, Ian Hanger QC, made it clear to the media that it was a fact finding inquiry and not a prosecution. Alec Shand QC appeared as counsel for Justice Vasta. Gibbs recommended that "reasonable costs of Mr Justice Vasta and Judge Pratt be paid by the Government of Queensland", and adjourned the hearing until February 1989.

Vasta's was the first parliamentary commission of inquiry into a judge in Queensland. It lasted three months, during which time everyone from Justice Vasta, straight-backed in the witness box, to former Police Commissioner Sir Terence Lewis (awaiting his own trial) gave evidence. The weeks went slowly by as the tangled skein of Vasta's activities slowly unravelled.

The normally indefatigable TV frontman, Quentin Dempster, covering the case for the ABC and *Sunday Mail*, occasionally dozed, head on hands, at his media table, while counsel expounded and the judges fired questions. In an article entitled "Truth and justice: the key issues facing the judges",

Dempster observed that it had been an intense battle of wits. "At stake here," he wrote, "is public confidence in the judiciary...perhaps in the system itself. Already there is a healthy scepticism and distrust about the motivation of the politicians, about the media and the power games they play. But we need to trust the judges."[6] In mid-May the Commission reported to the Legislative Assembly, finding that the removal from office of Justice Vasta was warranted on five counts, varying from false income tax statements, to giving false evidence, to making wrongful allegations. But the report observed, "There is not the slightest reason to believe that Justice Vasta was guilty of misconduct in his duties as a judge."

Two months later, Judge Pratt was cleared of any impropriety and returned to the District Court bench. Gibbs and his colleagues were concerned at the precedent the Vasta and Pratt Inquiries had set for media intrusion into judges' private affairs, and commented that they had:

> formed the clear opinion that the holding of an inquiry into the question whether "any behaviour" of a judge warrants removal is open to grave objection. It is one thing to inquire into specific allegations of impropriety but it is quite another to conduct an inquisition into all aspects of a judge's life. An inquiry of the latter kind exposes the judiciary to unacceptable risks that pressure will be applied to its members and becomes especially dangerous if instigated by pressure groups or as a result of media clamour.[7]

Lady Gibbs shared a widely felt sympathy for Justice Vasta. The next time Angelo Vasta appeared in court it was for the proud task of introducing and sponsoring his son to the Queensland Bar. It was an occasion the media and the public generally noted and applauded.

For Gibbs the years were now starting to exact their toll. After returning to Sydney to the new harbourside home at Cremorne, Sir Harry had an appointment with Andrew Menzies of the Attorney-General's Department in Canberra to discuss the review of the Criminal Code. During the meeting, Menzies noticed Sir Harry's extreme pallor and fatigue, and persuaded him to cut discussion short. On the way back to Sydney Gibbs suffered a heart attack. Gibbs mistook the severe chest pains which had caused him to collapse as a recurrence of some ulcer trouble. His doctors, however,

---

6 Quentin Dempster, "Truth and justice: the key issues facing the judges" in *Sunday Mail* 30 April 1989.
7 *The Courier-Mail* of 20 July 1989, "Pratt set to return to Bench". In April 1994, following the High Court's ruling that almost 200 hours of Australian Federal Police tapes were obtained illegally in this case, criminal charges against Vasta and his brother-in-law, Santo Coco, were dropped: see *The Courier-Mail* of 19 April 1994.

admitted him to St Vincent's hospital for quadruple bypass surgery for coronary artery stenosis.

Several months of convalescence followed. His exercise walks were now short and slow. He returned to work looking frail but feeling energetic. One of his first tasks was to write a foreword for Bruce McPherson's scholarly history, *The Supreme Court of Queensland., 1859-1960.* He found the "thorough nature of [McPherson's] research and the comprehensive scope of his work...remarkable". Gibbs quoted Francis Bacon:

> Histories do rather set forth the pomp of business than the true and inward resorts thereof. But Lives, if they be well written, propounding to themselves a person to represent, in whom actions both greater and smaller, public and private, have a commixture, must of necessity contain a more true, native and lively representation.

McPherson commented on his long writing labour and his emergence from being a "troglodyte figure inhabiting the lower reaches of the family home."

Governments saw good value in employing Gibbs, the retired supremo in the law, to conduct enquiries. The new decade saw him undertaking an investigation in an entirely new field. The New South Wales' Greiner Government appointed him to make an "Inquiry into Community Needs and High Voltage Transmission Line Development." This involved a wide range of technical matters relating to the supply of electricity, its impact on the environment, the siting of new transmission lines, their social and economic impact, and possible alternatives (wind, solar and hydro electric power). This engrossed him. The Minister for Mines and Energy, Neil Packard, asked Gibbs specifically to investigate "the questions of electromagnetic fields and their relationship to health." Reports of cancer and other health risks from proximity to high voltage power lines had been featured in the press. Gibbs found himself over several months examining 177 submissions from mayors and presidents of shire councils from all over the State. He held public hearings in Sydney, Grafton and Bathurst, and inspected, via helicopter or car, projected transmission lines between areas such as Lismore to Mullumbimby and Grafton to Coffs Harbour. Then it was necessary to consult with experts overseas.

Muriel Gibbs was somewhat alarmed to see her husband, so recently recovered from major heart surgery, once again swinging suitcases from airport roundabouts - in Tokyo, London, Oxford and then across in Toronto. A variety of hotel rooms saw Gibbs writing late into the night as he made his assessments. They finally made their way to the United States. He conferred again with professors and engineers in many centres, from Washington and Pittsburgh to Kansas, a city whose exceptional architecture, art and hospitable citizenry impressed them both.

Gibbs' 160 page report found that the Electricity Commission had made forecasts, "as accurate as humanly possible" for needs until the end of the century. He found that a transmission grid covering the whole State, or even wider, has substantial advantages over local generation; that it has not been established that electric fields or magnetic fields of power frequency are harmful to human health and there is no reason for concern as to their effects on animals or plants; that some community concern at the siting of easements is well founded and the Electricity Commission could involve the community in the selection of new transmission routes before deciding upon them. It was a well-reasoned and practical report. *The Bulletin* thought that "the Gibbs Inquiry...may be the first empirical test of whether communities and bureaucrats are willing to put aside their differences in an effort to preserve Australia's resources and curb environmental destruction."[8]

The New Year saw the Gibbs again at Hervey Bay. The desperately ill Gerald Patterson, who had lost his wife the previous year, had decreed that he be driven there from a Brisbane hospital to join his family. Sadly, heart failure forced him into hospital again. The Gibbs went to visit him as soon as they were permitted. They found him bright and alert, but he died within minutes of their leaving. Harry Gibbs had lost the closest and warmest of his old friends. He had from the earliest days enjoyed Gerald's irreverent and spirited intelligence, his relaxed but stimulating companionship. He had been larger than life and would leave a gap of similar proportions. But speaking at the formal service for Patterson in Brisbane, Gibbs told family and friend not to grieve. Here was a man who had lived his life to the full - and had lived it well. A few months later a rather happier time was spent in Brisbane - with Gibbs' old legal colleague and friend, Sir Walter Campbell, then Governor of Queensland and celebrating his 70th birthday. Gibbs and Campbell, both speaking on the occasion, drew from shared legal experiences over nearly five decades. They looked at light-hearted aspects of producing Queensland's first academic law journal, of Campbell's filling of the Supreme Court place left by Gibbs, of their continuing contact through court and university.

The Gibbs farewelled their son Harry, and his wife Jacinta, who were off to New York where Harry had been appointed to a New York clinic to practice his specialty, invasive cardiology. Their eldest daughter, Barbara, continued

8 Paige Barlow, "Power to the people" in *Bulletin* of 4 December 1990.

with her career in film production, the second daughter Margaret (wife of political pollster, Rod Cameron) was soon to present them with their first grandson, Harry Gibbs Cameron. Their youngest daughter, Mary, had divorced and happily remarried. To the family-oriented Gibbs senior, Sydney was to remain home, much as they would both have enjoyed retirement in Brisbane.

During these years, also, Gibbs presided over the Court of Appeal for Kiribati (formerly the Gilbert Islands). He had flown there for a week or two annually to hear appeal cases at the capital Tarawa, where Justice Maxwell, a Nigerian, administered an efficient court. There was invariably a large volume of work. In 1991, when Dame Roma Mitchell of South Australia (Australia's first female Supreme Court judge and then State Governor) and Sir Sydney Frost of Papua New Guinea retired from the judiciary at much the same time as Justice Connolly retired from the Queensland Supreme Court, Connolly was appointed, as also was Justice Raymond Reynolds of NSW. Gibbs, Reynolds and Connolly flew together from Sydney by Air Nauru and were taken to their accommodation - the Hotel OD N AIWO. Connolly was dismayed at the meagre facilities. The Gibbs, with their formidable luggage, had managed to get up to the first floor. Connolly insisted, as "a young fellow of merely 70", in helping to settle them in. Kiribati had a new Chief Justice, Fakir Muhammed, a British-born Indian. This amiable judge found the Australians' legal customs hard to fathom. He had offered them his Chambers - the Chief Justice's Chambers are air-conditioned. Gibbs'. face was a study when he walked in to the chambers and saw at a glance that the Australian judiciary's bible, the *Commonwealth Law Reports*, were stacked on the shelves, beginning at volume 79 and continuing in haphazard fashion thereafter (the current volume is 180). "He was too polite to comment," said Connolly, "but he couldn't bear to look at them and simply turned his back and worked." Connolly resolved to deal with the matter. He asked Chief Justice Muhammed the next morning, Saturday, for permission to rearrange the CLRs. Muhammed agreed, but evinced surprise. "You chaps don't need books here," he remarked. "You are probably right", replied Connolly, "but we feel more comfortable if we can say 'Somebody said this before'." "Absolutely incomprehensible," the Chief Justice muttered, as he left Connolly to it. On Monday, Gibbs' relief at the ordered shelves was visible. The work was expedited.

The Kiribati people are fine hosts to their Appeal Court friends from Australia. They provide open air feasts of omelettes cooked in gourds, fish baked in palm fronds and an abundance of luscious tropical fruit. Reynolds, described by his colleagues as "an accomplished judge and a fine historian", lined up happily with Gibbs and Connolly for the ceremonial placing of leis on their heads - "chaplets in the Roman fashion".

The Honourable Raymond Reynolds, the Right Honourable Sir Harry Gibbs and the Honourable Peter Connolly enjoying the festivities in Kiribati.

Earlier that year, Sir Harry had attended a legal seminar in Brisbane on a suitable basis for a uniform criminal law for Australia, a topic of considerable concern to him. Australia, with its relatively modest population, had nine separate criminal law jurisdictions. The Gibbs Committee's Third Interim Report on Criminal Responsibility was the starting point for the debate on uniformity. The Standing Committee of Attorneys-General met, upgraded the proposed Brisbane seminar to a full conference to include eminent judges and jurists from around the country, and made a political commitment to a uniform Criminal Code. At Brisbane's riverside Parliamentary Annex at Gardens Point, the ninety delegates included Queensland Attorney-General Dean Wells, Western Australian Chief Justice David Malcolm, and Canadian lawyer and President of their International Society, Vincent Del Buono. Del Buono's opening address dwelt upon the excellence of the Queensland Criminal Code initially drawn up by Sir Samuel Griffith and adopted by Western Australia, Tasmania and British New Guinea. Del Buono also emphasised the fundamental importance of detection and deterrence to the practical utility of the criminal law.

The conference reached a remarkable degree of acceptance of the Gibbs Committee's recommendations. The Standing Committee of Attorneys-General subsequently received a report from the Brisbane conference and formally appointed an interjurisdictional committee of criminal law experts to continue the work. Their aim was to unify and simplify Commonwealth, State and Territory criminal law. Auckland hosted the Fourth International Criminal Law Congress the following year. Gibbs chaired a session and wrote a chapter of the Report. Andrew Menzies commented:

> Sir Harry's chapter on the Principles of Criminal Responsibility is a fundamental and significant contribution. It is the first time in Australia that there has been an attempt to state these principles in a coherent form though it is true that the Gibbs Committee was assisted considerably by a Report of the United Kingdom Law Commission. That part of our Report has inspired the greatest interest in the legal profession - it is regarded as a landmark document.

Gibbs' work in this difficult area, which may be the basis of a Model Criminal Code, could prove to be one of his most enduring achievements.

But both at the High Court and on constitutional questions generally, events were moving in a direction in 1992 which caused Gibbs great concern. His actions and public pronouncements on these issues were to bring him before the public eye once more.

Chapter 13

CONTEMPORARY ISSUES

In April 1991 well-known constitutional law specialists, Professors James Crawford and Cheryl Saunders, organised a Constitutional Centenary Conference on the anniversary of that held by Sir Henry Parkes in 1891 to discuss the formation of a Federation. Delegates to Sydney included former Governor-General Sir Ninian Stephen, Justice Pincus of the Federal Court, Justice Kirby of the NSW Court of Appeal and *The Australian*'s well-known journalist Padraic McGuinness. They considered constitutional reform for the 10 years leading up to the centenary of Federation in 2001.

Prime Minister Robert Hawke and Opposition Leader Dr John Hewson attended the final day to discuss the question of an Australian republic. With the United Kingdom committed to becoming a member of the European Community, Hawke saw an Australian republic as inevitable. Also discussed at the conference was a guarantee of basic rights, whether the powers of all governments at all levels could be safeguarded and the possibility of a Bill of Rights. A possible mechanism to address the rights of the Aborigines as the indigenous people of the country, the Prime Minister hailed as "far sighted and imaginative". Hewson was committed to reform and change within Australia, saying "constitutional change would support economic change". He suggested that a four year term for the Commonwealth Parliament be put to a referendum. The Conference appointed Sir Ninian Stephen, the retired Governor-General, to chair the Constitution Centenary Foundation to examine the above questions. The Commonwealth Government injected a healthy allocation of funds, later boosted by State Government and private enterprise funding. The purpose of the Foundation was to encourage informed public debate and stir interest in the Constitution. Padraic McGuinness wrote that there was a "strong...undercurrent of patriotic feeling in the conference. Everybody cared deeply about our country and its future."

Gibbs watched these developments with great interest but also concern. He is a constitutional monarchist. He does not believe that a republic would be beneficial, or that it is inevitable in Australia. He is also opposed to a Bill of Rights, considering that basic human rights are upheld by Australia's present parliamentary and judicial systems. Fortunately, the Hawke government seemed prepared to hasten slowly. In regard to the protection of governments at all levels, a matter on which Gibbs felt strongly, the Prime Minister later in the year mooted a more equitable distribution of the tax revenue between the Commonwealth and the States, which he referred to as "the new federalism", that is, a modifying of central power and dominance.

This was very soon to be dropped. After machinations which were documented in the ABC's award-winning television program, *Labor in Power*, Hawke was followed as Prime Minister by his former Treasurer, Paul Keating, on 19 December 1991. Attitudes were now to be very different. The new Prime Minister was not only strongly centralist but keen for Australia to become a republic. He lent his support to the newly-formed Australian Republican Movement, launched by the acclaimed author, Thomas Keneally, earlier in the year. During the first half of 1992, Gibbs and others of like mind, saw the need for a society to give some balance to the debate. They formed *Leadership Beyond Politics - Australians for Constitutional Monarchy*, which had a widely diverse council membership, including Chancellor of Sydney University, Dame Leonie Kramer, president of the NSW Court of Appeal, Michael Kirby, former federal Liberal Party president, Sir John Atwill, former Labor Lord Mayor of Sydney, Doug Sutherland, and the president of the Australia-Britain Society (NSW), Lloyd Waddy QC. Gibbs regretted that the debate on changing the Constitution had been dominated by republicans. "I think it would have been better if there was no debate at all," he said. "But now the debate has been started, it is important it is balanced." He still feels that a majority of Australians favour the retention of the constitutional monarchy. Solid support emerged. Prominent Aborigine and former Liberal senator Mr Neville Bonner believed there were many Aborigines who supported the monarchy. "The country was taken over by the British, but if it had not been it would have been taken over by some other country; we could not have defended it," he commented. "As far as I am concerned we have done better under the present system than other indigenous people in other countries, although that is not to say everything is perfect. There is still room for change."[1]

Later that year, the High Court delivered its highly controversial decision in *Mabo v The State of Queensland (No 2)*[2] recognising Native Title to Torres Strait Islanders (specifically, to Murray Islanders) and holding that British colonisation had not, ipso facto, erased Aborigines' rights relating to land. To the High Court Justices, this threw open the whole question of the extent of native title on the Australian mainland. The ramifications of the *Mabo* ruling are still being felt. It led directly, 18 months later, to Commonwealth land rights legislation.

---

1 *The Australian* of 25 May 1992.
2 (1992) 175 CLR 1.

The High Court was attacked for exceeding its role as interpreter of the common law and, in effect, legislating. It had, indeed, taken an attitude such as it had with the *Tasmanian Dam* case in 1983,[3] when it broadened the scope of the External Affairs Power, using an International Treaty to which the current federal government had been a party, to rule on that intrinsically domestic matter. In *Mabo*, Sir Daryl Dawson in his dissenting judgment, concluded with the words: "If traditional land rights, or rights akin to them, are to be afforded to the inhabitants of the Murray Islands, the responsibility, both legal and moral, lies with the legislature and not the courts." Gibbs shared this belief.

He now joined a group who wished to preserve the Constitution as it stands and to provide a forum for such views. The Samuel Griffith Society was formed. Its members pledged to defend the Constitution and to oppose the further centralisation of power in Canberra. The Society's inaugural meeting was held in Melbourne in late July 1992. Gibbs, its first Chairman, wrote the major paper. He had to fly to London, however, and it was delivered on his behalf by Queensland National Party identity, David Russell QC. Among those attending were Melbourne QC, SEK Hulme, former chairman of MIM, Sir Bruce Watson, and Peter Connolly. Brisbane's *Sunday Mail* felt that the Society's objectives would "strike a chord with state leaders, businesses and farmers", who were concerned with "Canberra's ever-increasing grab for power and...the erosion of the role of Parliament". Other relevant matters mentioned were the reviewing of financial arrangements between the Commonwealth and the States in favour of the States; reducing duplication by eliminating Commonwealth influence in matters that should be the primary concern of the States (eg, education, health), and safeguarding judicial independence. Sir Ninian Stephen, speaking for the Centenary Foundation, welcomed this alternative organisation. So did McGuinness in *The Australian*. The Chief Justice, Sir Anthony Mason, commented, "The more *informed* debate about the Constitution there is the better for all concerned - in particular, the community."

Gibbs had regretted missing the inaugural meeting. He had been called to London to participate in a centuries old ceremony at St Paul's Cathedral; the unfurling and hanging of his heraldic banner as a Knight Grand Cross of the Order of St Michael and St George. Lady Gibbs accompanied him, as did their son, Harry, and his wife, Jacinta. Harry, over from New York, acted as his father's "Squire" and carried the banner. Sir Harry had been awarded the GCMG some years before, but the heraldic banners at St Paul's are not changed until the death of a holder, when a space becomes available: he now

---

3 *Commonwealth v Tasmania* (*Tasmanian Dam* case) (1983) 158 CLR 1; 46 ALR 625.

entered an exclusive circle. Sir Ninian Stephen, who was in Dublin as mediator between the UK and the Irish Republic, visited London and the two former colleagues, together with their wives, were guests at Privy Councillor, Lord Roskill's country home. Sir Anthony Mason was also in London to address the English, Scottish and Australian Bars Conference, and he and Sir Harry hosted a dinner for their English colleagues. Whatever their differences in judicial policy (Gibbs more federalist in outlook on constitutional matters than Mason), the friendship between the two men remained firm.

The Gibbs' extended their London trip to include a "Bed and Breakfast" tour through the English midlands up to Scotland with their son and his wife. Later they visited France with Sir Harry's brother Wylie and his wife, now living in Bedfordshire, and drove through the countryside, enjoying both the renewed companionship and the Chateau country. On returning to Paris, Gibbs decided they should experience the Arctic, another travelling challenge. He and Lady Gibbs, still with residual balance problems from her illness, flew to Bergen where they took a coastal cargo steamer up the coast of Norway to the Russian border.

Meanwhile, back in Australia, the ramifications of the *Mabo* judgment were being hotly debated. Phrases such as "High Court's Coup d'Etat" headed feature articles and editorials on the question. Gibbs prepared to write a foreword to a comprehensive analysis of the controversy, *Mabo: A Judicial Revolution*, edited by M A Stephenson and Suri Ratnapala and published by University of Queensland Press. This 1993 special issue of the *University of Queensland Law Journal* included articles by authoritative Aboriginal Affairs and constitutional law experts, such as Professor RD Lumb and Father Frank Brennan SJ (son of Justice Gerard Brennan). Sir Harry Gibbs' foreword indicates his views, as he questions the High Court *Mabo* majority's scholarship and impartiality:

> Many decisions of the High Court have resulted in controversy, but few, if any, have given rise to such a diversity of responses, ranging from euphoria to deep anxiety, as *Mabo v Queensland.*
>
> The case raises a number of questions of great public importance. Did the Court carry judicial activism too far in departing from principles that were thought to have been settled for well over a century, on the ground that those principles were contrary to international standards and the fundamental values of the common law? In doing so, the Court applied what some of its members perceived to be current values and the further question arises whether in fact those values are widely accepted in the community and whether, assuming that they are, it is right to apply

contemporary standards to overturn rules formulated at a time when community values were not necessarily the same. These issues become all the more significant if the decision has a wider operation than merely in relation to the title to, and use of, land and if it provides authority for the acceptance of Aboriginal customary law in relation to other matters - in respect of crime for instance. The further questions arise whether the decision casts any doubt on the rights of such persons as pastoral lessees, holders of mining leases and occupation licences and trustees of public reserves and whether the Crown is able to recover for itself, or provide for others, the unencumbered possession, occupation, use or enjoyment of lands long believed to be Crown lands without payment of compensation to persons not yet identified. A final question, of a practical, or perhaps moral, rather than a legal kind, is whether on the whole it will prove more beneficial for the Aboriginal people that they should be provided with what may be an uncertain basis for making legal claims which are likely to result in protracted controversy and litigation, rather than leaving it to the political process to do justice to them...

There is one matter which has puzzled me a little. In the judgments in *Mabo*, and in much public discussion which has followed, there are frequent references to the doctrine of *terra nullius*, which the Court has said to have rejected. The question whether land was *terra nullius* is relevant at international law in deciding whether a state has acquired sovereignty by attempted occupation. So far as I am aware, it was not the question asked at common law to determine whether a colony, admittedly under the sovereignty of Great Britain, was acquired by settlement. Indeed the expression "*terra nullius*" seems to have been unknown to the common law. I have found no trace of it in legal dictionaries ranging from *Cowel's Interpreter* (1701 ed.) to *Stroud's Judicial Dictionary* (1986 ed.). It is not mentioned in *Taring's Law Relating to the Colonies* (1913 ed.) which in its day was regarded as authoritative. It may have been thought that the expression was synonymous with the common law rule that if Englishmen establish themselves in "an uninhabited or barbarous country" the colony will be regarded as acquired as by settlement but that ignores the fact that it was enough to satisfy the common law that the land was "barbarous", by which was meant not under civilised government. Australia was certainly not unoccupied in 1788 but it is another thing to say that the social organisation of the Aboriginal inhabitants was of a kind which the nations of Europe in the eighteenth and nineteenth centuries recognised as civilised. Of course, the High Court understood the full extent of the common law principles but public understanding is not assisted when those principles are described by a phrase which is misleading and perhaps emotive.

The *Mabo* decision prompted the Keating government to draw up the Native Title Act, which was passed by Parliament in 1994. This controversial legislation took the High Court's decision a step further. Critics alleged that it was rushed through and should have been deferred to the following year for more detailed debate. It was opposed by the Hewson-led conservative Opposition, and passed through the Senate, after a brief but bitter debate, with the support of the Kernot-led Democrats and the two Green Senators from Western Australia. At the same time, the Western Australian Liberal Premier, Richard Court, was drawing up his own State legislation and making plans to challenge the Commonwealth Act. Meanwhile Chief Justice Mason had broken his silence. He claimed, in a speech at Cambridge University, that the High Court in the *Mabo* case, had done no more than the United States, Canada and New Zealand in regard to native title. Academic lawyers have disputed this point. As Peter Connolly pointed out in his paper, "Should the courts determine social policy?", delivered to the Samuel Griffith Society on 15 June 1993, the cases involved in those other countries concerned "not nomads [such as the Australian Aborigines], but indigenous people who occupied and exercised rights over defined areas of territory." Connolly also disputed Mason's assertion that the rejection of the doctrine of terra nullius by the *Mabo* Court was "entirely consistent with the rejection of the doctrine by the International Court in the Western Sahara" - the case also quoted as authoritative by Justice Brennan in his judgment in *Mabo*. Connolly maintained that the International Court rejected "not the doctrine of *terra nullius* but Spain's claim that the Western Sahara in 1884 answered that description". Historian, Geoffrey Blainey, author of *Triumph of the Nomads: A History of Ancient Australia* (1975), then entered the argument, suggesting that the High Court justices had misread their history and projecting that their decision could hurt the economy.

Chief Justice Mason put one important aspect to rest in December 1993 by striking out a claim made by the Wiradjuri Aborigines to a substantial portion of New South Wales. He did so primarily on the basis that the claim was not a genuine one. He also made it clear that claims that Aboriginal peoples have some sovereign independence from the rest of the Australian community have no legal basis. This same point was made by Frank Brennan SJ in his chapter in *Mabo: A Judicial Revolution*. The first week of 1994 saw Native Title Tribunals open in all the capital cities of Australia for the hearing of claims to unalienated Crown land. In Professor Leonie Kramer's apt Macbeth analogy, "the hurly-burly's yet to come". State governments are acting to clarify the repercussions of the case. For example, the Queensland Parliament had to legislate to declare that pastoral leases and constructed roads, granted or built prior to 1 January 1994, extinguished native title in Queensland. A new channel of work for lawyers - tenure history searching - has opened up.

In the interim, during 1993 Gibbs turned his attention to the vexed question of taxation, which he, like many others, considers to be in dire need of reform. As Chairman of the Australian Tax Research Foundation, he addressed the Taxation Institute of Australia's 11th National Convention. Since the Convention was to be held at Alice Springs, and Sir Walter Campbell was also to attend, the two friends and their wives met in Sydney, flew on to Adelaide and went via that well-equipped, symbolically-named train *The Ghan* (after the Afghan camel drivers of earlier years) over the vast desert country to the Centre.

At Alice Springs Gibbs opened the Convention, which also marked the Jubilee celebration of the foundation of the Taxation Institute. In a powerful speech, he suggested the tax system had "gone seriously wrong...and require[d] basic reform." He pointed out that reform in any area of law is likely to be slow and difficult, but more so in this area because "taxation is now, as it has been throughout history, one of the main sources of political controversy". He offered some historical instances where perceived unfairness in the imposition or collection of taxes had resulted in "great disturbances in society". Beginning with the peasants' revolt at the poll tax in 14th century England, which resulted in the Chief Justice having "his head cut off and carried round Bury St. Edmunds on a pike" (he acknowledged that misguided criticism towards lawyers still exists but "is not always expressed so vehemently"), he led them through the English Civil War, which arose partly through the attempted arbitrary imposition of taxes and resulted in the execution of King Charles I, to the 18th century rebellion of the American colonies against England, one of the root causes of which was taxes imposed from afar. He reminded his audience that the bloody French Revolution was "directly precipitated by the fact that the French courts frustrated attempts to reform a tax system which was oppressive and unjust", and that 19th century Australia had its example, too; "the rebellion at the Eureka Stockade was a protest against the unfairness of a tax and the manner of its collection". He particularly lashed out at the lack of clarity in the tax law:

> It is not an exaggeration to say that the Income Tax Assessment Act is obscure and uncertain in its operation, it is burdensome to comply with and to prevent avoidance it resorts to heavy penalties and to discretions so wide as to make it a gamble for a taxpayer to endeavour, quite legitimately, to reduce the tax payable. Such a law reflects no credit on the society which tolerates it.

These few sentences have been often quoted since.

Gibbs had been a member of the Barwick High Court which had lacerated several sections of the Australian tax statute. The anti-avoidance provision - s 260 - had been emasculated by a series of High Court decisions and Gibbs had occasionally featured in the majority, although he did not sit on the benches that decided such resounding defeats for the Commissioner of Taxation as the 1976-1977 cases of *Cridland*,[4] *Mullens Investments Pty Ltd*[5] and *Slutzkin*.[6] Noted commentators, such as Geoffrey Lehmann and Yuri Grbich, attacked the Barwick Court's anti-tax line, but did concede that Gibbs, Mason and Stephen JJ occasionally diverged from Barwick CJ's strong line on tax matters. The Commissioner of Taxation and the Federal Parliament reacted strongly and, regrettably, say legal academics and accountants, with some tortuous and long-winded legislation. One of the longest tax statutes of history resulted. To make matters worse it was badly written, since it was created in response to one weakness or another in the previous wording. A finger in the hole in the dyke drafting approach developed. It is widely recognised that after Barwick's departure the High Court under Gibbs' leadership mended its tax ways (and even restored s 260 as a meaningful provision). Gibbs' attack on verbosity and broad discretions in the tax statute was a pleasant relief for legislators who had struggled to dance to the High Court's tune of the Barwick years. No one doubts the accuracy of Gibbs' comments: there is popular accord with the denunciation of a ludicrously complex taxation system.

Gibbs also gave his support for a broad-based goods and services tax for Australia. Campaigning to install such a tax had defeated the Liberal push for power in the 1993 general election, although Australia remains only one of the very few OECD nations that do not have a GST. Gibbs commented at the Taxation Institute's National Convention:

> Income is in its nature an inappropriate base for a tax, and the Parliament should adopt the recommendation made by the Asprey Committee in 1975 that the weight of taxation should be shifted towards the taxation of goods and services and away from the taxation of income. A change of that kind would enable the marginal rates of income tax to be reduced to an extent that would lessen the incentive to avoid the tax, and would make it easier to reform the income tax laws.

Gibbs inveighed, too, against the imbalance between Commonwealth and State uses of taxing powers:

> The Commonwealth raises more than 75% of all the taxes levied in Australia. On the other hand, the Commonwealth's expenditure represents only about half of the total expenditure by governments in Australia. Clearly it raises many billions of dollars more than it needs for its own

---

4 76 ATC 4538.
5 76 ATC 4188.
6 76 ATC 4076.

purposes. On the other hand, the States' own revenues, from taxation and otherwise, are quite insufficient for their purposes...about 55 per cent of all revenue available to the States consists of grants made by the Commonwealth. At least half of those grants are made on condition that they be used for specific purposes.

Gibbs recognised the advantages of this system, principally an overall central policy for essential services in our democracy. But there are "grave disadvantages". For instance:

[P]ower of the States to control their own affairs is seriously diminished and the State governments are rendered less accountable, because they spend money which they are not responsible for raising. The system leads to a lack of efficiency. Forward planning is made difficult for the State...What is perhaps worse...is that the ability of the Commonwealth to pursue policies in matters which are strictly of State concern (eg health, education, urban renewal) has resulted in an expensive duplication of bureaucracies.

At the end of the Convention, while the press featured articles such as *The Australian*'s "Former judge lashes tax law", the Gibbs and Campbells hired a four-wheel drive to tour the beautiful Palm Valley. After visiting other gorges and rugged red range areas, they parted company, the Campbells setting off to view Uluru (Ayer's Rock) while the Gibbs flew over to the Kimberleys and the pearling town of Broome with its fascinating mix of races and exquisite turquoise waters.

On their return to Sydney, Gibbs wrote a paper for a seminar organised by Australians for Constitutional Monarchy held on 4 June at Parliament House, Sydney. There the debate on the formation of the Federation had been held exactly one hundred years before. Gibbs spoke strongly against the republican movement and with considerable authority.

There is no weakness in our Constitution that would be cured by making Australia a republic. Australia would not derive any material benefit from abolishing the monarchy...the only advantage of the change would be purely symbolic. The proposal raises serious constitutional questions. The current catch-phrase is that the change should be "minimalist"...it is difficult to take seriously the suggestion that Australia should become a republic only in part (ie, some States might retain their relationship with the Queen). The position of the States...will...need to be addressed before any proposal to create a republic is submitted to a referendum. A question only superficially addressed is that of which of the powers presently vested in the Governor-General should be conferred on a President. That question is central to the debate.

Gibbs branded as unconvincing the claims that Australians would think better of themselves and become more loyal and united and more respected by their

Asian neighbours as a republic. His arguments displayed his trademarks of logic and persuasiveness. He pointed out that today most constitutional monarchies are free and democratic - Australia has been a free and stable society since 1901 - whereas most republics are not, the exceptions being Switzerland and the United States. Analysis showed that "constitutional monarchies have proved in practice to be a more successful form of government than republicanism." He feels that it may be Australia's immaturity, rather than its maturity, that sees it become a republic.

Gibbs discussed the extensive powers of the Governor-General. He or she chooses the members of the Executive Council, appoints all Ministers of State, and is the Commander-in-Chief of the armed forces. These powers are usually exercised by the Ministers, but the Constitution does not require the Governor-General to rubber stamp every executive decision. The Governor-General almost invariably does so, however, in conformity with long established conventions originating in 17th century England and continuing in Australia. An essential component of his role is political impartiality. The same is true in general of State Governors. Occasions arise when the Governor-General or Governors must exercise their discretionary judgment and exercise reserve powers. Gibbs cited Tasmania's Governor Sir Phillip Bennett's solving a constitutional crisis in 1989 concerning Liberal Premier Gray, which resulted, in the interests of stability, in the appointment as Premier of the Leader of the Opposition (ie, of the Labor Party). He also recalled Queensland's Governor, Sir Walter Campbell, solving a crisis in 1987 when Sir Joh Bjelke-Petersen was forced to abandon a plan to rid himself of some of his ministers (by the device of resigning and seeking a fresh commission) when he discovered that Sir Walter would not necessarily recommission him as Premier.

Next, Gibbs warned of the dangers of executive power wielded with insufficient checks and controls.

> It would...be a most dangerous course to confer on a President the powers which are at present vested in the Governor-General...he would be legally free to exercise those powers independently, and would...be likely to do so in a political way, the result would be to give immense strength to the Executive Government. Already during this century there has been a marked increase in the power of the executive vis-a-vis that of the Parliament. That situation is not peculiar to Australia. In addition, within the Executive itself, there has been a considerable increase in the power of the Prime Minister vis-a-vis the other members of the Ministry. If we had a President who was given the present powers of the Governor-General, the strength of the President and the Prime Minister in conjunction could well enable them, if they were minded to do so, to proceed on the road to

dictatorship. We find a warning in the political history of India, whose Presidency is sometimes suggested as a possible model for ours. In June 1975 Mrs Indira Gandhi was found by a court to have committed electoral irregularities. Her position as Prime Minister was under threat. Without delay, and without first informing the Cabinet, she approached the President, who, at her request made a proclamation of internal emergency and by so doing enabled Mrs Ghandi to exercise dictatorial powers. By the next morning many of the Opposition party had been imprisoned; hundreds more were imprisoned later - habeas corpus was suspended. That is by no means the only example of the way in which a democracy can slide into a dictatorship if the Constitution does not sufficiently curb the power of the executive. Witness Nazi Germany and Mussolini's Italy. The framers of the United States' Constitution recognised that if the President was to have full executive power, it would be necessary to limit that power by an intricate arrangement of checks and balances.

He pointed out that, in the unlikely event of a President of Australia being given the executive power of the United States' Presidency (something not envisaged at present by the Republicans), it would be a disaster if the checks and balances of the United States' Constitution were not provided and if this were done it would greatly increase the status and power of the Senate. Gibbs discussed then what is at present more important, namely, the powers of the Governor-General. If these were to be conferred upon a President, it would be necessary to devise new and effective limits on the President's power (his/her appointment by a majority of both Houses of Parliament is known to be favoured by the Government Leader in the Senate, Gareth Evans). If the Governor-General's powers were not to be conferred on a President, then their re-allocation would mean a major constitutional change. In any event, Gibbs concluded "no mere minimal change will be involved."

When the Republican Advisory Committee, set up under the chairmanship of leading republican Malcolm Turnbull, set off round the country during the year, calling public meetings to test opinion, it did not uncover a groundswell of opinion urging any hurried adoption of republicanism. In Brisbane, Turnbull's meeting at the Parliamentary Annexe to discuss the topic drew only about 40 people, while another, to launch two Women's Legal Service publications on the status of women, in the same week drew 400. The public was, and is, much more concerned about social ills, unemployment and economic problems. Political analyst, Malcolm Mackerras, commented at the beginning of the decade that a referendum for a republic would be unlikely to be carried in Australia until about 2015 AD. He may well be accurate.

Gibbs concedes that younger people particularly have an emotional preference for the idea of an Australian head of State, a trend which has been strengthened by the sensationalised private lives of the next generation of British royalty. Also the federal Government is well aware of the need to spell out the manner in which it would build into a new Constitution the checks and balances which work so well under the present system. As Peter Connolly points out, there is much wisdom in Burke's words: "It is with infinite caution that any man ought to venture upon pulling down an edifice which has answered in any tolerable degree for ages the common purposes of society."

A number of Gibbs' former High Court colleagues do not see as many constitutional dangers and difficulties in a possible change to a republic as do Gibbs and Connolly. On the other hand, an unexpectedly severe blow to the republican movement was dealt by Governor-General Bill Hayden. He was reported to have held republican views, but, in his 1993 televised debate with former prime minister Bob Hawke, he stated that replacing a constitutional monarchy that works well with a republic could create "unstable government". Fortunately, the Australian public, not the executive of the federal parliament, will decide if and when that risk is worth taking.

Meanwhile, Sir Harry delivered an address to the first National Congress of Justices in Brisbane. He dismissed as nonsense claims made by a federal minister that the make-up of the High Court should reflect society. "It would be most unfortunate if appointments to the court were to be influenced by populist theories or by an attempt to curry favour with sectional interests," he said. "The policy...that more women and members of ethnic groups should be appointed to the Bench without regard to...whether they are the persons best qualified for appointment, must surely be misconceived." Merit, he emphasised again, should be the sole criterion for judicial appointment.[7]

Throughout 1994, Gibbs stayed in the public eye for his continued strong support for the constitutional monarchy cause. A convulsion at leadership level in the Liberal Party, still destabilised from its devastating (though marginal) 1993 electoral loss, saw John Hewson replaced as leader by Adelaide-based Alexander Downer, grandson of one of the founding fathers of the 1901 Constitution. Before some vacillations in articulating policy made his position uncertain, Downer's confident political persona, the legacy of generations of forebears who gave distinguished public service, resulted in a honeymoon surge of public support for him. Prime Minister Keating, perceiving that the republican issue would present Downer with the most thorny of problems, immediately stepped up his republican campaign, declaring that it would be a major issue at the next election. The debate

---

7 *The Courier-Mail* editorial of 28 September 1993.

received fresh impetus. Downer and his Shadow Treasurer and Deputy, Peter Costello, declared the Liberal Party's official policy to be support for the constitutional monarchy, accompanied by a willingness to listen to the republican proposals, which some Liberals favour. The new Opposition Leader, John Howard, who took over in February 1995, has a similar stance to Downer, only more vigorously expressed.

Gibbs was busy still. Apart from activities associated with his being patron of the two new criminal law organisations and his honorary membership of the Law Council, he was Chairman of the Taxation Reform Foundation, a prominent member of Australians for Constitutional Monarchy and had undertaken some work as a commercial arbitrator. He was taken up, too, with legal functions such as the inaugural dinner of the Queensland Law Graduates' Association, of which his old friend Peter Connolly is president. He also continued to hear appeal cases, with Connolly, at Kirabati as he has done since his retirement. Suitably preoccupied, he was stunned to find himself the subject of an unprovoked, personal attack. He had underestimated his importance as a pro-monarchist and thus the likelihood of becoming a target for political attacks.

In *The Weekend Australian* of 16-17 July 1994, columnist and republican Humphrey McQueen, an historian by training, wrote an article entitled "Sir Harry's not a constitutional man", in which he attacked Gibbs' reputation as a constitutional lawyer and generally denigrated his abilities and achievements. Gibbs was, McQueen added, an asset at the High Court (which "spends more of its time on commercial crudities than the deciding of constitutional niceties") because of his "intimacy with real estate and book-keeping". The columnist harked back to the National Hotel Royal Commission, distorted and exaggerated Gibbs' "dictatorship'" warning in regard to a republic, and also inferred that Sir Owen Dixon would have bracketed Gibbs with the other long-tenured, earlier Queensland member of the High Court, Charles Powers, the Bundaberg solicitor who had never practised at the Bar and who was derided as a cipher. It was unpleasant and ill-informed journalism. Fortuitously, in the same paper, there appeared a letter from Liberal politician, John Howard, in which he commented:

> The flavour of much republican rhetoric, and it is reflected in your editorials on the subject, is that nobody can be treated as being involved in the debate until he or she has conceded the threshold principle that Australia ought to become a republic. Apparently "the debate" is about the form of a future republic and not if there should be one. Such an attitude is deeply offensive to millions of Australians...I accept the integrity with which many republicans hold their views. My only request of them is that they afford the same respect to others without cheap and sneering putdowns designed to

paint those who support the present system as unfashionable, bereft of intellectual rigour and hopelessly shrouded in nostalgia.

The attack on Gibbs was a recognition of the influence of his support for the anti-republican movement. *The Australian* published the following week a letter from Francis M Douglas QC, a Sydney member of the Douglas Queensland legal family, friends of the Gibbs for two generations. It rebutted the McQueen article, in particular the attack on Gibbs' grasp of constitutional matters. Douglas went on to say:

> I believe I am well placed to say that amongst his contemporaries Sir Harry Gibbs was regarded as being the most able of his contemporaries in other States...The fact that he may hold views which are different from those held by some of the present members of the High Court, and is an opponent of republicanism is no reason to insult him...that *The Weekend Australian* should allow this to happen is a matter of considerable regret.

> As one who has had the pleasure of witnessing Sir Harry discharge the duties of the judicial office, from the time when I was my father's associate in 1967 (when Sir Harry was a member of the Queensland Supreme Court), up until the time when he retired from the bench, I have always been struck by his unfailing courtesy and modesty notwithstanding the enormous breadth of his intellect. In that, I think there is a lesson for all of us.

Gibbs' concerns about centralising of political power in Canberra received unexpected support from Queensland Labor Premier Wayne Goss several months later. Catching front page headlines, Goss warned: "Australia is on a course where the continuing shift of power to Canberra is leading to the de facto abolition of States...and I suspect [this] could be complete by 2001... If we continue as we have been, the States will cease to exist." Goss outlined the great loss in efficiency, competitiveness and accountability which could result and challenged the nation to seize the initiative before it was too late: "Reinvigorate and reform," he advised. "Put simply, we need to re-invent the States".[8]

To Gibbs, stressing as he always has the federal nature of the Constitution, this, coming from the Premier of his home State, was sweet music indeed. The preservation of Australia's stable democratic way of life in which the legal system, to which his own life has been dedicated, plays a vital part is Harry Gibbs' philosophy. The High Court, as the arbiter in deciding the limits of Commonwealth power, has great responsibility. Gibbs sought in his judgments to interpret the Australian Constitution as it is set forth, which is as a *federal* Commonwealth, favouring neither Commonwealth nor States,

---

8 See Peter Morley, "Canberra power grab", *The Courier-Mail* of 20 September 1994.

but preserving the balance between them. His peers consider his greatest strengths have been in the clarification and development of the Australian common law, equity, and criminal law. He is recognised internationally.

Renowned English judge, Lord Wilberforce, with whom Gibbs sat on the Privy Council in the 1970s, found that "a re-reading of his judgments show how valuable his contributions were". Lord Denning, writing from retirement, puts Gibbs in the Australian perspective: "His work as Chief Justice was of the first quality and I would rank him as one of the greatest of your Chief Justices rivalling even my good friend Sir Owen Dixon who was the greatest Chief Justice that Australia has ever had."

In Australia, there is the testimony of the *Commonwealth Law Reports,* which hold Gibbs' significant High Court judgments over 17 years. His judicial philosophy was to give due respect and scrupulous attention to precedent; to move the law forward by a gradual process, always remembering that such is the manner in which it evolved over the centuries.

He is a conservative man, some think too conservative. Gibbs, having made up his mind, will not be moved. Nonetheless, he has seen great changes and moved with them, as in the implementation of the Australia Act which gave the nation full judicial independence. His life has been one of great achievements, with few significant setbacks. It is the triumph of intelligence, tenacity and internal strength. By definition, anyone who reaches the apex of a nation's legal hierarchy has had a brilliant career. He was not a burning comet or a passionate reformer. Gibbs' brilliance was that of the master craftsman, who rarely falters, who moulds circumstances with forethought and anticipates dangers. With his self-discipline, the diversity of his experience, and the breadth of his knowledge, he brought to his high office the attributes of a great judge.

Since his retirement from the High Court, Australia has seen the flowering of his ideas as he felt more at liberty to express them. He calls for taxation reform, which affects every adult in the country. He advises vigilance in curbing both the present tendency to judicial activism in the High Court and its support for excessive Commonwealth government interpretation and use of its external affairs power. He puts the argument forcibly for the continuation of the status quo in the constitutional monarchy versus republic debate. Sir Harry Gibbs puts forward a reasoned, authoritative view to which people listen. They may or may not agree, but Australians want to hear all sides to these questions which will shape the nation at the bicentenary of federation in 2001AD. Gibbs provides leadership, he remains steadfast - a strong, balancing, national voice.

Appendix

THE YEARS ON THE HIGH COURT AND AFTER

By *Peter Connolly*

On 4 August 1970 Gibbs was appointed to the High Court of Australia. Eight days later argument commenced in a case of considerable constitutional significance.[1] It concerned the manner in which the jurisdiction of the courts of the States must be exercised where they are invested with federal jurisdiction. Gibbs took the view that, as the Commonwealth must take State courts as it finds them, federal jurisdiction is exercisable not only by the judges but by such other officers of State courts as ordinarily exercised jurisdiction of a like nature. The new judge found himself in dissent. The court had sat with seven and the majority comprised Barwick CJ, McTiernan, Menzies, Windeyer, Owen and Walsh JJ, a strong court indeed. Many of us would not have been hard to persuade that the collective wisdom and experience of the majority should carry the day. The dissenting judge was neither stubborn nor vain. He had, however, in the highest degree, two qualities which are essential to a great judge, total commitment to legal principle and a positive inability to compromise once persuaded what the law requires. It remains to note that twelve years later this dissenting judgment was to prevail, a new court accepting, with one dissentient only, the view he had there expressed.[2]

The High Court is now the nation's final court of appeal in all matters. For almost all the century it has been the ultimate court for all matters involving the division of power between the Commonwealth and the States. Such a division is, of course, of the essence of federalism and, as the very fact of divided power makes for a conscious and constant effort by the central government to enlarge its power base, so the arbiter, of necessity the court, must exercise the great authority and responsibility which are involved in deciding the limits of Commonwealth power. No one would dispute that since 1920 when the famous *Engineers'* case[3] started a massive enlargement of the powers and influence of the central government and parliament, the

---

1 *Kotsis v Kotsis* (1970) 122 CLR 69.
2 *Commonwealth v Hospital Contribution Fund* (1982) 140 CLR 49.
3 *Amalgamated Society of Engineers v Adelaide Steamship Co Ltd* (1920) 28 CLR 129.

High Court's social and legal philosophy has been unashamedly centralist. This may well be due, in part at least, to the fact that inevitably a majority of the court at any time come from the two most populous States. It is no accident that the capital is located approximately half way between Sydney and Melbourne.

It is natural enough that the inhabitants of those two great States, Victoria and New South Wales, see nothing disastrous in the enlargement of Commonwealth power, for, in their different ways, they feel confident of being able to cope with Canberra. It is otherwise for those who live in the outlying States. It is instructive, therefore, to examine the decisions to which Gibbs was a party in the constitutional field. One might have expected that, as a judge from an outlying State, he might well take a strongly anti-centralist approach. A dispassionate examination, however, will show that he saw constitutional law not as a political exercise (by which, of course, I do not mean to refer to party politics but rather to matters of social policy), favouring neither the Commonwealth nor the States but seeing the Constitution, in terms of its own preamble, as the legal embodiment of an "indissoluble *federal* Commonwealth".

The first such case arose within a few months of his appointment to the High Court.[4] The question raised was whether the Commonwealth might lawfully impose payroll tax upon the governments of the States. As Barwick CJ put it, expressed in its narrowest form, the question was whether the inclusion of the Crown in right of a State in the definition of employer was a valid exercise of the taxation power and stated in its broadest form it was whether the Commonwealth might, by a law of taxation not confined in its operation to States, impose a tax upon a State. Three of the judges, led by Barwick CJ, carefully confined themselves to identifying the legislation as being a law with respect to taxation. A majority of the court was concerned at the implications for the federal system. The court had held, back in 1947,[5] that a provision of the Banking Act which attempted to force the States and their instrumentalities to bank as directed by the Treasurer was not a valid exercise of Commonwealth power. All of the judges, as Gibbs put it, recognised that implications must be made in the Constitution because of its federal nature. Sir Owen Dixon had said in that case that the federal power of taxation would not support a law which placed a special burden upon the States, affirming that they cannot be singled out and taxed as States in respect of some exercise of their functions.

---

4 *Victoria v Commonwealth* (1971) 122 CLR 353.
5 *Melbourne Corporation v Commonwealth* (1947) 74 CLR 1.

Gibbs' conclusion, however, was that the authorities did not support the proposition that the power of the Commonwealth parliament to make laws with respect to taxation is subject to an implied limitation that excepts from the scope of the power any law that imposes taxation on the States. On the other hand he accepted Dixon's view that a Commonwealth law which discriminates against the States in the sense of imposing some special burden or disability upon them is bad. He added the further rider that a general law of the Commonwealth which would prevent a State from continuing to exist and function as such would also be invalid. His final conclusion on the case was that the Commonwealth had not transgressed against this implied restraint. The significance of this type of decision obviously lies in the future. It affirmed the implied restraint on Commonwealth power which qualifies the *Engineers'* case and which, it is plain enough, the minority led by Sir Garfield Barwick would have wished to scotch. It was, however, far from being what the journalists would call a "States' rights" decision, because it affirmed the power of the Commonwealth to tax the States themselves in relation to their employment of their own servants. The implied restraint was endorsed by a Full Court of the High Court in 1985[6] in which the court held invalid Commonwealth legislation passed during the pendency of a dispute between the Queensland Electricity Commission and the Electrical Trades Union, the effect which would have been to remove the dispute from the jurisdiction of the State industrial authorities and impose upon the State electricity authorities burdens not equally laid upon others subject to federal industrial law.

1975 saw a string of constitutional cases before the High Court. One of the most important decisions to come before the High Court in its history concerned what was called the Australian Assistance Plan[7] for the purpose of which a very large sum was appropriated by an Act of the Commonwealth Parliament for grants to Regional Councils for Social Development. The purposes for which such Regional Councils might disburse the funds so appropriated were not shown to be confined to matters within the legislative power of the Commonwealth.

The case examines the constitutional limits on the capacity of the Commonwealth to expend the Consolidated Revenue Fund. Section 83 of the Constitution provides that no money shall be drawn from the Commonwealth Treasury except under appropriation made by law and s 81 provides that the Consolidated Revenue Fund shall be appropriated for the purposes of the Commonwealth. The court differed widely as to the reach of

---

6 *Queensland Electricity Commission v Commonwealth* (1985) 159 CLR 192.
7 *Victoria v Commonwealth and Hayden* (1975) 134 CLR 338.

the expression "the purposes of the Commonwealth" in s 81. In the result the Chief Justice and Gibbs and Mason JJ, both future Chief Justices, held the appropriation to be invalid. McTiernan, Jacobs and Murphy JJ held it to be valid and the case against the appropriation failed because the seventh Justice, Stephen J, held that the State of Victoria and its Attorney-General, who had challenged the appropriation, had no standing.

Legal restraints on the expenditure of the revenues of the Commonwealth are sparse enough in all conscience. The mischief which has resulted from this failure of decision, by way of unrestrained spending over many years now, much of it for purposes of the most doubtful social utility, is notorious. Gibbs, after an examination of the previous decisions, observed:

> The balance of judicial opinion is heavily in favour of the view that the power of appropriation is not general and unlimited but may be exercised only for purposes which can in law properly be described as purposes of the Commonwealth - purposes which the Commonwealth can lawfully put into effect in the exercise of the powers and functions conferred upon it by the Constitution. Quite apart from authority I consider that view to be correct. It would be contrary to all principles of interpretation to treat the words "for the purposes of the Commonwealth" in section 81 as adding nothing to the meaning of the section. The words do not in their ordinary sense have the same meaning as "for any purpose whatever" or "for such purposes as the Commonwealth may think fit"....in this context the words "for purposes of the Commonwealth" in section 81 naturally refer to purposes for which the Commonwealth, as a political entity, is empowered by the Constitution to act. This construction is supported by section 83 - the power can only be exercised by a law validly passed.

If this view had prevailed it may well be that the Commonwealth would not have such a massive deficit on current account today.

1975 also saw legislation by the State of Queensland, whose government was chafing under the centralist tendencies, as it saw it, of the High Court. Accordingly a means was devised of obtaining rulings direct from the Privy Council upon references made to the Queen by the Supreme Court. One such provision would have enabled the reference of a question as to the respective powers of the Commonwealth and the State. Now s 74 of the Constitution provides that appeal does not lie from the High Court to the Privy Council on such a question without the certificate of the High Court itself. The Queensland legislation, if valid, would thus have bypassed the prohibition contained in s 74, for the case would never have gone to the High Court at all. A case was taken to the High Court[8] and Gibbs wrote the principal

---

8 *Commonwealth v Queensland* (1975) 134 CLR 298.

judgment which was agreed in by Barwick CJ, Stephen and Mason JJ. He held the legislation to be invalid as being "contrary to the inhibitions, which, if not expressed, are clearly implicit in Chapter III" of the Constitution. If a comment may be permitted, implications which preserve the integrity of the Constitution are not necessarily unwelcome to the centralist mind, provided always that they do not cut down central power.

1975 also saw constitutional cases which dealt with representation of federal territories in the parliament and the resolution of a deadlock between the Houses. The background to the first, at the risk of being repetitive, is that the six constituent colonies had agreed to federate on the basis that there should be a division of governmental and legislative powers on a basis hammered out at the Conventions and, equally important, that the interests of the smaller or outlying colonies (as against those of New South Wales and Victoria) should be protected by a Senate of equal standing in most matters with the House of Representatives and in which each of the new States should have equal representation. Now the territories, of the nature of things, have tended to be financially dependent upon the Commonwealth and, to a large extent, clients of Canberra. To give them full representation in either House would have a tendency to distort such balance as there is between the Commonwealth and the States: and this is particularly so in relation to the Senate.

Section 122 of the Constitution provides amongst other things that the Parliament may allow the representation of a territory in either House to the extent and on the terms which it thinks fit. This plainly contemplated limited representation and, indeed, the ACT and the Northern Territory had had restricted rights, first of all speaking rights and then voting rights with respect to matters affecting the territory in question in the House of Representatives. So far as the Senate was concerned the width of the provision in s 122 fell to be read with the particular provision of s 7 of the Constitution, which provides that the Senate is composed of senators for each State. However, in 1973 the Parliament provided for two senators representing each of those territories with full voting rights. In the resulting case[9] the majority read s 122 literally and as overriding, to that extent s 7, striking, as many would think, yet another blow at the federal compact. The minority, Barwick CJ, Gibbs and Stephen JJ held, in Gibbs' words, that the federal balance, which went to the very basis of federation, could not be destroyed by converting the senate from a House representing the States to a House in which the States might conceivably be in a minority, Gibbs pointing out that there was no theoretical limit to the number of senators who might, if the legislation was valid, be appointed to represent a territory.

---

9 *Western Australia v Commonwealth* (1975) 134 CLR 201.

This decision left open the validity of legislation which gave full voting rights to representatives of the territories in the House of Representatives. This latter situation fell for decision in 1977. The 1977 case[10] was brought by Queensland which had not been a party to the decision in 1975. Queensland sought to reopen the validity of the legislation which provided for representation of the territories in the Senate. On this occasion, Gibbs expressed himself as being of the same mind as before and therefore of the opinion that the previous decision was erroneous. The question then arose whether he should follow the decision of the majority in the 1975 case, notwithstanding that he believed it to be wrong. He acknowledged that it had been said that since the court has the duty of maintaining the Constitution, it has a duty to overrule an earlier decision if convinced that it is plainly wrong. He cited a dictum of Isaacs J which puts that point of view in plain and trenchant language.

> Our sworn loyalty is to the law itself, and to the organic law of the Constitution. If, then, we find the law to be plainly in conflict with what we or any of our predecessors erroneously thought it to be, we have, as I conceive, no right to chose between giving effect to the law and maintaining an incorrect interpretation. It is not, in my opinion, better that the court should be persistently wrong than that it should be ultimately right.

Gibbs put the contrary argument in equally plain language. He said that like most generalisations this statement can be misleading and went on:

> No Justice is entitled to ignore the decisions and reasoning of his predecessors, and to arrive at his own judgment as though the pages of the law reports were blank, or as though the authority of a decision did not survive beyond the rising of the court. A Justice, unlike a legislator, cannot introduce a programme of reform which sets at nought decisions formerly made and principles formerly established. It is only after the most careful and respectful consideration of the earlier decision, and after giving due weight to all the circumstances, that a Justice may give effect to his opinions in preference to an earlier decision of the court.

No statement more simply and uncompromisingly states Gibbs' judicial philosophy. Consistently with it, he subordinated his own view and accepted the ratio of the 1975 case, as did Stephen J.

This is not to compromise one's own opinion but to acknowledge that it has not prevailed. Except in the most unusual circumstances, to insist upon it can only lead to instability in the legal system and to a just impeachment of intellectual self-indulgence.

---

10 *Queensland v Commonwealth* (1977) 139 CLR 585.

The degree of self discipline involved was formidable. Of the former majority of four, McTiernan J had been replaced by Aickin J, who took what was then the minority view. Had Gibbs and Stephen JJ not accepted their duty to apply the decisions of the court rather than their personal views, the 1975 case would have been reversed. Respect for the High Court and confidence in the stability of the legal process, which in those days were regarded as important, would have been greatly disturbed if, after so short an interval, with no intervening change of circumstance, it had now been declared that the territories could be fully represented in neither of the Houses or in the House of Representatives only.

The question goes beyond the conscience of the individual judge. It is, indeed, of critical importance to the standing and general acceptance of our highest court. Since Gibbs' retirement, the High Court has, to use the language of the next Chief Justice, embarked on a course of judicial activism. Far from the decisions formerly made and principles formerly established being given careful and respectful consideration, they are tending to be brushed aside, or, indeed, ignored without consideration at all. A notable example was the decision in *Cole v Whitfield*[11] in 1988, in which the literally scores of decisions on s 92 of the Constitution were in effect overruled: and the settled doctrine of the court which had obtained since Federation that s 92 conferred an individual right on Australian citizens to trade freely interstate subject only to proper regulation, was dismissed as a mere theory. The reasoning which led to this decision may fairly be described as socio-economic, based upon a resort to the convention debates which, since 1920, have been rejected by the court in favour of the text of the Constitution.[3] But, so long as *Cole v Whitfield* stands it will be not only unnecessary but positively unhelpful ever again to refer to the text of s 92. True it is that the politicians and bureaucracies of the country applaud to a man the removal of restraints on government. The views of citizens who have been deprived of a personal right which they have enjoyed since Federation are unlikely to be of any interest, even to those who have taken to advocating an expansion of constitutionally guaranteed rights. Those who are interested in the constitutional implications of this decision might note that the Commonwealth and all six States were represented by their Attorneys-General who virtually in unison sang the same song, begging that the burden might be removed from them. The court obliged.

Gibbs' approach in the territories' cases had a celebrated precedent. Sir Owen Dixon had dissented from majority views on the effect of s 92 on interstate transport. He ultimately concluded that, whilst his personal

---

11 (1988) 165 CLR 360.

opinion remained unchanged, he should adhere to the majority view. It probably gave him little personal satisfaction that the Privy Council was to reverse the majority decisions and restore his own. Sir Harry Gibbs has had the same experience in the sense that, after a passage of years, a differently constituted High Court has, more than once, accepted his dissenting judgment. An instance has already been given in relation to State courts invested with federal jurisdiction.

Judges will, from time to time, be faced with the difficulty that their personal opinion on a question of law will be at variance with decisions of the court. On 18 March 1993 the High Court gave a decision[12] in which one of the Justices was faced with this problem. He observed[13] that there were weighty statements of authority which support the proposition that, in matters of fundamental constitutional importance, the members of the court are obliged to adhere to what they see as the requirements of the Constitution as opposed to settled authority on the point and in support of his resolve to do so he cited passages set out in the 1977 territories decision. He might, with advantage, have considered the passage from the judgment of Gibbs J in that case set out above.

We come now to a decision of major importance relating to the deadlock provisions which are contained in s 57 of the Constitution.[14] Section 57 provides first for a double dissolution in the event of two successive rejections or failures to pass a proposed law, the second occasion being three months after the first. This was alleged to have occurred. But in the High Court the question was whether there had in truth been a rejection or failure to pass on the first occasion. After the double dissolution the House passed the bill again and the Senate failed to pass it, whereupon the Governor-General convened a joint sitting of both Houses at which it was affirmed by a majority and presented for the royal assent. The State of Victoria challenged the validity of the legislation. The whole of the subsequent machinery depended, for the validity of the Act, on whether there had been a failure to pass or a rejection on the first occasion, which was on 13 December 1973. This was the last day of the spring session of parliament. The bill was adjourned to the autumn session in February 1974 and was ultimately rejected on 2 April 1974. The House of Representatives did not wait for three months to expire from the Senate's rejection but passed the bill again on 8 April, the contention being that there had been a failure to pass on 13 December 1973.

---

12 *Stevens v Head* (1993) 176 CLR 433.
13 Deane J, ibid at 461.
14 *Victoria v Commonwealth* (1975) 134 CLR 81.

The view of the majority, Barwick CJ, Gibbs, Stephen and Mason JJ, was that there was no failure to pass until the due deliberative processes of the Senate had occurred. The first requisite of this somewhat cumbrous machinery had therefore never occurred and the bill had never passed into law. Apart from resolving the proper meaning to be given to s 57, the court decided a number of other points of fundamental importance. The first was that the question whether a measure has been passed in accordance with s 57 is examinable by the High Court, and the second was that the Governor-General does not have an unexaminable power to decide whether the conditions of s 57 have been satisfied. Finally, whether the Senate has failed to pass depends upon the facts objectively viewed and not upon the statements of individual senators. One argument raised by the Commonwealth went, in Gibbs' judgment, to the function of the Senate and in his view disclosed a serious misconception of the place of the Senate as a legislative chamber. The Commonwealth's submission involved the proposition that if the Senate does not pass a bill originating in the House as soon as it has had an opportunity of doing so it will have failed to pass. In rejecting this view he said:

> Under the Constitution the Senate does not occupy a subordinate place in the exercise of legislative power. It is an essential part of the Parliament in which the legislative power of the Commonwealth is vested....It is expressly provided by s. 53 of the Constitution that except as provided in that section, the Senate shall have equal power with the House of Representatives in respect of all proposed laws....Clearly the Senate retains the power to amend any proposed law which is not within the specific prohibitions imposed by s. 53 (i.e. in relation to money bills)...the Senate may reject any proposed law, even one which it cannot amend. Moreover, under the Constitution the House of Representatives has no power to control the Senate in the exercise of its functions and, in particular cannot compel the Senate to give immediate or prompt consideration to any particular measure.

Prophetic words in late 1975 when the judgment was delivered! And Stephen J said of the Senate's powers, "These powers, unusual in a modern upper House, reflect the federal character of our polity....It would be a distortion of the history of the Constitutional Conventions to regard that solution which s 57 represents as involving no more than...that the will of the House should prevail and should do so without delay."

Since 1969, Barwick CJ had advanced the view that before Federation the colonies had no proprietary rights in the territorial waters which washed their shores nor in the land below those waters.[15] His Honour acknowledged that a large number of opinions of law officers of the Imperial Crown spoke of the

---

15 *Bonser v La Macchia* (1969) 122 CLR 177.

territorial seas of the colonies. But his Honour said that if they meant that such seas were either colonial property or under colonial dominion they had been under a basic misconception. In 1973 Commonwealth legislation asserted Commonwealth sovereignty over the Continental Shelf, the territorial sea and sea bed and certain internal waters. The legislation was passed in reliance in part at least on the International Convention on the Territorial Sea and the Contiguous Zone and the Convention on the Continental Shelf.

The States challenged the validity of the legislation in the *Territorial Seas case*.[16] The legislation in relation to the Continental Shelf was upheld by the whole court under placitum (xxix) of s 51 of the Constitution (the external affairs power). A majority of the court also sustained the legislation in relation to matters other than the continental shelf under the external affairs power and three of the judges, Barwick CJ and Mason and Jacobs JJ, further held that the external affairs power was not limited to authorising laws with respect to Australia's relationship with foreign countries but extended to any matter or thing external to or situated outside Australia.

To determine the validity of the Commonwealth legislation, it was also necessary for the court to determine whether the colonies before Federation had sovereign or proprietary rights in respect of the territorial sea or sea bed. By a majority the court decided against the States, Gibbs and Stephen JJ dissenting. Murphy J acknowledged that the colonies had exercised some jurisdiction over the territorial sea before Federation, but held that on Federation the territorial sea attached "as an attribute of international personality" to the Commonwealth. Stephen J, in holding that sovereignty over the colonial land mass carried with it ownership of and dominion over its league seas, said:

> The contrary view, that self-governing colonies, possessing very extensive shorelines and having absolute power of management and control over Crown lands within their land masses, were nevertheless deprived of ownership and control of league seas, those waters being outside their territory and remaining under the control of the Imperial Parliament and executive, is to my mind unacceptable. It is, moreover, a view which is shown by the extensive evidence which is before the court in this case, to have been at no time within the contemplation either of the Imperial authorities or of a colonial legislatures or executives. The numerous opinions of the Law Officers of the Imperial Crown throughout the 19th century touching league seas are in my view inconsistent with the title and control of those waters being retained by the Imperial Crown and executive, especially having regard for the then prevailing view that colonial legislatures had no extra territorial competence.

---

16 *New South Wales v Commonwealth* (1975) 135 CLR 337.

Gibbs, in one of the most powerful judgments he has written, analysed the legislation rigorously and exposed the domestic power-grab lying beneath what was piously claimed as a mere acceptance of international obligation. His historical summary points up the distortion of historical facts and long established law which can occur when lawyers who are entrusted with the protection of the Constitution, are basically unsympathetic to it. It is a process which has not yet ended, as the decision in the notorious *Mabo* case plainly indicates. Gibbs said:

> In fact, before Federation, the various colonies made laws for the establishment of harbours and the construction of wharves, jetties and breakwaters, the control of navigation and pilotage, the maintenance of lighthouses and lightships, the regulation of fishing, whaling and prawning, and of diving for pearl shell and beche-de-mer, the grant of oyster leases and licences to get marine fibres and sponges, and the grant of leases to enable mining to be carried out below low-water mark, and for customs and quarantine purposes. The validity of this legislation was not questioned by the courts or by the Imperial authorities in London. On the contrary, opinions given by the Law Officers in London, many of them lawyers of great distinction, consistently affirmed that the authority of the colonial legislatures, in Australia and elsewhere, extended for three marine miles from low-water mark: see O'Connell, Opinions on Imperial Constitutional Law (1971) esp. pp. 123-125, 159-160, 190-197. It might be possible to regard some of this legislation as extra-territorial but nevertheless sufficiently connected with the colony to be within power, but that cannot truly be said of all of it. For example it seems to me that if the doctrine of extra-territorial incompetence were logically applied, and unless the waters within the three mile limit were regarded as part of the colony, the colony would have no more right to prevent foreigners, in a foreign boat, from fishing in the territorial sea except under licence than it would to prevent them from hunting in the neighbouring colony. If the territorial sea is outside the colony how can one justify legislation regulating the exploitation of the minerals under the sea bed or the pearl shell upon it?

> Under the power conferred by colonial statutes the Crown, on the advice of its colonial ministers, did in fact dispose of interests in, and control the use of, the lands beneath the territorial sea. Leases were granted to enable mining to be carried out beneath the Pacific Ocean off the coast of New South Wales and licences were granted to fish for pearls and beche-de-mer in the Queensland and Western Australia. Hundreds of wharves and jetties extending below low-water mark were built - in the ocean, not only in internal waters - particularly along the coasts of Queensland and Western Australia. It would have been absurd if the Crown's right to control the sea bed adjoining a colony - for example the right to authorise the building of a pier or to grant an oyster lease - could only have been exercised on the advice of Her Majesty's Ministers 12,000 miles away in London. The practical administrators in Whitehall did not descend to such absurdity.

Once self-government had been granted to a colony, neither the Imperial Parliament nor the Imperial Government sought to fetter the decisions of local administrators as to the use of the territorial sea or the sea bed.

And he made a telling point in relation to the Commonwealth's powers over navigation and shipping, which had been held to deal with that subject insofar only as it is relevant to interstate trade and commerce. If this territorial sea were part of Commonwealth territory and subject to plenary Commonwealth power there would seem, he said with justice, to be no reason why the Parliament could not deal with any navigation shipping within the three mile belt including purely intrastate navigation and shipping.

The successful assertion of Commonwealth sovereignty over the territorial sea and sea bed on grounds which, to orthodox lawyers, seemed spurious proved in truth to be a mere fillip to the megalomania of the Commonwealth. Irrespective of where the sovereignty lies, activities in the territorial sea are of great concern to a littoral state and a nexus between such activities and the power to legislate for the peace order and good government of that state is readily found. The next year, 1976, saw Western Australian legislation forbidding the possession of undersized fish in Western Australian waters. The validity of this legislation was affirmed by the High Court,[17] for the decision in the 1975 *Territorial Seas* case had not denied the power of the States to give their legislation operation beyond their land territory. Gibbs observed:

> There is an intimate connection between the land territory of a State and its off-shore waters. Those waters had been popularly regarded as the waters of the State, and as vital to its trade. The people of the State have traditionally exploited the resources of the off-shore waters and used them for recreation. The enforcement of the laws of the State would be gravely impeded if a person could escape from the reach of the laws and the authority of the State by going below low-water mark. It does not appear that any law of a colony or State has ever been held invalid in its operation within the off-shore waters, only on the ground that it lacks sufficient connection with the colony or the State. Legislation of a kind accepted for over a hundred years as being validly enacted is not lightly to be overturned, with consequences gravely inconvenient for the administration of the laws of the States, and in some cases with disturbance to old-established proprietary rights. When after so many years we asked to declare for the first time that such legislation is ultra vires, we may well pause to consider what reason exists to deny the States power to enact legislation taking effect within their off-shore waters.

He went on to point out that, as a result of the *Territorial Seas* case those waters were now held to form part of the territory of the Commonwealth but

---

17 *Pearce v Florenca* (1976) 135 CLR 507.

that any conflict between the type of law traditionally passed by the States and a law of the Commonwealth for this regime would be solved by s 109 of the Constitution.

The sovereignty over the territorial sea proffered by the High Court to the Commonwealth would seem, after all, to have proved a poisoned chalice. Canberra was no more capable of administering the territorial sea regime than it is of any other of the useful and indeed essential but unexciting aspects of public administration in this country. Of the immense amounts of money which are expended annually by the Commonwealth, very little goes on everyday public administration which is essential to a civilised society. True it is that by the exercise of the powers given to it by the Constitution in s 96 to make grants to the States for specific purposes (ie tied grants), it is enabled to impose its views in such areas of essentially State concern as education. The net result has been that billions of dollars are expended in one of the most important services any State can give to its citizens and the net result has been an increasingly illiterate society for whom it is now perceived by those on high that the very statute book should be rewritten in ungrammatical language, giving currency to sociological fads and shibboleths, the end product being excruciating to read and totally lacking in precision. Vast expenditure of public funds to achieve such a disastrous result must surely mark a deep malaise in a society if not the likelihood that it is in its terminal phase.

To revert to the *Territorial Seas* case, the spurious nature of the whole exercise was revealed by its aftermath. In 1979 and 1980 the States requested the Parliament of the Commonwealth to make a law extending the legislative powers of the States in and in relation to the States' coastal waters and the Commonwealth passed the Coastal Waters (State Powers) Act 1980, allegedly under s 51 (xxxviii) of the Constitution. It also passed the Coastal Waters (State Title) Act 1980, vesting title to the sea bed of the territorial sea in the States. As Professor Lane observed in his commentary on the Australian Constitution at 203, the legislative aftermath of the court's decision strove to put the States back where they thought they were previously. It would seem obvious enough that the Commonwealth realised that the administrative burden involved in providing the necessary services in coastal waters around the entire continent was quite beyond it and, having established its sovereignty, for what that is worth, hastily passed the problems back to the States.

Before passing from Sir Harry Gibbs' contribution to Australian constitutional law, the writer is conscious that some explanations are called for. One is attempting to present a general view of the legal work of a great lawyer as it emerges from his judgments. The language in which it is evaluated in these pages is unlikely to be that which the Judge himself would have chosen. On the other hand, it is intended for a much wider audience than professional lawyers. Furthermore, the writer has been unable to restrain strong feelings about the role which the High Court has played in recent years. This view is well understood by lawyers although, of course, not all would agree that it is a bad thing.

These lines are being written in 1993. Those who wish to see the Constitution radically altered in the next seven years and the States replaced by agglomerations of large local authorities directly answerable to the Commonwealth would doubtless see the efforts of the High Court as pointed entirely in the right direction and find nothing unacceptable in the notion of a continental nation being governed in all respects from a make believe city on the banks of the Molonglo River. Perhaps one of the reasons why history is not being taught seriously is that a consideration of the history of other societies might lead to the conclusion that this is a pipedream. This particular model for a single parliament was first proposed, in the recollection of the writer, by a former prime minister, Mr EG Whitlam. Australians would do well to remember that the blessings of central government, even in relatively small countries, are not universally perceived. Thus, in the United Kingdom, many Scots and Welshmen resent being governed from London and the Swiss utterly decline to be wholly governed from Bern. Australia is a continent. In assessing the prospects for long term central administration, one could not do better than consider the examples of the Soviet empire and of Yugoslavia, both of which flew apart once the savage repression imposed by the Communist Party was removed.

The nature of the Constitution under which our descendants are to live is of fundamental importance for their future. It deserves to be considered as a question involving serious issues and subjected to rigorous analysis as occurred in the great constitutional debates which led to the present Constitution. Those who wish to manipulate the Australian people into accepting a highly centralised polity for this continent may well, consciously or unconsciously, see the increasing illiteracy of its people as a factor which will ease the realisation of the pipedream. History, however, teaches us that human beings will not tolerate indefinitely being governed by people who are remote from them. If the wrong decisions are made in this generation it is certain that sooner or later the proposed monolith will collapse in disorder and bitterness.

CRIMINAL LAW

Most lawyers whose practice has been largely on the civil side, find, on appointment to the Bench, that the criminal law is a challenging experience.

No doubt this is partly because of its novelty but, more importantly, because they are conscious that they are playing an important role in the administration of an area of the law which is critical to the continuance of an orderly society, seen as such by their fellow citizens and, in its essentials at least, well understood by them. Gibbs was no exception. By the time he was appointed to the High Court he had of course had extensive experience as a trial Judge in the criminal jurisdiction, both on the Supreme Court of Queensland and in the Australian Capital Territory and, as an appellate Judge, on the Court of Criminal Appeal. One of the tensions which criminal investigation involves is that between the interests of the accused person in having only true and reliable evidence presented against him at his trial and the frustration felt by investigating police officers, who are confident that they have detected the person responsible for an offence but whose investigations have fallen short of obtaining admissible and convincing evidence of each element of the offence. It has been known for investigators in such a situation to supply the missing proof by the fabrication of confessional evidence.

Such an exercise is obviously far more difficult if the accused person's solicitor is present while he is being interviewed. There had been those who had considered that the refusal to allow the solicitor to have access at the critical time was not admissible as going merely to the credit of the police. In 1977, Gibbs,[18] with the concurrence of a majority of the Court, held *first* that evidence that the accused's solicitor has been excluded from an interview with investigating police at which a verbal confession is alleged to have been made does not go merely with the credit of the police witness but is relevant to the question whether the confession was in fact made; and *second* that, while an unsigned record of interview is admissible, if there is evidence that the accused acknowledged it to be correct, a trial judge may exclude it in the exercise of his discretion, which is particularly called for if the evidence has little or no weight but may be gravely prejudicial. He gave reasons for suggesting that "the most careful consideration" should be given to the exercise of the discretion in cases of unsigned records of interview. It is fair to say that, except in quite unusual circumstances, the tendering of such documents at a trial has ceased. They are merely used these days for the refreshing of the memory of the police witness. This means that it is still a matter for the jury to consider whether the confession was in fact made or not, but they do not have with them in the jury room the alleged written record prepared for the signature of the accused which may have a weight in their minds which is out of all proportion to its true value.

---

18 *Driscoll v The Queen* (1977) 137 CLR 517.

When Sir Samuel Griffith, drawing heavily on the code drafted by Sir James Stephen in the 19th century, codified the criminal law for Queensland in 1901, he was not to know, though no doubt he intended, that the exercise would relieve Queenslanders of the constant vicissitudes and anomalies of interpretation which had been visited by the courts on the common law principles relating to crime.

Fundamental to the notion of criminal responsibility is the question whether a person who does not intend that a given event should occur may nevertheless be answerable for it. The drunken motorist, unable properly to control his vehicle, may cause death or grievous harm. The sportsman or the soldier on a rifle range may fire a rifle and unwittingly kill or wound another. In what circumstances are they criminally responsible? Common law requires a culpable state of mind, which common lawyers call mens rea from the Latin for that phrase. The appropriate mens rea varies according to the offence which is charged. The solution adopted in Griffith's Criminal Code for offences which do not require a specific intent was a general proposition applicable to virtually all such situations, which may be shortly and not too inaccurately stated as being that a person is not criminally responsible for an act which is not a deliberate act or a result which he did not foresee and which a reasonable man would not have foreseen. Particular rules were adopted to cover cases of intoxication, insanity, mistake and duress. Lawyers being lawyers there has been disagreement from time to time as to what constituted the act as against the event, counsel for the accused naturally contending that the end result is the act so as to entitle him to an acquittal if it is not shown that that result itself was "willed".

Gibbs had been on the High Court some two years when a case from Queensland came up in which the accused, allegedly under provocation, forced a glass against the victim's eye causing him grievous bodily harm.[19] In relation to voluntariness, the defence was exactly what one would have expected, namely that it must be shown that the causing of the grievous bodily harm was the willed or deliberate act. Gibbs pointed out that this was very close indeed to a submission that the Crown must show that the accused had an intention to cause grievous bodily harm, a question which was, of course, quite irrelevant to the charge which contained no allegation of specific intent.

In that case the pushing of the glass and the infliction of the harm were very close in point of time, but the distinction must be maintained, as Gibbs pointed

---

19 *Kaporonovski v The Queen* (1973) 133 CLR 209.

out. Thus in an earlier case an accused man, in the darkness in a fit of anger, had aimed a blow with a stick at his wife and unwittingly struck their child whom she was carrying and of whose presence he was unaware. In that case the act was the aiming of the blow with the stick and the event was the striking and killing of the child. So, in the case in 1973, it was the pushing of the glass which was the act of the accused. It was quite deliberate and could not be described as unwilled. The event or result was the doing of grievous bodily harm and the accused man was guilty of the offence, unless that result was both unintended and would not reasonably have been foreseen. No such conclusion was open and he was therefore properly convicted.

Observance of this distinction, which is, of course, required by the language of s 23 of the Queensland Criminal Code, made the direction of juries where this sort of question arose simple in the extreme. Equally important, it is clear from the judgment of Gibbs in the 1973 case that whenever an accused person seeks to contend that an act occurred independently of the exercise of his will, he must bring himself within s 23 of the Criminal Code which deals with that situation. Thus an accused person who claims that his will was inoperative by reason of the intoxication will find his case governed by the provision which deals with intoxication under which this contention is not available; and if he sets up insanity he must bring himself within the provision which deals with insanity and accept its consequences if he succeeds, namely indefinite detention. In 1990, after Gibbs' retirement from the High Court, the court dealt with the interaction of the various provisions of the Queensland Criminal Code within which s 23 falls[20] and in the course of extensive judgments came to no conclusion which is inconsistent with Gibbs' judgment in the case now under consideration.

In 1978, the decision of the High Court in the case of *Viro*[21] plunged the common law of Australia into a morass of tortuous reasoning on the subject of self-defence. The Privy Council had decided that anyone who is attacked may defend himself, doing what is reasonably necessary for that purpose but no more. It was held that the defence will fail only if the prosecution shows beyond reasonable doubt that what the accused did was not done in self-defence.[22] Their Lordships held that once the jury reaches that conclusion the issue of self-defence vanishes and there is no half-way house. By 1978 decisions of the High Court were no longer subject to appeal to the Privy Council. It followed that the High Court was no longer bound by Privy Council decisions, although naturally according them great respect. Now in

---

20 *The Queen v Falconer* (1990) 171 CLR 30.
21 *Viro v The Queen* (1978) 141 CLR 88.
22 *Palmer v The Queen* [1971] AC 814.

Howe v The Queen, a case decided in 1958,[23] the High Court had engrafted a qualification on the common law principle to the effect that if the defence failed only because the force used was excessive, the accused was guilty of manslaughter only. In its 1971 decision in *Palmer* the Privy Council rejected this qualification. The 1978 decision in *Viro* formulated a view of this defence which required six separate propositions to be put to a jury.

Gibbs' judgment in *Viro* rejected the *Howe* formulation as likely to lead a jury to confusion and error and as being unsound in legal theory. Specifically, he considered that the decision of the Privy Council in *Palmer* should be preferred to that of the High Court in *Howe*. However, in a characteristic affirmation of the responsibility which a judge owes to the community, he continued:

> But since writing the foregoing I have had an opportunity to read the reasons prepared by the other members of the Court. It is apparent that we hold a diversity of opinions. It seems to me that we should be failing in our function if we did not make it clear what principle commands the support of the majority of the Court. The task of judges presiding at criminal trials becomes almost impossible if they are left in doubt what this Court has decided.

It being apparent that a majority of the court supported the *Howe* doctrine, he agreed with the majority, contrary to his personal opinion but in a desire to achieve a measure of certainty.

Gibbs' prediction proved only too right. In 1987 the court recognised that *Howe* and therefore *Viro* had imposed an onerous burden on judges and juries. Three of the judges in the 1987 decision[24] said:

> It is apparent, we think, from the difficulties which appear to have been experienced in the application of *Viro* that there is wisdom in the observation of the Privy Council in *Palmer* that an explanation of the law of self-defence requires no set words or formula. The question to be asked in the end is quite simple. It is whether the accused believed upon reasonable grounds that it was necessary in self-defence to do what he did.

This is a convenient point at which to say something at which offence may be taken although none is intended. It is however a simple fact that the High Court has not, for many years, been overburdened with judges who had had during their earlier careers constant experience of the conduct of trials, especially in the criminal jurisdiction. When *Viro* was decided there were

---

23 *Howe v The Queen* (1958) 100 CLR 448.
24 *Zecevic v Director of Public Prosecutions* (1987) 162 CLR 645.

only two judges with that type of experience, Stephen J who formed part of the majority and Gibbs. Until recent years the High Court, to which appeal lay by special leave only in criminal cases, granted such leave only where matters of real principle, as distinct from practice points and questions of fact, were involved. It is fair to say that it is a common criticism of the court that it has made the task of trial judges in the criminal jurisdiction onerous, while the subtle and complex reasoning which it is the duty of the judges to seek to apply in directing juries is, in most cases, unlikely to make any significant impact on the mind of the criminal jury. One last word needs to be said about Gibbs' judgment in *Viro*. He insisted that, when a specific intent must be proved (in that case an intention to kill or do grievous bodily harm), the jury may consider the fact that the accused was intoxicated by liquor or drugs for the purpose of deciding whether the specific intent in fact existed.

Gibbs' contribution to the common law in relation to crime is exemplified by two other cases. A view had grown up that in cases of importation of prohibited imports knowledge by the person charged that the imports were in fact being brought into the country was not an element of the offence. In 1985 he affirmed the common law presumption that mens rea is required for grave criminal offences and held that the mens rea for importation of prohibited imports was that the offender knew he was importing or, where he was charged with possession, knew that the goods were in his possession.[25] In the same year he decided that an offence of aiding and abetting the commission of a crime required proof of a deliberate act with full knowledge of the essential facts or at least wilful blindness to them so that neither negligence nor recklessness is sufficient for conviction of such an offence.[26]

When Sir Samuel Griffith codified the criminal law for Queensland he was, speaking generally, putting into statutory form the common law as it was then understood. He provided, consistently with the common law as it then stood, that intoxication is no defence but that it may be taken into account by the jury in determining whether a specific intent exists. In *O'Connor* in 1980,[27] the High Court decided by a majority of four to three that self-induced intoxication is relevant on a charge of a criminal offence which does not involve a specific intent. In so doing the court departed from the common law as it had long been understood and as it had recently been affirmed by the House of Lords in *Majewski*.[28] Indeed the formulation in the criminal codes of Australia (Western Australia and Tasmania having followed

---

25 *He Kaw Teh v The Queen* (1985) 157 CLR 523.
26 *Giorgianni v The Queen* (1985) 156 CLR 473.
27 *O'Connor v The Queen* (1980) 146 CLR 64.
28 [1977] AC 443.

Queensland in codifying this field of the law) accepts the old common law on this subject. Gibbs dissented, agreeing with the observation of Lord Salmon in *Majewski* that "if there be no penal sanction for any injury unlawfully inflicted under the complete mastery of drink or drugs voluntarily taken, the social consequences could be appalling." The *O'Connor* decision, unhappily, has remained the law for the common law States but it was quickly rejected in Queensland by the Court of Criminal Appeal as being inconsistent with the explicit provisions in this behalf of the Criminal Code. However, in *The Queen v Martin* in 1984[29] *O'Connor* was applied, Gibbs characteristically joining in the unanimous decision of the court, despite his personal belief to the contrary.

A feature which distinguishes the common law from the civil law which obtains in most countries on the continent of Europe, is that the previous criminal history of the accused person is rigorously excluded from consideration by the jury. The philosophies of the two systems are poles apart, civil lawyers pointing out that the jury is thus deprived of evidence which in a logical sense may be most compelling and common lawyers pointing out the extreme danger that an accused person may be convicted of a criminal offence merely because in the past he has committed an offence or offences of the nature of that presently charged.

However, the common law admits of an exception when the circumstances of the offence charged are so strikingly similar to those of another offence as to be highly persuasive that both were committed by the same person. The House of Lords had adopted the requirement of striking similarity before such evidence was admitted. There is, in truth, no similarity at all between two instances of the same offence which have nothing in common save the fact that the elements required by law are present. In a judgment in 1984 Gibbs, generally acknowledged as a master of the law of evidence, accepted the English formulation.

Many criminal offences are committed by persons well known to the victims. On the other hand, it frequently happens that the offender is not previously known to the victim or to other witnesses and that a suspect is not apprehended for a considerable period after the commission of the offence. The difficulties which attend identification in such circumstances are well known to lawyers and the courts have by their decisions built a variety of safeguards into the system.

---

29 58 ALJR 217.

A decision in 1981 which came before the High Court[30] concerned identification of an accused by eyewitnesses who had seen the likely offender in circumstances associated with the offence (including in one case a witness who could not identify him at the trial). The witnesses had identified the suspect from a group of photographs. Gibbs, then Chief Justice, affirmed that such evidence is admissible with the rider that the judge has the discretion to exclude it if its evidentiary value is outweighed by its prejudicial effect. Evidence by persons who observed the identification (that is to say, who were present when the identification from the photographs was made) is hearsay and therefore inadmissible, unless the identifying witness himself gives evidence and it is then admitted to show that the identification in court is neither a mistake nor an afterthought. In the case of the witness who cannot say whom he identified without refreshing his memory, the evidence is admissible as original evidence from a witness who observed the identification. Any other conclusion would have made an ass of the law. But the Chief Justice was able to demonstrate by strict application of the principles of the law of evidence that this approach was not only pragmatically sound but intellectually impeccable.

Some Contributions on the Civil Side

The law as developed by the judges over the centuries differs from statute law in one important respect. The former resembles a biological process like the building of a coral reef. It grows by incremental additions and time and circumstance dislodge the weaker tentative growths. It is thus the product of hundreds of years of trial and error. The uncertainties in areas of judge-made law are, largely speaking, peripheral or, if important, so well known that the profession is able to chart a course which enables the lay world to avoid the problem. An act of parliament is a new and instantaneous creation. If it has not been satisfactorily thought through - and the sheer volume of the annual additions to the statute law in this country make this quite impossible - the courts are constantly faced with the need to avoid an unintended injustice by drastic surgery. It is at this stage that some knowing commentator may be expected to announce to his admiring public that the law is an ass. Nothing can be done about the legislative process except to try to make its products work. We are about to turn to an area in which Sir Harry Gibbs played his part in clarification and development of common law and equitable rules.

Many of the legal problems with which citizens are placed in a complex modern society involve their relations with government. Again a central difficulty involved in dealing with government is to find out just what has

---

30 *Alexander v The Queen* 145 CLR 395.

happened. Freedom of information legislation is a step in the right direction. However powerful departments manage to have themselves excluded to a greater or lesser extent and such legislation will never provide the whole answer. One means of obtaining the necessary facts is through the process of discovery in litigation. Where a government department is involved the process of disclosure of relevant documents in the possession of the department applies as it would in litigation between a large corporation and the would-be litigant. Now, for many years it was thought to be the law that if the relevant minister or his departmental head swore an affidavit claiming Crown privilege for the document on the basis that it would be contrary to the public interest for it to be disclosed, the court would treat the affidavit as conclusive of the point. At one time this approach by government was so inflexible and so determined that when the victim of a motor car accident sought to discover what the police investigation had revealed he was faced by an affidavit by a minister or some great official to the effect that it was contrary to public policy for the record of what was really a routine administration of an accident to be made available. When the House of Lords decided *Conway v Rimmer*,[31] the general rule was that the court would not order the production of a document, although relevant and otherwise admissible, if it would be injurious to the public interest to disclose it. Lord Reid, however, pointed out what is now obvious and that is that, while there is a public interest in preserving the secrecy of matters of high public importance (such as national security), there is also a public interest in the administration of justice; that there may be a conflict between the two; and that the resolution of that conflict calls for a balancing exercise which obviously can only be performed by the courts.

In Australia this question arose in a dramatic case brought against a former prime minister[32] alleging breach on his part of the Financial Agreement of 1927. Amongst the documents, of which discovery was sought and which the defendant objected to produce, were Executive Council papers and memoranda from senior Treasury officials to senior officers of a department, including one such paper which had already been published in both a periodical and a book. Gibbs, then Acting Chief Justice, recognised that it had been repeatedly asserted that there were certain documents which by their nature fall into a class which ought not to be disclosed, no matter what the documents individually contain. But he pointed out that, although that statement was repeated in the case in 1968 in the House of Lords, "it accords ill with the principles affirmed in that case". He insisted that all the circumstances have to be considered in deciding whether the papers in

---

31 [1968] AC 910.
32 *Sankey v Whitlam* (1978) 142 CLR 1.

question are entitled to be withheld from production, no matter what they individually contain. The logic of this judgment has never been questioned. It represented a courageous advance on the law as stated in *Conway v Rimmer* in 1968 by the House of Lords, forcing the logic of the reasoning of their Lordships to its proper and ultimate conclusion.

Sankey v Whitlam[31] dealt with a point of almost equal importance in relation to committal proceedings. These are criminal proceedings in which the evidence is examined before a magistrate to determine whether there is a case fit to be placed before a judge and jury. There was a supposed rule of long standing that the court would not interfere by prerogative writ with the conduct of committal proceedings. The High Court, however, held that declaratory relief is available in relation to the conduct of committal proceedings, although sparingly granted for the reason that such applications could be made for the purposes of delay and to fragment the criminal process, which is already time consuming and open to abuse. In coming to that conclusion, Gibbs applied his earlier decision on the High Court in *Foster v Jododex Australia Pty Ltd*,[33] in which he had demonstrated the width of the power to grant declaratory relief and its availability in criminal proceedings.

Gibbs has sometimes been described as conservative, a word which in populist jargon has come to mean someone who adheres to views of which the speaker disapproves (no matter how recently he has been converted to that attitude of mind). Thus the extreme hard core left-wing members of the Communist Party of the old Soviet empire are now called "conservatives" by the fellow travellers, who previously could see nothing at all distasteful in any of their wickedness. In some legal circles the word "conservative" is applied to one who insists that the law is more important than one's personal preferences and that the hard logic of legal principle should not be overborne by sociological considerations. It was this type of legal conservatism which led to the next two decisions to which reference should be made.

The first of these two cases was decided in 1981 and involved an Aboriginal land claim in the Northern Territory.[34] Such claims could only be made to unalienated Crown land. By a statutory definition land in a town was not unalienated Crown land. The land in question was declared a town by a planning regulation made by the Administrator of the Northern Territory and there were strong suspicions that this declaration had been made to defeat the Aboriginal claim. Toohey J, sitting as an aboriginal land commissioner, held

---

33 (1972) 127 CLR 424.
34 *Reg v Toohey, exp Northern Land Council* (1981) 151 CLR 170.

himself bound to treat the declaration as valid and thus as excluding his jurisdiction. A majority of the High Court held that the Administrator represented the Crown in the Northern Territory. Although Gibbs did not agree with this view he held that, assuming it to be correct, that the principle that a statutory power may be exercised only for the purpose for which it is conferred applies even when the power is vested in the Crown itself, saying: "It seems fundamental to the rule of law that the Crown has no more power than any subordinate official to enlarge by its own act the scope of a power that has been conferred on it by the Parliament." He noted however that there are expressions of opinion which are entitled to great weight in support of the view that acts of the Crown in Council apparently regular in form, cannot be examined on the ground that they were done with the intention of achieving an unauthorised purpose. Those opinions had been expressed by such giants of the legal system as Sir Owen Dixon, Sir Wilfred Fullagar, Sir Isaac Isaacs, Sir John Latham and Sir Hayden Starke, but Gibbs nonetheless concluded that there was no binding authority and stated the principle as follows:

> If a statutory power is given to the Crown for one purpose, it is clear that it is not lawfully exercised if it is used for another. The courts have the power and duty to ensure that statutory powers are exercised only in accordance with law. They can in my opinion inquire whether the Crown has exercised a power granted to it by statute for a purpose which the statute does not authorise.

As the power to make regulations was exercisable for planning purposes and not to defeat traditional aboriginal land claims, mandamus issued to Toohey J to determine the purpose for which the power had been exercised and therefore the validity of the regulation which, if invalid, would of course not have prevented his exercising his jurisdiction as an aboriginal land commissioner. This is true legal conservatism for it asserts the supremacy of the law itself and corrects misconceptions based on an imperfect understanding of the maxim that the Monarch can do no wrong. Such an attitude of mind does not involve an unthinking application of previous dicta if they are perceived to be inconsistent with fundamental legal principle. It has however nothing to do with sociological or political preconceptions which have been seen to influence some recent decisions of the High Court, notably the *Mabo* case.

The second of these cases was decided in 1982. The court was faced with the refusal of the Governor in Council of Victoria to renew the licence of a workers' compensation insurer which had been in the business for some twenty years. The insurer had been refused a hearing which it sought in order to answer whatever allegations had been made against it. If the decision has not been made by the Crown it would have been bad for failure to afford natural justice. Mason J, now Chief Justice of the High Court, acknowledged that a dictum of Sir Owen Dixon in the *Communist Party* case[35] affirmed that the acts of the Crown and its agents are immune from challenge. Despite such observations from so persuasive a source, in this case, as in the *Northern Land Council* case, the court held[36] that the Crown like any other authority is bound in exercising a statutory power by the rules of natural justice. Gibbs emphasised that the Governor was not acting personally or as a representative of the Crown exercising the prerogative, but was acting on the advice of ministers. The court had been pressed with technical difficulties in that there was binding authority that certiorari and mandamus do not lie to the Crown, but Gibbs was able yet again to draw on the *Jododex* decision, which enables a declaration to be made against the Attorney-General by which the Crown would be bound.

The genius of the common law has been the case by case approach. Its advantage lies in its gradualism which enables new aspects of a given legal problem to be quietly accommodated and the unsatisfactory features of a past decision to be quietly modified. The attempt to formulate general statements which will cover satisfactorily aspects of a particular problem which have never materialised, is virtually certain to be unsatisfactory. In our society, this sort of effort is ordinarily made only by the parliaments. Those who doubt this are welcome to look at the statute book and see how often an act of parliament, which its makers hoped would cover the problem area satisfactorily, has had to be amended as its imperfections became apparent. This is not to criticise the parliaments, but to point out that the attempt to formulate wide all-embracing general propositions in advance is beyond the wit of mortal man. But there are those who will not face this reality. The academic world tends to be impatient at the slow development of both law and equity and to hail as heroic those who attempt the impossible. Gibbs has always been one who accepted the orthodox approach. A couple of important decisions in which he participated in the field of equity will illustrate the point.

In 1983 the court set aside a guarantee given by the parents of the governing director of a building company to a bank to secure the indebtedness of the company to the bank.[37] It emerged that the bank had a wholly owned subsidiary, a finance company, which was engaged in a joint venture with the building company. It also emerged that the building company was insolvent and that indeed, to maintain an appearance of prosperity, the bank and the building company's directors had jointly adopted a policy of selectively

---

35 *Australian Communist Party v Commonwealth* (1951) 83 CLR 1.
36 *FAI Insurances Ltd v Winneke* (1982) 151 CLR 342.
37 *Commercial Bank of Australia Ltd v Amadio* (1983) 151 CLR 447.

---

dishonouring the company's cheques. The company was desperately short of money to pay creditors and a short term arrangement was made between the bank and the company for an increase in the company's overdraft on condition that the overdraft be cleared within a short time. To support this arrangement the son induced his parents to execute a mortgage over property which they owned, the mortgage containing a guarantee of the company's indebtedness. The mortgage document was taken to the parents' home by the manager of the bank. The security was of indefinite duration, although the manager was well aware that the parents believed it to be for a short term. If it matters, the parents were elderly and were migrants with an imperfect understanding of written English. It is clear enough that a self-respecting legal system should have some mechanism to give relief to persons in the position of the parents against the security which they have given. To put it bluntly, the bank by its officers was well aware of the true situation and of the virtual certainty that the property over which the parents gave security would be swallowed up in a relatively short time in payment of the liabilities of the company.

Gibbs rested his conclusion that the case was one in which the security should be set aside on the principle, for which there was ample authority, that there is a duty of disclosure in the case of banker and customer where there is a special arrangement between the bank and the customer of a kind which the surety would not expect. Other members of the court seized the opportunity to categorise the case as one of unconscionable conduct. So indeed it was, but the rubric can be applied to an enormous range of behaviour and little guidance is offered for the future if the courts abandon the sure touchstone of a precise statement of the situation or situations which will give rise to a claim for equitable relief, based on past decisions, in favour of a generalisation the limits of which can be but dimly perceived. The Irish courts had accepted the generalised approach of the Irish Master of the Rolls in *Slator v Nolan*[38] in 1876, but it had not been widely adopted elsewhere.

The next year the court was faced with the problem of a company which had contracted, on a commercial basis, to promote the sale of an American company's products, the whole purpose from the point of view of the operating company being to make a profit, and the possibility of a conflict between the interests of the two being likely and not necessarily to be resolved in favour of the manufacturer.[39] The manufacturer sought to establish that the operating company was a fiduciary and the case raised the still difficult question of the criteria by reference to which the existence of a

---

38 IR 11 Eq 367.
39 *Hospital Products Ltd v United States Surgical Corporation* (1984) 156 CLR 41.

fiduciary relationship may be established as distinct from the established categories in which that relationship is acknowledged to exist.

Gibbs, characteristically, resisted the invitation to formulate a general statement pointing out that such relationships are of different types carrying different obligations and that what might seem an appropriate test for one purpose might be quite inappropriate for another. The possibility of a single over-arching principle which will yield the answer of equity to all situations of this type had been denied by Lord Upjohn who said:[40] "Rules of equity have to be applied to such a great diversity of circumstances that they can be stated only in the most general terms and applied with particular attention to the exact circumstances of each case." The Privy Council has recently[41] applied a passage from the judgment of Mason J in *Hospital Products*. The present Chief Justice had emphasised the vital role of the underlying contract in determining the extent of a fiduciary obligation. The English case involved the alleged fiduciary obligation of a real estate agent to disclose to one vendor the intention of another which might have borne on the price. It is obvious that real estate agents, acting as they do for a variety of vendors, cannot owe a fiduciary obligation of total disclosure to one which could be against the interest of another. The result in *Hospital Products* was that, by a majority which included Gibbs CJ, the court held that while the conduct of the distributor was fraudulent and in gross breach of contract, there is no fiduciary relationship between the parties and that commercial morality could be vindicated by the ordinary remedies of damages for fraud and breach of contract.

The two decisions which have just been discussed reveal a distrust of generalisation the reach of which cannot be foreseen and a preference for specific rule where it has been found to serve well. In 1979, as Acting Chief Justice, Gibbs led the court[42] to reject an approach to the appellate jurisdiction which would have had the effect of limiting rather severely the usefulness of the appellate process. Under the influence of Barwick CJ, some of the judges had adopted a view that the inferences drawn from facts admitted and proved before the court of trial should not be disturbed unless they were shown to be positively wrong. In other words, the judges were not to be free to prefer another inference to the one which had been adopted in the court below. This, of course, was perilously close to equating such conclusions to the verdict of a jury, although Barwick CJ, the author of the proposition, had rejected that view. The doctrine was called by the former Chief Justice the doctrine of "judicial restraint". It was, however,

---

40 *Phipps v Boardman* [1967] 2 AC 46.
41 *Kelly v Cooper* [1993] AC 205.
42 *Warren v Coombes* (1979) 142 CLR 531.

inconsistent with a long line of authority going back to the 1920s if not before. A passage from the joint judgment of Gibbs ACJ, Jacobs and Murphy JJ is worth citing here as an example of orthodox judicial philosophy:

> There is in our respectful opinion no authority that entitles us to depart from the doctrine expounded in this Court in cases (going back to 1953 and earlier) and in the House of Lords in (a case decided in 1955). The balance of opinion...inclines in favour of adherence to that doctrine. Shortly expressed, the established principles are, we think, that in general an appellate court is in as good a position as the trial Judge to decide on the proper inference to be drawn from facts which are undisputed or which, having been disputed, are established by the findings of the trial Judge. In deciding what is the proper inference to be drawn, the appellate court will give respect and weight to the conclusion of the trial Judge, but, once having reached its own conclusion, will not shrink from giving effect to it. These principles, we venture to think, are not only sound in law but beneficial in their operation.

The reader will note again the voice of self-discipline.

On the other hand, where previous decisions, even of the highest authority, have been widely perceived to work injustice and to be inconsistent with fundamental legal principle, he never hesitated to set the law back on its proper course. In 1983 the question arose whether purchasers could be relieved against the forfeiture of their equity by rescission of the contract for their failure to perform strictly on time where time was of the essence. The Privy Council had held in two cases that the making of time of the essence operates to exclude the jurisdiction to specific performance in favour of the purchaser who is in default. The High Court was no longer bound by the decisions of the Privy Council. Gibbs, in a joint judgment with Murphy J,[43] stated the law as being that specific performance will be an exception in such circumstances, but, in principle, such an order may be made when it will not cause injustice but in fact prevent it. The decision was influential in what is now a leading case[44] in which the law of equitable estoppel received, after Gibbs' retirement, a vigorous impetus.

The sixty odd years since the famous case[45] about the snail in the bottle of ginger beer have seen an almost incessant explosion of the law relating to negligence, at least in so far as personal injury is concerned. Not only has the motor car caused the transformation of the landscape but its merciless

---

43 *Legione v Hateley* (1983) 152 CLR 405.
44 *Waltons Stores (Interstate) Ltd v Maher* (1988) 164 CLR 387.
45 *Donoghue v Stevenson* [1932] AC 562.

progress has left countless thousands of human beings dead or disabled in varying degrees. This in turn led to the compulsory insurance of owners and drivers and as a consequence to exquisite refinements of the law of negligence. It is not, however, confined to the areas of human activity affected by the motor vehicle.

When a person suffered injury, of whatever sort, it came to be seen as natural that the victim should look around for someone, preferably of ample means, to blame for his misfortune. The sacrificial victim thus selected tended not to be co-operative. The contests which ensued provide a good deal of the income of the legal profession and sharpened the wits of the common law judges in progressively extending the principles upon which damages for negligence could be recovered.

The law, however, resisted the notion that purely economic loss not associated with personal injury was recoverable in negligence as opposed to breach of contract. Behind this attitude lay the sheer uncertainty and unpredictability of the number of potential claimants. Where economic loss was suffered as a result of breach of contract no such injustice was perceived, for the claimant was the innocent party to the contract. But when we turn to careless behaviour in a situation not governed by a contract the possible range of persons who may suffer as a result may be very great. This led the courts to lean heavily against the recovery in tort of damages by way of economic loss which was not sustained as a result of personal injury or damage to property of the victim.

In 1989 a fearful calamity occurred at Hillsborough Stadium in England when a crowd stampeded at a football match cutting down and crushing to death some 95 people and injuring hundreds of others. Apart from the claims of the injured and of the dependants of the dead, claims materialised from persons who had suffered nervous shock through being close to these terrible events, through hearing of them, although at a distance from Hillsborough, either by radio or from those who had seen them or who had heard of them, and claims from persons who observed the events on television. The line below which claims would not be entertained by the courts was drawn rapidly and, of course, arbitrarily by the House of Lords.[46] There were to be no claims by persons who suffered nervous shock as a result of what they saw or heard on the television or radio and the relatives and friends who suffered such shock, even if present at Hillsborough, had no claims unless they had been very close to the victim.

---

46 *Alcock v Chief Constable of South Yorkshire Police* [1992] AC 310.

This line drawing exercise is known as the requirement of proximity. Once it is acceptably drawn for a class of case it will provide the yardstick for others of that class. Essentially it is not an intellectual exercise but an exercise of ordinary good sense. When people say that the judges do not merely interpret the existing law but make law, this is the sort of thing they have in mind.

During the last ten years or so the law of England had been bedevilled by a flood of cases which arose from negligent design or construction of buildings, often on unsatisfactory foundations; and from efforts to fix local authorities with liability on the ground that they had been careless in the exercise of their powers of inspection of buildings in the course of construction. The High Court of Australia resisted the temptation to follow the English Courts, wisely as it turned out, for the House of Lords was constrained, ultimately, to overrule most of the decisions which had given damages for economic loss in these circumstances.

The point of departure for the High Court was the decision in the *Caltex* case.[47] In that case a dredge fractured a pipeline which was not the property of Caltex but which connected its terminal to a refinery and through which Caltex passed crude oil for processing and received refined product. Caltex claimed the cost of transporting refined product while the pipeline was out of use. This was clearly economic loss and it was not a consequence of physical damage to Caltex's property. The question, therefore, was whether there was the necessary proximity between it and the owners of the dredge for an action in tort for economic loss. It was accepted by Gibbs, Stephen and Mason JJ that, although as a general rule damages are not recoverable for economic loss which is not consequential upon injury to person or property, even if the loss is foreseeable, damages are recoverable in a case in which the defendant has knowledge or the means of knowledge that a particular person, not merely as a member of an unascertained class, would be likely to suffer economic loss as a consequence of his negligence. The decision is one of potentially wide application. The potentiality will exist in cases in which a number of actors with varying roles take part in a composite activity such as a building operation and where the nature and degree of interdependence of all of them is common knowledge.

In *Candlewood Corporation v Mitsui OSK Lines Ltd*, Lord Fraser of Tullybelton, delivering the judgment of the Privy Council, was critical of *Caltex* saying that their Lordships had difficulty in seeing how to distinguish between a plaintiff as an individual and a plaintiff as a member of an

---

47 *Caltex Oil (Australia) Pty Ltd v The Dredge "Willemstad"* (1976) 136 CLR 529.

unascertained class.[48]   But, with all respect, the decision to accept the requisite proximity is a policy one and behind that decision lurks the constant fear of opening the tortious liability of an individual to a wide and indeterminate mass of claimants. The *Caltex* criterion meets this head on. It should also be recognised that, as is pointed out in *Candlewood,* the judgment of Stephen J set out five features of the case which demonstrated a close degree of proximity between the defendant's conduct in severing the pipeline and the economic loss which Caltex suffered.

Once it is recognised as, one would think, it now must be, that proximity falls to be identified on a case by case basis, it may be predicted that *Caltex* will provide a sound point of departure in many situations. Thus it may well be that cases in which the English courts have been unable to find the necessary proximity, (such as cases of nominated suppliers and sub-contractors, who, by faulty workmanship cause economic loss to the building owner or head contractor) may, in Australia, be brought under the umbrella of Caltex. To date the High Court has shown commendable caution in avoiding the pitfalls which so embarrassed the English Courts including the House of Lords. Gibbs retired in 1987 from the Bench of the High Court. By then the centralist tendency which is always close to the surface in the High Court was to divide it on an issue which was, and is, of central importance to the federation and to expose the frailty of the Constitution as a defence for the constituent States against the encroachments of Commonwealth power.

THE EXTERNAL AFFAIRS POWER

In all the leading cases up to *Koowarta v Bjelke-Petersen,*[49] in which placitum (xxix) was held to sustain legislation of the Commonwealth to give effect to a treaty, there was an international element in the sense that the subject matter of the treaty directly affected our relations with other countries. Such an element was obviously present in the cases involving the regulation of international air traffic.[50] The domestic legislation had been passed to give effect to international treaty obligations but the treaties themselves had regulated an aspect of Australia's external relations. Thus the rights of external sovereignty over the continental shelf, regulated by a treaty, provided a subject matter within placitum (xxix) which authorised the passing of domestic legislation. Again the expropriation of enemy alien property for the benefit of the international allied powers and their subjects

---

48 [1986] AC 1 at 24.
49 (1982) 153 CLR 165.
50 *R v Burgess ex parte Henry* (1936) 55 CLR 608; *R v Poole ex parte Henry (No 2)* (1929) 61 CLR 634; *Airlines of NSW Pty Ltd v NSW (No 2)* (1965) 113 CLR 54.

was held to fall within the subject matter of placitum (xxix)[51] and the prohibition of publication of matter calculated to promote disaffection against a friendly power was sustained under placitum (xxix).[52] The general approach of the court was to treat placitum (xxix) as dealing with "the regulation of relations between Australia and other countries".[53] However, from the beginning of the Federation it has been recognised that placitum (xxix) creates grave difficulties of interpretation.

It was in *Koowarta* that the question first arose whether the Parliament of the Commonwealth can enact laws for the execution of any treaty to which it is a party, whatever its subject matter; and, in particular, for the execution of a treaty which deals with matters that are purely domestic and in themselves involve no relationship with other countries or their inhabitants. As Gibbs pointed out in that case it had never been doubted that placitum (xxix) is wide enough to empower the Parliament to pass a law which carried into effect within Australia the provisions of an international agreement. But all of the treaty cases had been ones in which the subject matter of the international agreement was itself an "external international affair" in the sense of involving relations between Australia and other countries.

Koowarta presented, for the first time, legislation to give effect to an international treaty which had no conceivable bearing on the relations between Australia and other countries but rather called for the imposition of a particular standard of conduct upon Australian citizens. The treaty called for the elimination of all forms of racial discrimination, not in the dealings amongst member States but in dealings by governments with their own people and dealings amongst those people. It was plainly, therefore, not directed to or founded upon any external matter or external relationship, unless it is possible to say that the mere fact of an international treaty is in itself and without more an "external affair". Gibbs, of course, perceived the danger of holding that such a situation was within placitum (xxix). The danger was, as he put it simply and directly that:[54]

> If the Parliament is empowered to make laws to carry into effect within Australia any treaty which the Governor-General may make, the result would be that the Executive can, by its own act, determine the scope of Commonwealth power... The Executive could, by making an agreement, formal or informal, with another country, arrogate to the Parliament power to make laws on any subject whatsoever.

---

51 *Roche v Kronheimer* (1921) 29 CLR 329.
52 *R v Sharkey* (1949) 79 CLR 121.
53 See, eg, per Latham CJ in *Burgess* (1936) 55 CLR 608 at 643.
54 (1982) 153 CLR 165 at 198.

He pointed out that to qualify such a doctrine, by requiring that the treaty be not merely a colourable device, would provide no safeguard, for the Executive Government would, of the nature of things, ordinarily have in mind an object which many might think beneficial. The majority of the court in Koowarta (Stephen, Aickin and Wilson JJ as well as the Chief Justice) was of the opinion that placitum (xxix) does not support legislation to give effect to treaty obligations, unless the treaty "was made in reference to some matter international in character," as Dixon J had put it in *Burgess*.[55] The Commonwealth's answer to this was that the question of racial discrimination had become a matter of international debate and concern. However, as Gibbs pointed out,[56] the fact that many nations are concerned that other nations should eliminate racial discrimination within their own boundaries does not mean that the domestic or internal affairs of any one country thereby become converted into international affairs. It was at this point that a fatal rift occurred in what otherwise would have been the majority in *Koowarta*. Stephen J was persuaded that a subject matter of international concern "necessarily" possesses a capacity to affect a country's relations with other nations and that this capacity was sufficient to attract placitum (xxix). With all respect, the history of the 20th century reveals that international relations, founded on the self-interest of the participating countries, is usually not in the slightest degree affected even by monstrous internal behaviour on the part of the participating States. Stephen J's view, added to the view of Mason, Murphy and Brennan JJ that the international treaty was in itself an "external affair," resulted in a majority of the court sustaining the legislation, the operation of which was entirely internal, as an exercise by the Parliament of the power to make laws with respect to external affairs. The worst fears of all those who had seen placitum (xxix) as potentially the source of unlimited enlargement of the legislative power of the Commonwealth were soon to be realised.

The *Koowarta* decision led directly to what has proved to be the most socially divisive decision ever handed down by the High Court of Australia. This of course was the *Tasmanian Dam* case in 1983.[57] Tasmania was proposing to construct a dam for hydro-electric purposes in the south-west of that State. This excited the disapproval of a vociferous minority who have come to be called the Greenies. Perhaps drawing on European experience, the Commonwealth government of the day sought to attract the Greenie vote in reliance on the International Convention for the Protection of the World Cultural and Natural Heritage, which required a party to endeavour to take

---

55 (1936) 55 CLR 608 at 669.
56 (1982) 153 CLR 165 at 202.
57 (1983) 158 CLR 1.

---

appropriate measures for the protection of that heritage. The Commonwealth Government procured the entry of nearly 800,000 hectares of south-west Tasmania, including the dam site onto the World Heritage list. The subject matter of the Convention had no conceivable bearing on Australia's relations with other countries, but the High Court, by a slender majority, upheld the validity of legislation passed by the Parliament of the Commonwealth to prevent the construction of the dam. The common thread in the majority judgments (Mason, Murphy, Brennan and Deane JJ) was that a law is within placitum (xxix) if it gives effect to a treaty obligation, although some of the Justices would have gone even further. Gibbs' judgment[58] identified the central question in relation to placitum (xxix) as being whether it enables the Parliament to legislate to give effect to any treaty to which Australia is a party, even though the law deals with matters which occur, and can occur only, within Australia and even though the performance of the treaty in its relevant aspects involves no reciprocity or mutuality of relationship between Australia and the other parties to the treaty. A simple lawyer would have thought that this question had been decided in the negative by *Koowarta*. On the same page the Chief Justice pointed out that another aspect of the question was "Whether the power to implement treaty obligations is subject to any, and if so, what overriding qualifications derived from the Federal nature of the Constitution" using the language of Stephen J in *Koowarta*.[59] As has been seen, the majority in Tasmanian Dam did not accept the ratio of the majority in *Koowarta*. Gibbs, with Wilson and Dawson JJ, took the orthodox view, while the majority opted for the most extensive of the possible views of the power of the Commonwealth Parliament to make laws under placitum (xxix).

The consequences are of incalculable consequence to the Australian Federal system. As Gibbs pointed out[60] the external affairs power differs from the other powers conferred by s 51 in its capacity for almost unlimited expansion. He pointed out that there is almost no aspect of life which under modern conditions may not be the subject of an international agreement, and therefore the possible subject of Commonwealth legislative power. Moreover, whether Australia enters into a particular international agreement is entirely a matter for decision by the Executive. A consequence of the view of placitum (xxix) which was adopted by the majority in *Tasmanian Dam* is, as the Chief Justice pointed out, that the division of powers between the Commonwealth and the States which the Constitution effects could be rendered quite meaningless, if the Federal Government could, by entering

---

58 (1983) 158 CLR 1 at 97.
59 (1982) 153 CLR 165 at 212.
60 (1983) 158 CLR 1 at 100.

into treaties with foreign governments on matters of domestic concern, enlarge the legislative powers of the Parliament so that they embraced literally all fields of activity.

In holding that placitum (xxix) should be given a construction that will, so far as possible, avoid the consequence that the Federal balance of the Constitution can be destroyed at the will of the Executive, Gibbs was doing no more than giving effect to the proposition stated by Sir John Latham in the *Banking* case[61] that "no single power should be construed in such a way as to give the Commonwealth Parliament a universal power of legislation which would render absurd the assignment of particular carefully defined powers to that Parliament". The enormity of the potential for destruction of the Federal system which was freely proffered to the Commonwealth by the majority in *Tasmanian Dam* must have become apparent to government at all levels. To the Commonwealth indeed, it may well have been perceived to be another poisoned chalice. Almost none of the general administration of this country is done by the Commonwealth, all the donkey work which is necessary to the administration of an orderly society being the responsibility of the States. Members of the Parliament of the Commonwealth are thus in a position to raise almost unlimited funds and to use them for any cause, worthy or unworthy, which may appeal to them. Except in war time, there is relatively little apart from tax gathering, social services, the peace-time armed forces and its own vast bureaucracy which is the direct responsibility of the Commonwealth. On the other hand, by the expedient of tied grants and the general use of the power of the purse Federal politicians are able to implement their social policies through the agency of the States. The Federal system may well appear therefore to the Commonwealth a convenient symbiotic relationship which it is not in their interest to weaken unnecessarily. At any rate, at the Premier's Conference in June 1982 it was agreed that the Commonwealth would consult with the States before entering into further international agreements. This was endorsed by the Commonwealth in October 1983, a few months after *Tasmanian Dam* was decided. This may momentarily have allayed the concern of the States at the almost unlimited implications of *Tasmanian Dam* but of course such agreements have no binding effect.

In *Queensland v The Commonwealth*[62] the Court held that inclusion of an area in the World Heritage List by the World Heritage Committee was conclusive of Australia's international duty to protect and conserve it and

---

61 (1948) 76 CLR 1 at 184.
62 (1989) 167 CLR 232.

thus of the constitutional support for a proclamation with that object under Commonwealth legislation. The court held that no municipal court, including the High Court, could therefore decide for itself whether the area in question is in fact part of Australia's natural heritage. In other words, the constitutional balance between the Commonwealth and the States is at the mercy of the Executive Government in Canberra and an international bureaucracy - an alarming conclusion for Australians who are urged to "walk tall" and to be beholden to no external authority.

Then came *Polyukhovich v Commonwealth*.[63] It was there held that an Act of the Commonwealth Parliament passed in 1988, making certain conduct in Europe during the Second World War a criminal offence against the law of the Commonwealth, was a valid exercise of the power under placitum (xxix) in relation to an Australian citizen who had migrated since the events in question. Logically this seems to mean that anything is within the legislative power of the Parliament of the Commonwealth provided that it has nothing to do with Australia. Brennan J appears to have had some after-thoughts for he dissented, essentially on the basis that the "external affairs" subject to placitum (xxix) must be the external affairs of Australia.

Finally, we must come to *Mabo v Queensland* (No 1).[64] Much has been written and said about the Aboriginal land rights decision in *Mabo* (No 2),[65] which overturned retrospectively 200 years of settled law so as to divest from the Crown in right of the former colonies, now the States of Australia, the property in the wastelands (that is to say the unsettled lands) of Australia and subject them to as yet uncertain claims to native title. The financial consequences for our descendants will be felt for generations. This is not the place to enlarge on the social disaster which faces our country, particularly as recent Commonwealth legislation would appear to have enlarged the conception of Aboriginal land rights beyond anything the High Court had in mind. For present purposes, the important point is that this social revolution was made possible by the external affairs power.

The High Court in *Mabo* (No 2) acknowledged that the new found Aboriginal land rights had been subject to extinction by the exercise of sovereign powers until the passing by the Commonwealth of the Racial Discrimination Act 1975. This is the Act which, as we have seen, was upheld by a slender majority in *Koowarta*. It is this which denies to the States the right to exercise their powers of sovereignty so as to extinguish these nebulous

---

63 (1991) 172 CLR 501.
64 (1988) 166 CLR 186.
65 (1992) 175 CLR 1.

claims, except upon payment of compensation, claims the magnitude of which is likely to be in inverse proportion to the tenuous nature of the "land rights" in question. Thus this socially divisive and immensely costly disaster is the direct product of the external affairs power. What had happened in *Mabo* (No 1) was that the Murray Island people were to have been given, in place of their uncertain land claims, Crown leaseholds to be held by their Council as trustee for them. By a curious process of reasoning which defeated the minority of the court, this was held to be discriminatory against them. It was therefore invalidated by s 10(1) of the Racial Discrimination Act. The rest is history. The result, at the moment of writing, is that the Commonwealth has passed complex legislation which is almost universally regarded as unsatisfactory, setting up a great mass of tribunals which are, so far as one can understand the legislation, to be empowered and indeed required to act upon evidence which is in truth no evidence at all, regarding the findings in previous decisions of tribunals as themselves evidence. No-one could predict what the outcome will ultimately be.

DUTIES OF EXCISE AND TAXATION OF CROWN PROPERTY

One of the last critical decisions of the High Court on duties of excise in which Gibbs was involved was *Hematite Petroleum Pty Ltd v Victoria*.[66] The companies which carried on the business of exploiting Bass Strait oil used a pipeline to carry the hydrocarbons from the Bass Strait wells to a plant at which they were separated into different petroleum products; another pipeline by which the products were moved to another plant and, in the case of natural gas, a third pipeline to convey the product to Melbourne for consumption. From 1981 Victoria imposed fees for the use of the crude oil pipeline, the liquefied petroleum gas pipeline and the natural gas pipeline of 10 million dollars annually, to be adjusted in subsequent years by reference to the Consumer Price Index. If the fees so imposed were duties of excise, they were beyond the powers of the Parliament of Victoria, for s 90 of the Constitution gives the Commonwealth Parliament the exclusive power to impose duties of customs and excise.

The Victorian legislation obviously imposed a tax and a tax which of necessity would be passed on as part of the price of each of the Bass Strait products. Did this mean that it was a duty of excise? Chief Justice Gibbs pointed out that there are many taxes which have a tendency to enter into the price of commodities but which are not excises, and which are accordingly within the power of the States to impose. He gave the instance of payroll tax. Wilson J at 650 pointed out that if in seeking to determine the true character

---

66 (1983) 151 CLR 599.

---

of a tax one is unable to rely on the legal operation of the statute which imposes it, the constitutional distinction between taxes which are the subject of s 90 and other taxes must inevitably be eroded. His point was that if the term "duties of excise" is to be extended to cover any impost which in a practical sense may be seen to increase the cost of production or distribution of goods, then the powers of taxation hitherto conceded to State legislatures would be seriously diminished and, of course, the exclusive taxing power of the Commonwealth massively increased. The Chief Justice observed that the inability of the States to impose duties of excise had already created greater difficulties for them since the uniform tax arrangements had virtually prevented them from imposing income taxes. He noted that one view of experts in the field of public finance is that the wide extension made by the High Court to the definition of excise is "one of the greatest impediments preventing the achievement of a rational and lasting division of financial powers in the Australian Federal system". He predicted that one result must surely tend to be that the States would impose some forms of taxation which, although constitutionally permissible, are less economically desirable than taxes now categorised as duties of excise.

The wisdom by which the High Court had been guided up to the *Hematite* decision involved two widely accepted principles. The first was that excise is a tax directly related to goods and imposed at some step in their production or distribution. The second was that whether the tax is a duty of excise must be determined having regard to the legal effect of the taxing statute, it not being enough that it produces the same economic and practical effect as an excise. The Chief Justice observed that the conclusion that the grant to the Commonwealth of the exclusive power to impose duties of excise gravely hampers the States in the conduct of their financial affairs without conferring any corresponding benefit on the Commonwealth does not mean that the prohibition which s 90 contains must be disregarded, but that it does suggest that there is no good reason for giving a wide and loose construction to its provisions.[67]

He referred to *Browns Transport Pty Ltd v Kropp*[68] and *Bolton v Madsen*,[69] saying that each was "entitled to be regarded as authoritative",[70] on the footing that in each case the decision was given by all available members of the Court and was unanimous and that the correctness of their results had, so as he was aware, never been doubted. These unanimous decisions were

---

67 (1983) 151 CLR 599 at 618.
68 (1958) 100 CLR 117.
69 (1963) 110 CLR 864.
70 (1983) 151 CLR 599 at 620-621.

authority for the view that the question whether a tax is directly related to goods depends on the provisions of the legislation which imposes the tax, rather than on the practical effect of the tax. The Court which decided *Bolton v Madsen* consisted of Dixon CJ, Kitto, Taylor, Menzies, Windeyer and Owen JJ, surely one of the strongest courts ever to grace the High Court Bench. The only member of the then court who was absent was McTiernan J, who had been a party to *Browns Transport Ltd v Kropp*. The Chief Justice's suggestion that these decisions were entitled to be regarded as authoritative was doubtless ironical. He, of all people, was obviously aware that a chapter in the legal history of Australia was opening which would see unanimous decisions of the court's predecessors, no matter what their personal eminence, not as calling for respect but rather as a challenge to the new breed to show that they had nothing to learn from the past and that their own unaided wit was a surer guide.

On the traditional approach, which was applied by the Chief Justice and Wilson J, who dissented, a fee for the right to carry on a business may or may not be a duty of excise. Thus in the transport cases taxes on the carrier not fixed by reference to the goods in fact carried were held not to be excises and in the business licence cases, the failure of the legislation to relate the tax to the quantity of goods bought or sold had led to the same result. On the other hand an abattoir fee payable to defray the cost of inspection and charged in terms of the quantity of meat processed was held to be an excise. This principle came to be called the *Bolton v Madsen* formula. In *Hematite* the pipeline tax was completely unrelated to the quantity of hydrocarbons carried by the pipelines. Gibbs' conclusion was that the pipeline operation fee was not a tax upon or directly affecting goods; it was what it purported to be, a fee for a licence to use the pipeline and was thus not a duty of excise. Mason J, as he then was, sufficiently demonstrated the view of the majority in saying that the pipeline operation fee was a tax imposed on a step in production which was so large that it would inevitably increase the price of products. This was, of course, precisely the argument which had been rejected in the transport cases. The brave new world had dawned. In the course of his judgment, Mason J expressed his "profound disagreement" with the strict criterion of liability test, that is to say, the testing of the question in terms of its strict legal operation. Thus, curiously enough from our highest court, the legal operation of a statute was to become an unacceptable approach to the solution of the legal problems raised by that statute under the constitution. Time was to tell whether the practical operation test would serve the country as well.

The next year was to see *Gosford Meats Pty Ltd v New South Wales*,[71] in which a licence fee calculated on the basis of previous production was struck

---

71 (1984) 144 CLR 368.

down as a duty of excise, contrary to *Dennis Hotels Pty Ltd v Victoria*,[72] and this although the whole court had refused to allow *Dennis Hotels* to be re-opened six months earlier in *Evda Nominees Pty Ltd v Victoria*.[73] In *Gosford Meats* Gibbs CJ, Wilson and Dawson JJ dissented.

The new revelation was to be tested dramatically in *Queensland v Commonwealth*.[74] The decision was handed down on 3 February 1987, two days before Gibbs retired as Chief Justice. It has come to be called the First Fringe Benefits Tax case. Section 114 of the Constitution forbids the Commonwealth to impose tax "on property belonging to a State". The question was whether the State could be taxed on its provision of cars and houses which it owned as part of the emolument of its servants. It seems not to have been doubted by any member of the Court that tax on the ownership or use of the property of a State was forbidden by s 114. It was said however that the fringe benefits tax was imposed on the State in respect of the private use by its servants of State housing and cars. The Chief Justice, however, concluded that tax was imposed on the State by reason of the particular manner in which it had used its property and that this was the substance as well as the form of the legislation. Why the use to which an owner puts his property does not embrace its being made available to his servants to encourage their efforts does not appear.

Section 114 was to arise again in *South Australia v Commonwealth*.[75] The question was whether a Crown instrumentality was liable to income tax on the income on its invested funds and to capital gains tax on its investments. The latter was clearly a tax on the ownership or holding of the capital and was held by the Court to be within the protection of s 114. However, if one may say so with respect, the Court turned handsprings to demonstrate to its own satisfaction that the interest earned was not "property belonging to the State" and the tax on the interest was not imposed as a result of the holding or ownership of the capital. The Court was of course committed to its "substance rather than form" approach to constitutional interpretation. How anyone could contend that interest received or receivable on invested capital is not itself property is beyond the understanding of the writer. The argument advanced was that "income" for the purposes of the Income Tax Assessment Act is a statutory concept and therefore "a subject 'relevantly' different from the ownership or holding of property". What had happened to the substantial operation approach? The fact that the interest received or receivable is the

---

72 (1960) 104 CLR 589.
73 (1984) 154 CLR 311.
74 (1987) 162 CLR 74.
75 (1992) 174 CLR 240.

property of the State and that by virtue of s 114 it should not, as a matter either of form or of substance, have entered into the labyrinthine process of the ascertainment of income under that notorious statute seems not to have been worthy of attention. The object sought to be achieved was frankly stated as being to maximise the legislative freedom of choice of the Commonwealth Parliament.[76] It is, one supposes, of no moment that s 114 seems be wholly inconsistent with such an object.

On the same day the Court gave judgment in *Deputy Commissioner v State Bank of New South Wales*.[77] The Bank had manufactured printed material for its own use and was assessed to sales tax under s 17 of the Sales Tax Assessment Act of the Commonwealth as upon goods manufactured by it and applied to its own use. The Court acknowledged that it had been accepted in *Queensland v Commonwealth* that tax on the use of State property was forbidden by s 114 as being a tax on the holding or ownership of that property. The Bank therefore succeeded. The decision seems plainly correct but it is not altogether easy to see how as a matter of practical operation the decision is to be reconciled with *Queensland v Commonwealth*.

The Years After Retirement

During the years which have elapsed since his retirement in February 1987 from the office of Chief Justice, Gibbs has made a signal contribution to public affairs in bringing the clarity of his thinking and the strength of his reputation to bear on a feature of Australian public life on which he is particularly equipped to speak, namely the maintenance of the Constitution. At the time of writing, there is a determined effort by the Commonwealth Government to induce in the people a frame of mind in which they may accept amendments which will further weaken the States and enlarge the power of the Commonwealth and, above all, by abandoning our Constitutional Monarchy, remove all restraints from the Executive Government.

The main vehicle for the expression of Gibbs' views on these subjects has been the Samuel Griffith Society, set up in 1992, of which he was the founding President. The forces seeking massive change include the party in government and their adherents, the academic left, the products of the trendier law schools and the mass media, the support of which that party has acquired by the expedient, inexpensive to itself, but exposing our society to a danger which was once perceived and acknowledged by all parties, of permitting concentration of media ownership. This danger is a present

---

76 (1992) 174 CLR 240 at 248.
77 (1992) 174 CLR 219.

reality. Views which turn against the proposed changes remain largely unreported, no matter how eminent in their fields their authors may be. The main vehicle for Government propaganda in this area would seem to be the Constitutional Centenary Foundation, which proudly affirms its independence, absence of preconceived views and firmly non-partisan attitudes.

If it were not for the Samuel Griffith Society, most Australians would not know where to begin in identifying what lies beneath the sheep's clothing. The proceedings of this Society, in the form of papers by some of the best minds in our community, all carefully sourced and documented, identify the falsity of much of the current politically correct propaganda; the hypocrisy of these protestations by the Foundation; and the absence of principled reasoning to support the more bizarre decisions of our courts. It is not surprising that Sir Anthony Mason referred to the Society in a somewhat patronising fashion as, "a Society which chooses to call itself the Samuel Griffith Society". Griffith, after all, was a founding father of the Constitution and they are out of fashion. He was the first Chief Justice of Sir Anthony's Court, one who established the Court on a basis of strict principle, but principle must now, we are told, yield to contemporary sociological values.[78]

It would not be useful to restate in less adequate language the content or even the thrust of the papers which are freely available in the proceedings of the conferences of the Society, published in four separate volumes under the title "Upholding the Australian Constitution". But I shall summarise a part of Mr John Stone's paper "WhiteAnting the Constitution" on the Constitutional Centenary Foundation.[79] I do this to enable the reader to judge the claims of its founders that the Foundation is non-partisan and has no preconceived views, for we may be about to face a tidal wave of propaganda from this and related sources and it may be helpful to point the reader to the material which will assist in the formation of a judgment, material which is not easily assembled.

In 1988 the Australian people rejected overwhelmingly and in all States referendum proposals which came from the now defunct Constitutional Commission set up by Mr Lionel Bowen when Attorney-General. These proposals were for 4 year parliamentary terms; constitutional recognition of local government; trial by jury, freedom of religion; acquisition by any government to be in just terms. Some of them have an air of simplicity designed to attract the electorate, but the people must have been profoundly suspicious.

---

78 *Mabo v The State of Queensland (No 2)* (1992) 175 CLR 1 at 42.
79 (1994) vol 4 of the Society's Proceedings at 183.

The innocent might have expected that this expression of the people's will would naturally have ended any thought of constitutional change along these lines for a generation. The elitist left wing intellectual fringe, which thrives in the hot house atmosphere of Canberra, prates a great deal about democracy, but is notable for its complete rejection of popular opinion.

Thus in December 1988 a Centre for Comparative Constitutional Studies was established within the law school of the University of Melbourne and by 1992 it was justifying its program for change by reason of, amongst other considerations, "the dissatisfaction traditionally expressed with the Australian Constitutional system!". Traditionally? Not by the people, for they had in 1988 affirmed their satisfaction with it.

The Director of the Centre was Professor Cheryl Saunders, who was to play the leading role in the Constitutional Centenary Foundation. A public meeting to set up this body was convened in Sydney in April 1991 by Professor Saunders and Professor Crawford of the Sydney University Law School on the date of the first constitutional convention in 1891. The Chairman, Sir Ninian Stephen, permitted himself to compare the two occasions, a curious licence, as the constitutional conventions of the 1890s were a body of elected Statesmen whereas, ostensibly at least, the Constitutional Centenary Foundation is a group of self appointed and non-elected persons, although it had been revealed a month earlier by Mr Peter Charlton that the Federal Government "supported the conference and the processes of review which follow".

Mr Stone's paper names the 85 persons who attended. Anyone who cares to read the list can satisfy himself as to the preponderance of "true believers". The conference was conducted, apart from formalities, in camera. Ultimately it issued "an Agenda for the Decade" identifying key issues to be pursued in the coming decade. The very first item of this Agenda reads: "(1) The Head of State: Provisions should be made...to define the powers of, and to consider the appropriate method of selection of, the Head of State." This item is meaningless except in a republican context. Now this statement, as Mr Stone points out, was a year before Mr Keating launched the republican push, but the Foundation was established.

I chose to mention item 1 as being easily understood and being, far from impartial and uncommitted, a clear statement that the agenda of the Foundation assumed a new republican constitution and concerned itself merely with detail. Nonetheless, it has persistently claimed to have been established as an impartial body, to be independent, to be dedicated merely to a public process of education, to having no preconceived views, to being firmly non-partisan and indeed as having no predetermined view either on the need to change or the form which changes might take (see its first Annual Report 1992).

On the other hand the Sydney conference was "generously funded by the Commonwealth", according to Sir Ninian Stephen at the Official Launch on 14 April 1992. In fact it received $234,000 from Government to 30 June 1992 and its budget for 1992/93 looked forward to $500,000 from all government sources. The Foundation needs generous funding for it pays $100,000 per annum to Professor Saunders' Centre for Comparative Constitutional Studies for consulting advice.

Readers will judge for themselves whether the Foundation is really the disinterested body it claims to be, or whether in reality it is a creature of the Commonwealth Government and, more importantly, whether the "Agenda" also is not, in truth, that of the Government.

Gibbs delivered the launching address to the Samuel Griffith Society on 24 July 1992. A proposal for a new constitution to mark the approaching millennium was then being canvassed and he reminded those present that no practical need was apparent for re-moulding our constitutional principles in a way not yet made clear. Moreover, as he pointed out, the United States framed its constitution, on which ours is modelled, in 1787 and no politician in that country would dare to suggest that it should be consigned to the scrap heap.

He went on to deal with certain specific proposals which were being floated, putting first one which, he predicted, would be among the most contentious, threatening the very basis of the ideal of "one nation for one continent". That was the proposal for a treaty which should secure special constitutional rights for the Aboriginal people and Torres Straits Islanders as the indigenous people of Australia (a proposal which is in fact item 10 of the Foundation's Agenda, referred to above). The proposal, as canvassed in 1992, also included international recognition of the indigenous people as a sovereign people, with the possibility that some areas of Australia might become separate nations. Of this he said that "it must be obvious that the security of Australia would be threatened if any of those parts of Australia which are nearest to neighbouring countries, or at the very heart of the continent, acquired separate nationhood".

Among the ideas which came out of Canberra in those days was one which had the strong support of the Prime Minister. This was that the projected constitutional changes should be of a "minimalist" character, changing the constitutional monarchy of the country to a republic by the simple expedient of substituting a reference to "President" for all references to the Sovereign.

Gibbs pointed out what should have been clear to all involved, but which up to that date obviously had not been, that extensive powers are given by the constitution to the Governor-General as the Queen's representative including the office of Commander in Chief of the Armed Forces. The long history of the relations between the Monarch and the Parliament in England and the conventions which now govern the exercise of the Royal authority are also part of the constitutional history of Australia. In particular, it is now well understood that the powers of the Head of State (in Australia exercised by the Governor-General) are, except in most extreme circumstances, exercisable on the advice of Minsters. There is no constitutional history of the relations between a President and the Parliament and there are no conventions to govern those relations. The "minimalist" solution, if adopted, will create a Head of State of truly frightening power and authority. Public opinion polls at that time had revealed that, if the Constitution were to be changed by substituting a President for the Monarch or her representative, overwhelming public opinion favoured the election of the President by popular vote rather than by the Parliament (which of course in modern times means the Prime Minister).

If the Constitution were to be amended to provide for an elected President with the powers of the Head of the State presently set out in the Constitution, the exercise of those powers not being subject to the conventions which presently limit the practical authority of the Head of State, the political consequences would be enormous. We would, in truth, have a polity which resembles the present French Republic. The President would be very much the more powerful figure and the Prime Minister would be relegated very much to second place. There are, of course, those who would think this not an unattractive outcome, but one must look beyond the present personalities. Australia has thrived under a system in which power is carefully divided and the possibility of autocratic rule is minimised. It is unthinkable that a Prime Minister would favour a system in which a President created by the "minimalist" technique was popularly elected. So, indeed, it has proved. The present Prime Minister is known to favour the appointment of the proposed President by the Parliament. It is known, however, from the public opinion polls that the people are overwhelmingly opposed to this expedient.

A possible alternative, of course, for those who still cherish the dream of a "minimalist" constitutional amendment would be to provide that the President is to be subject to the conventions relating to the exercise of his power and authority which obtain at the date of the Constitutional amendment. This, however, would give the game away entirely. It would be apparent that the change which the Prime Minister has thought important enough to divide the nation was in fact no change at all, of no practical significance and merely a symbolic one. In the result, therefore, the "minimalist" dream really did not survive Gibbs' launching address to the newly formed Samuel Griffith Society in 1992, in which he pointed out that it is simply not true to say that all that would be involved would be the substitution of a President for the Governor-General.

In the same address he made the further point, which is of very great importance, and that is that the Constitutions of the States also provide for a representative of the Head of State as part of the legislative process and Head of the Executive Government of the States. In this connection he pointed out that the reserve powers of the Crown had, in fact, been exercised in recent years by the Governors of both Tasmania and Queensland and observed: "If the powers were abolished in relation to the States, responsible government would be diminished; if a President could exercise them in relation to the States that would further weaken Federalism in Australia".

The more one thinks about the proposal for a republican form of government, the more the hidden agenda become apparent. Our Constitution, like that of the United States, is fundamentally based on division of power. A federal system is a potent means of dividing power between central and regional authorities. The other great mechanism for dividing power in a society is the separation of the legislative and executive powers on the one hand and the judicial power on the other. Our highest court is enthusiastic about the latter, and rightly so, though for reasons which may not be hard to identify but, for whatever reason, is far from enthusiastic about the former. Indeed, with its current program of implying in the Constitution fundamental rights to which the legislative power of the Commonwealth itself is subject, the High Court may fairly be said to be at least seeking to establish itself as the apex of the political process. The Supreme Court of the United States had this role thrust upon it by what is known as the Bill of Rights which is, however, contained in their Constitution in explicit terms. By inventing a set of fundamental rights which were, as is well known, rejected by the founding fathers of the Constitution, the Court will, if it is successful, in practical terms amend the Constitution as the people refuse to do, and create for itself a pre-eminent position in the Australian polity. Much could be said and much obviously will be said about this unbalancing of the Constitution but, for the moment, what is relevant in relation to the contribution of Gibbs to the law of this country is that it is at least unlikely that the program of implying fundamental rights would have got off were he still Chief Justice. I say this with full realisation that he did not carry the Court with him in the *Tasmanian Dam* case, but he would certainly have exposed the shoddy reasoning which was held to justify the implication of freedom of political communication. There were, indeed, justices who did so, notably Dawson and McHugh JJ.

At the conference of the Samuel Griffith Society in Melbourne in 1993, Gibbs presented a paper headed "The Threat to Federalism". In it he pointed out that, while the attack on the Monarchy was at that stage the more vociferous, it could hardly be doubted that the ultimate aim of many of those seeking change was to destroy federalism. After referring to the fact that the clear intention of those who framed the Constitution was to establish a federal system of government and after alluding to the poor record of governments and courts in defending the federal principle, he made the significant statement[80] that there is no more effective way to curb abuses of political power than to divide it. So he continued, in words which deserve the widest of circulation:

> Australia has been a notably free and tolerant country, but it cannot be taken for granted that those conditions will always prevail. Already legislation is passed which appears to limit unnecessarily the freedom of the individual, and already citizens incur public obloquy if not punishment, for speaking truths which offend against political and social orthodoxy. A federal system cannot guarantee freedom and tolerance, but it can help to protect them.

In the same paper he made the telling point that, while true Federations are rare, because a State cannot be called Federal where the central authority dominates the constituent States, those Federations that do succeed are amongst the most liberal and wealthy countries of the world.

I turn finally to Gibbs' concluding remarks as President to the fourth conference of the Society in July 1994. He observed that for some years there has been a movement, hardly noticed by the general public, directed towards the achievement of increased Commonwealth power and increased executive power. He expressed the view that those who are urging that we become a republic are simply the vanguard before the main offensive. He reiterated that an important aim of the Society is that questions of this kind should be fully and openly debated. The operation of the external affairs power, as he pointed out, continues to be one of the major factors which destabilises the Constitution, but he identified a new one. That is the subordination of Australian sovereignty to some of the organs of the United Nations. He said, at 330:

> It would be a matter of amusement, if it were not so serious, that our Government, after abolishing appeals to the Privy Council, should thereafter give Australians the right to appeal to nondescript bodies composed of persons who may have no particular qualifications, and who may be citizens of regimes which pay no respect to human rights or the rule of law.

---

80 (1994) vol 2 of the Society's Proceedings at 191.

An instance of this practice, which was examined at the Fourth Conference by Senator Rod Kemp, was the effect of the ratification in 1991 by the Hawke Government of the First Optional Protocol to the UN International Covenant on Civil and Political Rights, which allowed individual Australians to take complaints to the UN Human Rights Committee. This allowed one Toonen to complain to the UN Human Rights Committee that the Criminal Code of Tasmania, under which sodomy is a criminal offence (as it has always been at common law), was in this respect an infringement of the right of privacy under the International Covenant. This committee is, of course, not a court and it is extraordinary that important questions of the domestic law of Australia should be able to be submitted to such a committee. The states of Australia are not parties to treaties and conventions, the only international person for the purposes of international relations being the Commonwealth. A weird anomaly occurs in cases such as Toonen's. The Committee heard Toonen, doubtless pursuant to the Protocol, and the Commonwealth which gave its own views. Those views supported Toonen's. The only way in which the State of Tasmania, whose legislation was being considered, could present its views was for the Commonwealth (already identified as the State's opponent) to include representations of Tasmanian views in its general submissions. The government of Tasmania, whose laws were the subject of the complaint, had no standing to present the case for that State.

It is only a few short years since Australians were urged to stand tall and no longer submit to the legal problems of this country being solved by an outside court such as the Privy Council. Under this protocol they are now being resolved by a committee which is not a court, has no necessary legal knowledge, and no particularly high credibility in terms of the constituent nations which have representatives on the Committee or indeed the Committee itself. The 18 members of the Committee include Ecuador, Costa Rica, Egypt, Hungary, Jordan, Senegal, Mauritius, Yugoslavia and Venezuela. The countries concerned include five which have not even signed and ratified the Protocol. The Committee does not give a reasoned decision. One has no way of knowing why criminal acts which occur in private are therefore to be exempt from the operation of the criminal law. Are counterfeiting and forgery no longer to be offences if they are carried out in private? What of crimes of violence committed within the privacy of the household? To return to the area of sexual offences, what is to be said about rape in marriage which of its nature is likely to occur in private? Finally, a question which the Commonwealth Attorney-General is having the greatest difficulty facing up to, what of incest whether consensual or involuntary, which is an essentially private offence?

Internationalism is being touted as the light on the hill. It follows that a questioning of this essentially dubious assumption is politically incorrect and worthy of public castigation or, if the editor is in a charitable mood, is simply passed over as the opinion of one past his use-by-date. On the domestic scene, there is general agreement that there is widespread ignorance of the nature of the Australian Constitution and of the principles upon which it is based. This, as Gibbs pointed out in his preface to *The Australian Constitutional Monarchy*[81] is due, in part, to the fact that the Constitution has worked so smoothly, and has given so little cause for public concern. In the same preface he had this to say:

> Ever since Federation, the great majority of the Australian people have enjoyed a degree of freedom, and of social justice, which has been envied by most of the world. We have enjoyed internal peace and stability, while other nations have experienced oppression, torture, genocide and civil war. Some people claim that our traditions, which have developed on the foundations laid by our British heritage, should be abandoned, because our society is now multicultural. Surely, most of our immigrants have come here because they have seen the benefits which our society can afford, and would wish to retain the traditions that have helped to shape a free and just society.

The constitution of the Samuel Griffith Society, in stating its purposes, includes a passage which reflects the same views:

> Australia has an unbroken record of constitutional government, and rule of law. It was one of the first nations to establish universal suffrage. It has been entirely free from any hint of civil war. Up until the Great War of 1914-18 Australia was also in per capita terms, the richest country in the world.

> The strength of our parliamentary and legal institutions, of our political conventions and modes of behaviour is, arguably, Australian's greatest asset. The Constitution which Australians drafted and accepted in the 1890's, and which established the framework of the Australian nation as a sovereign federal state, is the keystone of this structure and has served us well. It has protected our democracy, and our liberties, by providing for independent centres of political authority and the diffusion of power which flows from it.

Anyone who wonders why a man who has served with distinction the highest judicial office in Australia should, in his retirement, undertake the burden of opposing the fashionable trends which obviously have all the resources of government behind them will perhaps find an answer in Gibbs' 1995 Australia Day Message to the Society:

> In a society such as Australia a reasonable degree of freedom is taken for granted. It tends to be forgotten that in the history of the world there have been few free societies and that even today there are comparatively few countries that can truly be described as free. It is dangerous to be complacent and to take the continuance of freedom for granted.

---

81 G Grainger and K Jones (eds), (1994).

It is against these undeniable truths that Australians should evaluate the claim of Professor Saunders' Centre, referred to above, that dissatisfaction is traditionally expressed with the Australian Constitution.

CONCLUSION

We have seen above that the traditional view of s 90 of the Constitution, a view to which Gibbs adhered, was that it invalidated State legislation only if the duty in question went beyond imposing a burden which might be expected to find its way by one means or another into the ultimate cost of a product and that it must be directly imposed on the production or distribution of the goods in question, on the proper construction of the legislation (the "criterion of liability" test). As a consequence, licence fees for the carrying on of such businesses as the retailing of tobacco and the sale of alcohol and petrol were held to be within the power of the States.[82] In later cases the Court rejected the "criterion of liability" test, preferring to look to the "practical" rather than the "legal" operation of the taxing statute, as it claims to have done in relation to s 92 in *Cole v Whitfield*.[83] This approach is described as having regard to matters of substance rather than form in *Capital Duplicators Pty Ltd v ACT* (No 2).[84] In this case the Court held that an advance fee "payable in relation to the supply or offer for retail sale" of videos was an exaction made in a step in the process of distribution and therefore an excise. The fee was payable as a term of a statutory licence to sell the goods and charged at the rate of 40% of their wholesale value. The Court rejected the argument that the scheme was regulatory involving as it did no restriction on the sale of videos, no matter how violent or pornographic, goods of this character obviously being regarded by the government of the ACT as fit material (or perhaps eminently fit) for sale in that area. The legislation itself (s 21) identified the true nature of the exaction as being payable in relation to the supply or offer for sale of the goods (per Mason CJ, Brennan, Deane and McHugh JJ). In other and less fashionable words, this was the criterion of liability. On any view the legislation affected to impose a duty of excise and there was nothing remarkable about the conclusion that it did so.

However, some interests before the Court, notably the ACT, sought a reopening of the whole approach to s 90 with a view to confining it to duties imposed at the point of manufacture or production. Indeed this type of approach appealed to the minority (Dawson, Toohey and Gaudron JJ). It is becoming generally apparent that the Court's wide approach to s 90 threatens

---

82 *Dickenson's Arcade Pty Ltd v Tasmania* (1974) 130 CLR 177; *HC Sleigh Ltd v South Australia* (1977) 136 CLR 475.
83 (1988) 165 CLR 360.
84 (1993) 178 CLR 561.

to distort the financial balance between the Commonwealth and the States to an extent which will destroy the federal nature of the Constitution. Even the Commonwealth seems to have been alarmed, for it was said that the Treasurer was preparing to raise such taxes and distribute the proceeds to the States and Territories if the Court extended the grasp of s 90 further. This would obviously have been highly unsatisfactory to the Commonwealth. In the result the Court declined yet again to re-examine the decisions on liquor, petrol and tobacco outlets although they are plainly inconsistent with its current doctrine.

The Court's response was thus to abandon any attempt at a reasoned approach. The major sources of State revenue which were at risk if the doctrine that the "practical" rather than the "legal" effect of taxing statutes should be the criterion in all cases were, of course, licence fees for the carrying on of these businesses. Plainly enough their "practical" effect is to increase the price. The statutory criterion of liability however is the carrying on of the business, a legal if not an economic distinction, but a workable one. The majority solution to the dilemma was worthy of King Solomon. The statutory criterion of liability was anathema, but its rejection in these areas would produce chaos! The areas were therefore to be corralled off as a no-go area in which skirts would not be lifted to reveal the hidden "excise" beneath.

It will be recalled that in *Hematite* in 1983,[85] Gibbs had pointed out the danger to the Federal system if the orthodox view of s 90 were abandoned. Unfortunately his view did not prevail. He returned to this topic at the Second Conference of the Samuel Griffith Society held at the Windsor Hotel Melbourne from 30 July to 1 August 1993[86] and again, in the same year, at the Eleventh National Convention of the Taxation Institute of Australia held at Alice Springs. The present system continues to be workable, but at the expense of coherence in the case law. Can it be said that the doctrine of "practical effect" is an improvement on the previously established law?

Sir Harry Gibbs is by nature a private man. One would ordinarily have supposed that in his retirement from the Court he would happily have avoided areas of controversy. He has certainly managed to avoid criticism of the Court. However, facts speak for themselves. The Court is at present said to be engaged in "judicial activism" which would seem to mean fundamental change to the legal system initiated by the Court itself. When hardy souls express disquiet, they are told that the Courts have always played a role in changing the law. So indeed they have, but the changes have been

---

85 (1983) 151 CLR 599.
86 *Upholding the Australian Constitution* (The Sir Samuel Griffith Society 1993 vol 2).

incremental, interstitial and gradual, or, as Professor Colin Howard has observed,[87] "The philosophy of the common law is, above all, evolutionary not revolutionary. *Mabo* is, above all, revolutionary, not evolutionary." Even the cursory examination of Gibbs' contribution made in this discussion points to a sharp contrast. Above all it shows that change can be made within the traditional structure of the legal system when it is plainly called for. Gibbs has played a significant part in that process and the fact that the changes in which he participated have been widely perceived as called for is evidenced by the fact that the writer is aware of no disquiet occasioned by any decision of the Court in which his approach prevailed.

He has continued, in his retirement, to be heavily engaged with the legal system, making himself available whenever persuaded that he has a worthwhile contribution to make to the system generally or to the profession in particular. The obvious detachment and good sense with which he expresses himself have made a strong and, on occasions, decisive impression in areas of public concern. Thus the proposal for a republic was, in its early days, accompanied by a suggestion that it would need only a "minimalist" amendment of the Constitution, substituting the word "President" for reference to the Queen and the Governor-General. From the day Gibbs pointed out that the conventions which enable immense powers to be vested in the Governor-General with the certainty that in almost every situation they will be exercised on the advice of Ministers, whereas there are simply no conventions governing relations between a President and the Parliament and Ministry, this proposal has obviously and rightly collapsed. In the immediate aftermath of *Mabo* (No 2), there were suggestions that the Aboriginal people should have sovereignty over some part or parts of the continent. Since Gibbs pointed out in his launching to the Samuel Griffith Society[88] that the security of Australia would be threatened if any parts of the continent nearest to neighbouring countries acquired separate nationhood, the suggestion would seem to have died. A populist sentiment currently dear to the heart of politicians and journalists is that women and members of ethnic groups should be appointed to the Courts and in particular to the High Court. At the first Australasian Congress of Justices at Brisbane on 26 September 1993, Gibbs pointed out that the sole criterion for appointment should be merit (including character, as well as learning, experience and ability). Women are now increasingly available and therefore increasingly appointed without any concern being apparent in the community. Gibbs went on to describe as simply nonsense to say that the composition of the Bench should reflect the composition of society as a whole. This could never be achieved. Moreover

---

87 "The Consequences of the *Mabo* Case" Vol 46 No 1 IPA Review.
88 *Upholding the Australian Constitution* (The Samuel Griffith Society 1992).

it is a poor compliment to women and to the members of the wider ethnic community to suggest that they should be appointed irrespective of merit. Implicit in such a suggestion is the notion that such appointees will perform their functions on idiosyncratic lines whereas what the community requires is what the judge is sworn to give - justice according to law.

An attempt such as this to distil the essential features of a lifetime of service to the great but necessarily complex profession of the law, culminating in the Chief Justiceship of Australia is unlikely to be wholly successful. The writer has tried to bring out the essential features of a lawyer, who combined great learning with good sense, the exercise of great authority with modesty and a total absence of vanity with a refusal to compromise on questions of principle. It need scarcely be added that the opinions which are expressed in this paper, and the style in which they are expressed are entirely those of the writer.

POSTSCRIPT

While the printing of this book was underway the court gave its decision in *Teoh's* case a decision so full of inconsistencies that a professor at the University of Macquarie's Law School described it as "quite explosive in potential". A heroin runner was to be deported but the Court stopped the deportation because of its effect on his children's "rights" under the Convention on the Rights of the Child. As the Convention has not been enacted by the Parliament it had no legal standing in Australia and they had no such rights. Nevertheless the courts were required to have regard to it as raising "legitimate expectations" [89]. Professor P H Lane, Emeritus Professor at Sydney University identified the process as being the judges taking the convention on board when the Parliament failed to do so, in other words deliberately supplanting the Parliament. The Court is reported as saying that the fact that the convention has not been incorporated into Australian law does not mean that it has no significance for Australian law! Is this not sheer casuistry?

---

89 *The Weekend Australian* 8-9 April 1995 p3

INDEX